"Mundane astro[...] , as a vocation, than perhap[...] [...]ology. This book is a wonderful pla[...] [...] some of the best astrologers we have practicing in this field."

—Michael Munkasey

*The Astrology of the Macrocosm*—just what exactly does that mean? Well, the astrology that most of us are familiar with deals with ourselves as distinct individuals. It's *personal*. But astrology has much more to offer on a different level. Enter the worldly realm of *mundane* astrology.

Here you will discover astrology's place in predicting the weather or in revealing the relationship between celestial aspects and earthquakes.

Perhaps you'd rather learn about world leaders. Read a fascinating study of the disappearance of the Romanovs of Russia, and many authors of this anthology mention such American political figures as George Bush, Michael Dukakis, FDR and Harry Truman. Discover an astrological explanation of the American and Japanese involvement in World War II.

Such astrological tools as the Ingress chart (seasonal chart), the SuperMoon alignment (complete with listings of this event through 1999), and the Geodetic Equivalent method, used to predict or understand events at a specific geographic location, are thoroughly explained.

A chapter devoted to the philosophy of mundane astrology puts all this information into perspective, along with a discussion of the Age of Aquarius and its correlation with millenarianism.

Probe the astrological quatrains of Nostradamus for relevance to 20th-century man, or explore a projection of life in the 21st century according to major planetary configurations of the outer planets.

All this is yours on this astrological journey of the world!

## Other Books in This Series

## Forthcoming Books

Llewellyn's New World Astrology Series

# The Astrology of the Macrocosm

## New Directions in Mundane Astrology

Edited by

**Joan McEvers**

1990
Llewellyn Publications
St. Paul, Minnesota 55164-0383, U.S.A.

First Edition
First Printing

**Cover Design: Terry Buske**
**Marbled paper by Theresa Nordby**

Charts calculated and printed utilizing Matrix Blue Star Software, copyright © 1989 Matrix Software.

**Library of Congress Cataloging-in-Publication Data**

The Astrology of the macrocosm : new directions in mun-
    dane astrology / edited by Joan McEvers.
            p.    cm. — (Llewellyn's new world astrology series)
        Includes bibliographical references.
        ISBN 0–87542–384–1
        1. Mundane astrology.    I. McEvers, Joan.    II. Series
BF1720.A88   1990                                    90-35088
133.5—dc20                                           CIP

Llewellyn Publications
A Division of Llewellyn Worldwide, Ltd.
P.O. Box 64383, St. Paul, MN 55164-0383

# THE NEW WORLD ASTROLOGY SERIES

This series is designed to give all people who are interested and involved in astrology the latest information on a variety of subjects. Llewellyn has given much thought to the prevailing trends and to the topics that will be most important to our readers.

Future books will include such topics as vocational astrology, various relationships and astrology, electional astrology, astrology and past lives, astrological counseling, and many other subjects of interest to a wide range of people. This project has evolved because of the lack of information on these subjects and because we wanted to offer our readers the viewpoints of the best experts in each field in one volume.

We anticipate publishing approximately four books per year on varying topics and updating previous editions when new material becomes available. We know this series will fill a gap in your astrological library. We look only for the best writers and article topics when planning the new books and appreciate any feedback from our readers on subjects you would like to see covered.

*Llewellyn's New World Astrology Series* will be a welcome addition to the novice, student and professional alike. It will provide introductory as well as advanced information on all the topics listed above—and more.

Enjoy, and feel free to write to Llewellyn with your suggestions or comments.

**Joan McEvers**

Author of *12 Times 12* and co-author with Marion March of the highly acclaimed teaching series *The Only Way to . . . Learn Astrology*, Joan McEvers is a busy practicing astrologer in Coeur d'Alene, Idaho.

Born and raised in Chicago where she majored in art and worked as a model and illustrator for an art studio, she moved to the Los Angeles area in 1948 and continued her professional career in the sales field. This is where she met her husband Dean and raised their children.

Self-taught, Joan began her serious study of astrology in 1965 and in 1969 studied with Ruth Hale Oliver. About this time she started to counsel and teach astrology. She has since achieved an international reputation as a teacher and lecturer, speaking for many groups in the U.S. and Canada. An AFAN coordinator and member of NCGR, her articles have been published in several national and international astrological magazines.

In 1975 Joan and Marion founded Aquarius Workshops, Inc., with Joan as President. She also helped establish its quarterly publication *Aspects*, which is widely recognized for the wealth of astrological information packed in each issue. She continues to contribute to this periodical.

*12 Times 12* details each of the 144 possible Sun/Ascendant combinations. Each description includes information about personality, appearance, health, likely vocational areas, interests and attitudes. Having always been intrigued with astrological/vocational potential, Joan and Marion presently are conducting a "Vocational Probe," seeking to establish a computer program which can be given to schools to assist young people in selecting work and career fields. They are collecting myriad types of vocational data for this program.

Co-winner with Marion March of the Regulus Award for contribution to Astrological Education, Joan also has been presented a Special Commemorative Bicentennial Award for the excellence of her published works from the *Astrological Monthly Review*.

Currently, she is editing a series of anthologies entitled *The New World Astrology Series* of Llewellyn Publications, working on a Horary Astrology book, and preparing for the fifth book in the March/McEvers ongoing series. She also reviews books and cassettes for Astro-Analytics Publications and writes their bi-monthly newsletter.

A double Aquarius with Moon in Leo, when she isn't preoccupied with astrological activities, Joan enjoys spending time with her husband, four children and five grandchildren, quilting and playing bridge.

# CONTENTS

# INTRODUCTION

According to Nicholas DeVore, Mundane Astrology interprets charts in terms of world trends, the destinies of nations, and large groups of individuals based on an analysis of the effects of equinoxes, solstices, New Moons, eclipses, planetary conjunctions and similar celestial phenomena. *Webster's International Dictionary* defines *mundane* as "relating to the world, universe, heavens and heavenly bodies; of or pertaining to the world (mundo), worldly."

In this, the fifth in Llewellyn's New World Astrology Anthologies, we present a broad view of this type of astrology as it applies to all the above-mentioned subjects as well as weather forecasting, earthquake prediction and the actual philosophy of Mundane Astrology. There are articles on Ingress charts; the predictions of Michel de Notre Dame, more familiarly known as Nostradamus; the Age of Aquarius; the Geodetic chart; the SuperMoon alignment; an educated look at what the 21st century offers; the mystery of the Russian Royal Family; and the use of Astro*Carto*Graphy to bring Mundane Astrology down to Earth.

Combined with some diligent application, a careful perusal of this book offers the reader a broad perspective of political, social and economic astrology and the opportunity to learn how to make it work. Each of the authors is a specialist in the field, and no matter what your astrological interest, you are sure to find something that piques your curiosity.

*1*

Before you can start working with Mundane charts, you need to know something of the history and philosophy of this profound subject. **Jimm Erickson** of Portland, Oregon explains the background of this astrological field—how Mundane Astrology came into being and the principles on which it is based. Jimm may be familiar to you as the author of the political, world and mundane forecasts in *American Astrology* magazine.

Many of you may know **Judy Johns** as a contributor to the Financial book in this series. Here she outlines the use of the Ingress chart and how it relates to countries, their capitals and their leaders. Her choice of the 1941 Libra Ingress chart and the way it impacted the charts of the United States and Japan, as well as those of President Franklin D. Roosevelt and Emperor Hirohito, is intriguing, to say the least, even bordering on mind-boggling.

As Judy comments in her article, Ingress charts are set for the exact moment the Sun enters each Cardinal sign and can be done for any location on Earth. You may want to try tracking the four yearly ingresses for your immediate area, watching political, social and economic developments as they occur. Judy hails from Southern California.

All astrologers owe a great deal of gratitude to **Jim Lewis** for his development of the Astro*Carto*Graphy map. With this remarkable system, you are able to see at a glance where your planets are angular (where they have the greatest impact) throughout the world. In applying this system to Mundane Astrology, Jim uses the planetary placements of the United States, Japan and Harry S Truman, the president who decided to drop the atom bomb on Hiroshima and Nagasaki in 1945. The picture presented is stunning, and you will certainly want to apply the Astro*Carto*Graphy Mundane maps to your study of this fascinating area of astrology.

**Richard Nolle** from Tempe, Arizona introduces a

most provocative theory with his SuperMoon alignment. This is a New or Full Moon that occurs when the Moon is at its closest approach to the Earth. Richard feels this alignment relates to geophysical upheavals and may herald weather and seismic activity. He was able to foresee Hurricane David in September 1979, as well as other climactic phenomena. He includes a table of SuperMoon alignments for the 20th century. This tool, however, is not only related to weather and seismic forecasts but also may be placed in Ingress charts to point out other areas of possible upheaval.

Using Greenwich as the starting point at 0° Aries and moving eastward at 30° intervals, placing each succeeding sign of the zodiac at that point (30° east is Taurus, 60° east relates to Gemini, and so on), you can set up the Geodetic World Map. **Chris McRae** of Edmonton, Alberta, Canada explains the function of this truly remarkable device for watching transits impact various world areas. She describes how to set these charts for locations throughout the world. It is simple, easy, and above all, so informative.

English astrologer **Nicholas Campion** debunks the myths relating to the Age of Aquarius. A superb astrologer and an erudite writer, Campion points out how so many of the things astrologers say or predict come to be taken for granted or accepted as truth, when in actual fact they are fiction at best, and fantasy at worst. His analysis of New Age beliefs is perspicacious, discriminating and educational.

Since most TV weather forecasters openly admit they are often guessing about weather patterns, the concept of using astrology to predict meteorological trends seems fitting. **Nancy Soller** from Indianapolis, Indiana explains how by using Ingress charts, transits and New and Full Moons you too can predict weather patterns with at least as much, and maybe more, accuracy than your local weatherperson. Her perspective is clear, her rules readily understandable, and her track record respectable. Nancy writes the weather predictions for Llewellyn's *Moon Sign Book*.

**Marc Penfield**, besides being an astrologer, is also a historian and demonstrates his expertise in both fields with a discerning and profound dissertation on the disappearance of the Romanovs of Russia in 1918. Using both timed and speculative charts, Marc follows the path of the Royal Family from Moscow to Ekaterinburg and makes an interesting case for what actually (or fictionally) became of them.

When **Steve Cozzi** suggested he write a segment interpreting the quatrains of Michel Nostradamus, I had second thoughts. But I was pleasantly surprised by Steve's perception and definition of the prophecies of the French physician and astrologer who published a book of rhymed prophecies titled *Centuries* in 1555. Many of his predictions appear to have come true in the past, and Cozzi offers his meanings of the seer's quatrains relating to the current decade.

Earthquakes seem to be occurring with more frequency these days, or maybe it is just that the world has gotten smaller and we are able to view the devastation in our living rooms on TV. New York astrologer **Diana K. Rosenberg** presents her rules for determining possible Earth movement. Using eclipses, fixed stars, solstice points, antiscions, asteroids, and many other astrological devices, Diana maps out potential areas for devastating earthquakes and focuses on nodal activity as being instrumental in the timing of such phenomena.

**Caroline W. Casey**, a professional astrologer practicing in Washington, D.C., presents "Dreams and Disasters: Patterns of Cultural and Mythological Evolution into the 21st Century" in which she visualizes what life will be like as the outer planets continue their passage through the latter signs of the zodiac. As Saturn, Uranus and Neptune proceed through Capricorn, Aquarius and Pisces, and Pluto moves into Sagittarius, Capricorn and Aquarius, Caroline tells us how she foresees their effect on the world of the future.

These Mundane astrologers follow in the footsteps of some giants who have preceded them, including Ruth Hale Oliver, Olive Adele Pryor, Paul Grell, Charles Jayne, Barbara Watters, Edward Johndro and Donald Bradley, to mention just a few. This is a very specialized astrological field, and our authors serve it well.

In view of the major Earth-shaking events that have occurred in the latter half of 1989 and the early months of 1990, I thought that perhaps you would like to track these events by applying some of the astrological techniques suggested by our authors.

The following pages provide information, dates and horoscopes of various countries, 1988-90 Ingress charts, and Geodetic maps for auspicious time periods. Here is an opportunity for you to sharpen your skills in this area. All charts utilize Koch houses.

You may wish to put significant transits into the Geodetic maps, compare the charts of prominent people to those of their countries, or obtain Astro*Carto*Graphy maps to see what was occurring in each global area when major changes were taking place.

## Hungary Declares Its Freedom

Hungary, November 13, 1918, 12:00 p.m. MET
Budapest 47N30 19E05

| | |
|---|---|
| January 11, 1989 | Parliament allowed legal assembly and freedom of association. |
| February 11, 1989 | The Social Workers' Party approved the creation of an independent political party. |
| May 2, 1989 | Troops began dismantling the barbed wire fence on the Austrian border. Hungary was the first Soviet bloc nation to open the border to the West. |
| October 23, 1989 | The church bells rang . . . a free Republic was proclaimed. |

See the 1988 Capricorn Ingress, the 1989 Aries Ingress, the 1989 Libra Ingress, and the Geodetic chart for Budapest.

## Bulgaria Breaks with Communism

Bulgaria Autonomy, July 13, 1878, 1:37 p.m. GMT
Sofia 42N41 23E19
Bulgaria Independence, Oct. 5, 1908, 12:00 p.m. EET
Tirnovo 43N04 25E39
Bulgaria Communist Rule, Sept. 9, 1944, 12:00 p.m. MET
Sofia 42N41 23E19

You may want to look at all three of these charts when following progressions and transits for the current events taking place in Bulgaria.

| | |
|---|---|
| May 4, 1989 | Todor Zhivkov outlined the plan to break up collective farms and admitted the growing problem in food production. |
| November 10, 1989 | Todor Zhivkov resigned after 35 years in power; he was replaced by Petar Mladenov, who was born August 22, 1936. |
| December 10/11, 1989 | 50,000 people rallied and demanded an end to the Communist monopoly. The regime promised free elections by June 1990. |

See the 1989 Aries and Libra Ingress charts of Hungary as well as the 1990 Aries Ingress chart and Geodetic map for Sofia.

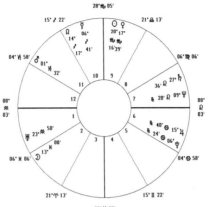

**Hungary**
**Nov. 13, 1918   12:00 P.M. MET**
**47N30   19E05**
**Budapest**

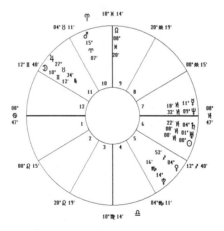

**1988 Capricorn Ingress**
**Dec. 21, 1988   3:29 P.M. GMT**
**47N30   19E05**
**Budapest, Hungary**

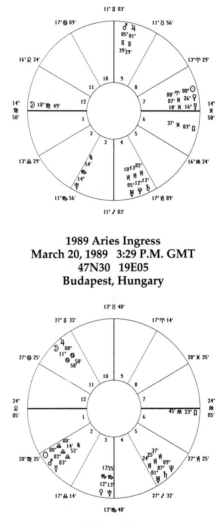

**1989 Aries Ingress**
**March 20, 1989   3:29 P.M. GMT**
**47N30   19E05**
**Budapest, Hungary**

**1989 Libra Ingress**
**Sept. 23, 1989   1:21 A.M. GMT**
**47N30   19E05**
**Budapest, Hungary**

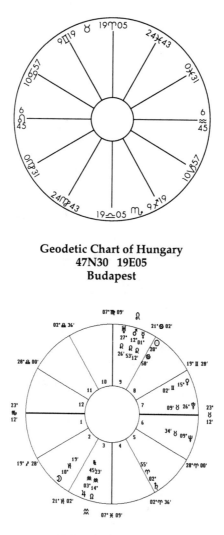

**Geodetic Chart of Hungary**
**47N30   19E05**
**Budapest**

**Bulgaria Autonomy**
**July 13, 1878   1:37 P.M. GMT**
**42N41   23E19**
**Sofia**

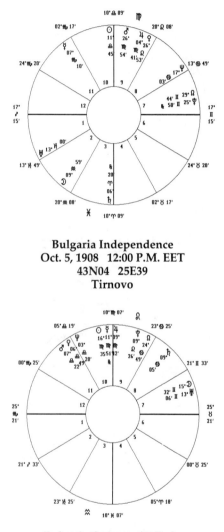

**Bulgaria Independence**
**Oct. 5, 1908   12:00 P.M. EET**
**43N04   25E39**
**Tirnovo**

**Bulgaria Communist Rule**
**Sept. 9, 1944   12:00 P.M. MET**
**42N41   23E19**
**Sofia**

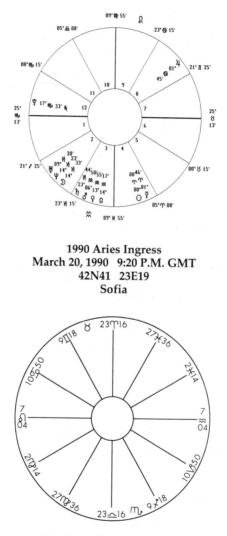

**1990 Aries Ingress**
**March 20, 1990   9:20 P.M. GMT**
**42N41   23E19**
**Sofia**

**Geodetic Chart of Bulgaria**
**42N41   23E19**
**Sofia**

## Poland Makes a Move

Poland, November 5, 1916, 12:00 p.m. MET
Warsaw 52N15 21E00

May 17, 1989            Poland granted legal status to the Roman Catholic Church, the first Eastern bloc nation to do so.

See the 1989 Aries Ingress chart of Hungary and the Geodetic chart for Warsaw.

## Chinese Students Revolt

China Republic, January 1, 1912, 4:05 a.m. GMT
Nanking 32N03 118E47

There are two charts for the establishment of the Communist People's Republic in 1949. Mao Tse-tung opened the Conference September 21, 1949, 12:00 p.m. WST, Peking 39N55 116E25. There was a massive rally in Peking October 1, 1949 around noon. Either chart may be valid. They are quite similar.

June 4, 1989            There was an uprising in Tiananmen Square in Beijing, which is the Chinese word for Peking. It resulted in the massacre of many of the protesting students.

See the 1989 Aries Ingress for Beijing and the Geodetic chart for Beijing.

## Hurricane Hugo

Charleston, SC, August 13, 1783, 12:00 p.m. EST
32N42 79W53
Source: *Horoscopes of U.S. States & Cities* by Carolyn Dodson

September 22, 1989            Hurricane Hugo touched land just after midnight.

See 1989 Cancer Ingress chart for Charleston and the Geodetic chart. Read Nancy Soller's weather-watching tips. You may also wish to consider the SuperMoon alignment in effect at this time. See Richard Nolle's chapter.

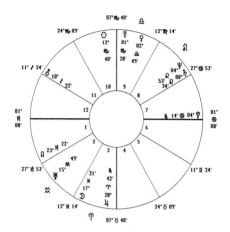

**Poland**
**Nov. 5, 1916   12:00 P.M. MET**
**52N15   21E00**
**Warsaw**

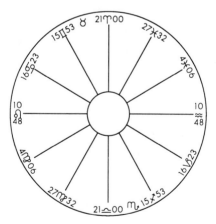

**Geodetic Chart of Poland**
**52N15   21E00**
**Warsaw**

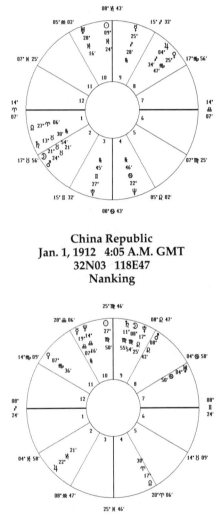

**China Republic**
**Jan. 1, 1912   4:05 A.M. GMT**
**32N03   118E47**
**Nanking**

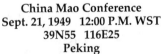

**China Mao Conference**
**Sept. 21, 1949   12:00 P.M. WST**
**39N55   116E25**
**Peking**

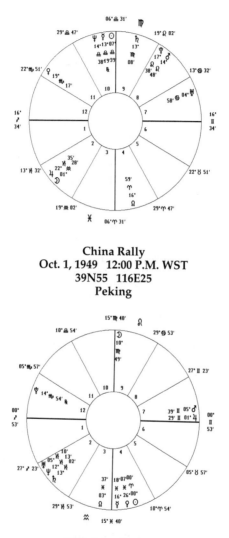

**China Rally**
**Oct. 1, 1949   12:00 P.M. WST**
**39N55   116E25**
**Peking**

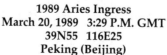

**1989 Aries Ingress**
**March 20, 1989   3:29 P.M. GMT**
**39N55   116E25**
**Peking (Beijing)**

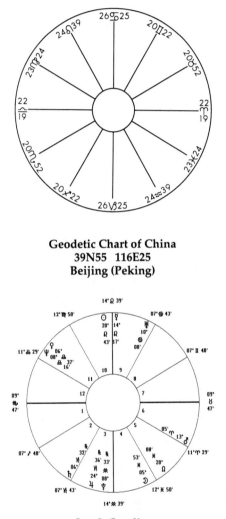

**Geodetic Chart of China**
**39N55   116E25**
**Beijing (Peking)**

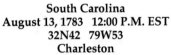

**South Carolina**
**August 13, 1783   12:00 P.M. EST**
**32N42   79W53**
**Charleston**

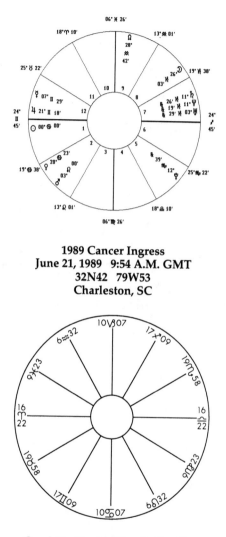

**1989 Cancer Ingress**
**June 21, 1989   9:54 A.M. GMT**
**32N42   79W53**
**Charleston, SC**

**Geodetic Chart of South Carolina**
**32N42   79W53**
**Charleston**

## Berlin Wall Falls

There are many charts for Germany, but we are providing:

Empire Proclamation chart: January 18, 1871, 11:51 a.m. GMT
Versailles, France 48N48 2E08
West Germany: May 23, 1949, 12:00 a.m. MET
Bonn 50N44 7E05
East Germany: March 25, 1954, 10:30 p.m. GMT
Berlin 52N30 13E22

November 9, 1989     The fall of the Berlin Wall occurred at 9:00 p.m. MET.
Egon Krenz ordered the wall opened. He was in
power for six days. He was born March 19, 1937.

Unification of Germany: October 3, 1990, 12:00 a.m. MET
Berlin 52N30 13E22

Birth Data for Helmut Kohl: April 3, 1930, 6:30 a.m.
MET, Ludwig Shafen, Germany 49N29, 8E26. Source:
Birth registry from Steinbrecher, AA.

See also the Geodetic chart of Berlin.

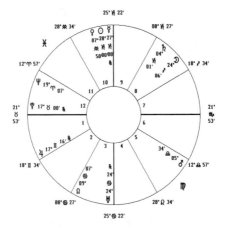

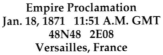

**Empire Proclamation**
**Jan. 18, 1871   11:51 A.M. GMT**
**48N48   2E08**
**Versailles, France**

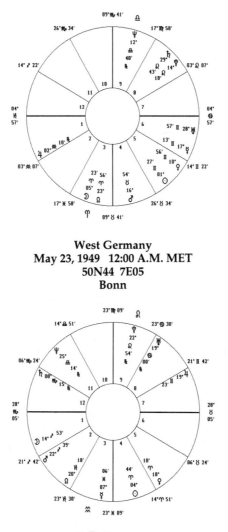

**West Germany**
**May 23, 1949   12:00 A.M. MET**
**50N44   7E05**
**Bonn**

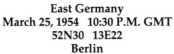

**East Germany**
**March 25, 1954   10:30 P.M. GMT**
**52N30   13E22**
**Berlin**

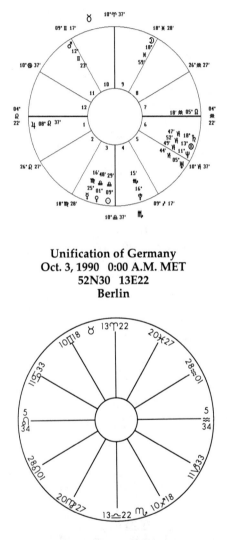

**Unification of Germany**
**Oct. 3, 1990   0:00 A.M. MET**
**52N30   13E22**
**Berlin**

**Geodetic Chart of Germany**
**52N30   13E22**
**Berlin**

## Romania Revolts

Romania Independence, May 21, 1877, 10:16 a.m. GMT
Bucharest 44N26 26E06

On March 2, 1945, Romania fell to the Communists, but the king did not abdicate until December 30, 1947. On April 13, 1948, the Soviet constitution was adopted. Probably all three charts should be considered.

November 24, 1989    Communists ended Congress, re-elected Nicolae Ceausescu as leader and rejected reform.

December 25, 1989    Ceausescu and wife were shot to death at approximately 4:00 p.m. He was born Jan. 26, 1918; her birthday was Jan. 7, 1917. See the solar equilibrium chart for each.*

See the 1989 Libra Ingress chart of Hungary and the 1989 Capricorn Ingress chart and Geodetic chart for Bucharest.

## The Invasion of Panama

Panama, November 3, 1903, 6:00 p.m. LMT
Panama City 8N58 79W32

December 20, 1989    United States troops invaded Panama.

January 3, 1990    Manuel Noriega, Panamanian dictator, captured. Noreiga was born Feb. 11, 1935, 5:00 a.m. EST in Panama City.

See 1989 Libra and Capricorn Ingress charts and the Geodetic chart for Panama City.

When you are using these charts, be sure to implement many of the other concepts presented by the authors represented in this book. I especially want to thank Judy

---

* This type of chart is prepared when the time of birth is unknown. The Sun is situated on the Ascendant and the degree and minute of the Sun is placed on each cusp with the signs following in order around the wheel. Using an ephemeris, the planets are positioned within the houses encompassing their sign, degree and minute.

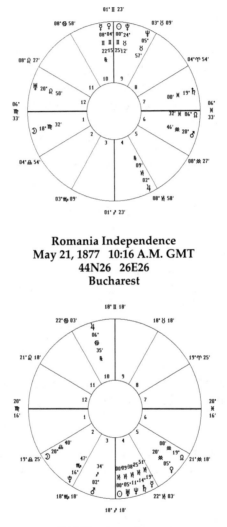

**Romania Independence**
**May 21, 1877   10:16 A.M. GMT**
**44N26   26E26**
**Bucharest**

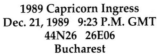

**1989 Capricorn Ingress**
**Dec. 21, 1989   9:23 P.M. GMT**
**44N26   26E06**
**Bucharest**

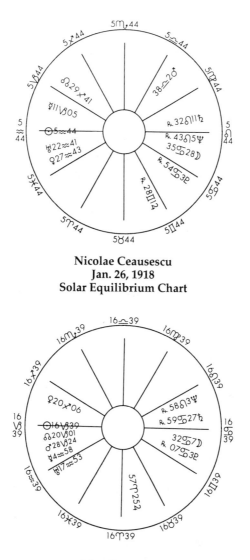

**Nicolae Ceausescu**
**Jan. 26, 1918**
**Solar Equilibrium Chart**

**Mrs. Ceausescu**
**Jan. 7, 1917**
**Solar Equilibrium Chart**

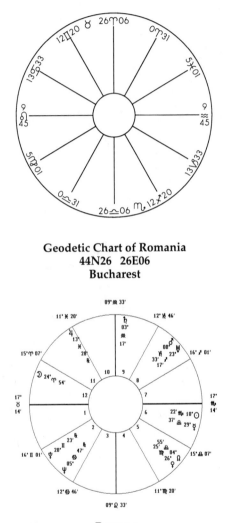

**Geodetic Chart of Romania**
**44N26   26E06**
**Bucharest**

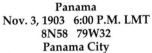

**Panama**
**Nov. 3, 1903   6:00 P.M. LMT**
**8N58   79W32**
**Panama City**

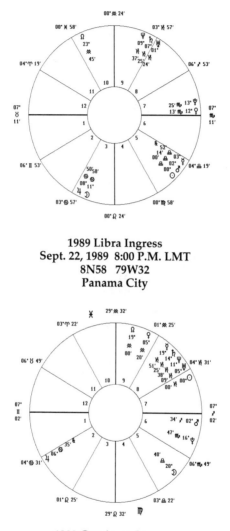

**1989 Libra Ingress**
**Sept. 22, 1989  8:00 P.M. LMT**
**8N58   79W32**
**Panama City**

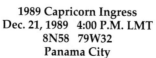

**1989 Capricorn Ingress**
**Dec. 21, 1989   4:00 P.M. LMT**
**8N58   79W32**
**Panama City**

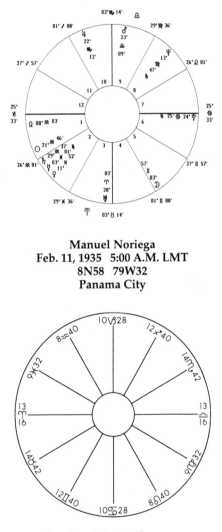

**Manuel Noriega**
**Feb. 11, 1935   5:00 A.M. LMT**
**8N58   79W32**
**Panama City**

**Geodetic Chart of Panama**
**8N58   79W32**
**Panama City**

Johns, who so kindly shared data and event information with me and made helpful suggestions.

The European charts and the ones for Japan and Panama are from *The Book of World Horoscopes* by Nicholas Campion, who is one of our authors. Manuel Noriega's birth information is from Zip Dobyns by way of Lois Rodden. The Geodetic charts are from Chris McRae's book *The Geodetic World Map*. I also wish to thank Jim Lewis for allowing us to reproduce the Astro*Carto*Graphy maps.

Joan McEvers
Coeur d'Alene, Idaho
October 1990

# A PHILOSOPHY OF
# MUNDANE ASTROLOGY

## Jimm Erickson

The greatest controversies spring from the simplest disagreements. Disagreements, however, tend to emerge out of dichotomous paradigms; no matter how wide the argument roams, usually the differences between those walking its various paths barely disguise preferences for one or the other of two directions. But the concept of dichotomy or complementary viewpoints presupposes that the scope of an argument's basic structure has already been determined. In other words, the terms of an argument are seen as defining the scope of the argument, and there is little disagreement as to the finality or precedence of those terms.

On the other hand, there's no shortage of controversy even when the central issue of a discussion is unarguable. For example, in the study of behavior (animal and human) there's a concept called the "sensitive period hypothesis." This hypothesis is simply that learning and experience have more impact during certain stages of development than they do in other stages. A two year old, for example, learns a new language more easily than a 20 year old because the former is in the midst of a "language sensitive period" and the latter isn't. This is an obvious hypothesis that of itself fosters no disagreement, but being political animals, people of every ideological bent have attempted to demonstrate that the sensitive period hypothesis supports their particular world view. Nature vs. nurture, social responsibility vs. individual blame, socialism vs. capitalism, determinism vs. freedom, form vs. content—the sensitive period hypothesis has been used in defense of each side of these and countless other arguments.

It's always possible, though, that more is taken for granted in an essentially dichotomous argument than in even a "self-evident" hypothesis; whereas the self-evident is merely another item of information, the dichotomy often disguises an implicit (but not necessarily self-evident) common ground. The *theme* of the dichotomy is taken for granted. (This is why clever historians pay attention to what is *not said* in the primary documentation of an era; the unstated is the true, common ideological bias of a given period.)

In approaching a theory of astrology, one dichotomous argument in need of a little thematic deconstruction is that of *Free Will vs. Determinism*. Basically, the problem can be summed up this way: Everything that happens is caused by something else, which in turn was caused by something else, and so on; therefore, all events are predetermined due to their implicit connection to an ancient causal chain; therefore, free will is an illusion. How can we simultaneously believe in causal law *and* personal freedom? Obviously, an extensive review of the answers to this question would be a book in itself; still, the causalist assumption is so inextricably embedded in modern Western thought, so central to all arbitration over which ideas may be allowed entrance into the canon of respectable establishment dogma, that a treatment of this issue is essential in confronting the main problem posed by astrology: *Astrology is completely ridiculous*, and yet it works.

Before proceeding, it's important to extract philosophy from the study of astrology. As Plato put it, "Philosophy begins with wonder." The wondrous aspect of astrology is the fact that it works; it really shouldn't, you know—at least not according to the dominant intellectual assumptions of our era. There's no point to astrology if, after an intelligent and reasonably skeptical apprenticeship in it, one fails to realize that its veracity (however great or limited) contradicts much of the reality model we've been force-fed by dominant ideology. Astrology should lead to a crisis of confidence regarding how much we should depend on authority structures in deciding what we do and do not believe. Unfortunately, people tend to either ignore chinks in the armor of conventional wisdom or go to the opposite extreme and accept an anything-goes intellectual anarchy. The goal should be dialectical progress, with astrology's apparently inexplicable validity as the *impetus*—not end—of the dialogue. After all, most of what has been determined scientifically, and most of the implications of these determinations, are true. But so is astrology—and here the philosophical development begins. What *specific* flaws in the modern/Western/establishment world view are revealed by its erroneous condemnation of astrology? That is the question.

## The Birth of Causal Law

Returning to the determinism debate, much of what has been written on this question was anticipated, in prototypical form, by the immediate intellectual heirs of Aristotle and Democritus. Reviewing the opinions of these Hellenistic philosophers, we get a sense of what we're up against throughout the history of Western philosophy; in fact, the Free Will controversy entered Western history in the two primary post-Aristotelian schools, the Stoics and the Epicureans.

Aristotle set the stage for the great debate. Whereas Socrates emphasized ethics (deriving from the fact that everything we take for granted is, once we overcome intellectual laziness, open to question) and Plato emphasized contemplation of the non-material (because wisdom is possible only when we transcend the obsessive tendency to analyze the incomprehensively chaotic material world), Aristotle taught that classification of things and phenomena, based on common characteristics, provides a model for understanding natural law. Because of this down-to-earth focus (unsubtly depicted in Raphael's *School of Athens* in which as Plato points to the sky, Aristotle is literally pointing down to Earth), Aristotle has assumed the role of prophet in the religion of scientism. Indeed, the rediscovery of his works in the late Middle Ages was an important catalyst in ushering in the Age of Science.

In developing a proto-scientific method, Aristotle thus dealt with causality as a *practical* rather than a metaphysical question. If any of his conclusions regarding these matters may be termed a theology, then it's essentially an animistic one—and here again he was a prophet, for here was the view of God that emerged during the Enlightenment. "God" is seen as adhering in all substance, and, more specifically, the spark of divinity in humanity is the ability to reason. We should thus seek the divine within and without by applying reason to observations of nature, finding God (or rather, god) in the orderly patterns of natural law. God is the Prime Mover, which created both the bodies and *potentials* of all material entities and set them in motion; hence, after this first cause, things merely behave and interrelate according to their potentials. In defining this variety of determinism, Aristotle arrived at attitudes quite prevalent in our own era, including the tendency to replace religion with science and the denial of an "afterlife" based on the apparently material foundations (brain, pineal gland, or whatever) of consciousness and the "soul."

Though Aristotle clearly developed a determinist

view, he was mostly interested in the practical issues related to it, so he didn't pursue the determinist dilemma much beyond his tidy First Mover idea; generally, Plato and Aristotle dealt with the question of "cause" as having to do with *explanation*, which is a limited category too crude to bear on cosmology. In the 3rd century B.C., however, "cause" came to mean much what it does in modern disciplines—cause (*aition*) is "the thing responsible," or that which brings about an effect. This shift in emphasis is crucial. Instead of looking for a cause (explanation) for this or that event, now all events were *characterized as effects of past causes.*

The Atomism of Democritus, in which reality is divisible only to the "atomic" level, which in turn is defined as the limit of divisibility, led to the profoundly reductivist views only hinted at by Aristotle. The Atomists accepted complete determinism as the logical correlate to a world of atoms combining and relating in strictly mechanical ways; an atom couldn't possibly move without being pushed, but whatever does the pushing was itself pushed, and so on. Obviously, this is simply the abstract causal principle translated into material terms, where the word "cause" becomes the word "atom" and causal chains are represented as material objects moving about due to the movements of the atoms comprising them.

From Democritus sprang the two great schools of Hellenistic philosophy, the Stoics and the Epicureans. With Democritus as the source of then-prevailing and established dogma, both schools accepted his atomic model. Though both dealt with a broad range of issues, the question of determinism was central to all their concerns.

The Stoics accepted unconditional determinism but also saw this as being reconcilable with an ethical outlook based on a "free will" of sorts. Their main arguments numbered three. The first as stated near the beginning of this chapter: Nothing happens without a prior cause; there is no uncaused event.

The second derives from a standard moralistic totalization of past/present/future: Any statement of fact is either true or not true. For example, since it is true that, say, Lincoln died in 1865, this statement was equally true a thousand years ago; therefore, it has *always* been true that Lincoln died in 1865, so that event was fated.

The third argument was later reiterated by Boethius and Descartes, but in different contexts: If one were "omniscient," knowing absolutely everything there is to know, one could deduce from present material reality the cause-and-effect patterns operative from now till doomsday, knowing the (inevitable) future. As Cicero put it, "If there were some human being who could see with his mind the connection of all causes he would certainly . . . grasp all that will be."

However, the Stoics were disturbed by the moral relativism contingent upon determinism. As Diogenes of Oenoanda put it, "If fate is believed in, that is the end of all censure and admonition, and even the wicked will not be open to blame." (This is particularly troublesome for those whose business it is to name "the wicked" and define their "censure and admonition"! I think the reader can see the beginnings of the nature vs. nurture argument here . . . .)

Their solution to this dilemma is perhaps too succinctly stated in an old joke about Zeno, usually considered the founder of Stoicism. According to Diogenes Laertius, Zeno caught a slave stealing and flogged him; the slave, who'd apparently been listening in during debate night, complained, "I was fated to steal." Zeno, to the delight of his thigh-slapping audience, responded, "And to be flogged."

And that pretty much sums it up. The Stoics decided there are "principle" causes and "auxiliary" causes. Basically, this was an ingenuous (or maybe disingenuous) camouflaging of the "form vs. content" argument. *Auxiliary* causes are mechanical catalysts acting on things that possess yet more crucial *principle* causes, i.e., their structural nature and its mode of action and reaction. In other words, all things (such as thieving slaves) have a "nature," which kicks in when something auxiliary comes along to stir things up and, in effect, "channels" the auxiliary cause. Reactions are thus seen as a function of both the transitory stimuli and the more permanent nature of whatever is being stimulated; but the "causal" chain involved in primary (principle) causes is seen as somehow liberated from purely mechanistic reaction. Hence, we are free to choose . . . and free, as one Stoic philosopher exulted in a work called "On Fate," to be punished.

Chrysippus, who tried to be impartial but was ultimately an apologist for the Stoics, saw causes as being "active" or "passive," and allowed for what he called "complex fate." His passive causes included objects whose natures were mostly similar to the elements Earth and Water, and his active causes partook largely of Air and Fire. Because Air was seen as a dominant element in anything living, generally active causes were simply all living things; more generally, active causes partook more of "god," and passive causes were more akin to "matter." Further, many fates are "complex" in that they necessitate a variety of different causal complexes to bring them about; if Hercules is fated to wrestle tomorrow, then someone else must be fated to be his opponent, the two of them must be fated to be together, the wrestling match must occur, etc.

To tie some of their ideas together, the Stoics developed a very peculiar creation myth. God created the world and eventually it will come to an end; then God creates it again—but because God is perfect and was absolutely right in how s/he went about the previous creation, the world is created again exactly the same way. The Stoics taught that we all go through our lives again and again in precisely the same way, creation after creation. However, it occurred to them that if things were *exactly* the same, then there'd be no way to say one creation took place during different moments than did other creations; therefore, they decided, there could be minor differences from one world to the next—the next creation Chrysippus might have a better haircut. Seriously.

The point of this creation myth was to illustrate the logical [sic] conclusions of their optimistic determinism. Like Aristotle, they saw God as beginning creation and then, as First Mover and structural architect, adhering within it; however, they also believed this to be "the best of all possible worlds," with a perfectly wise First Mover and a perfectly harmonious design. Finally, they decided that anything having a given nature and affected by a given cause would, time and again, react the same way. Put it all together with an axiomatic belief in the inevitable end of creation and you have the Stoic creation myth, weird as it is. Still, in their deterministic corollary that cause X plus nature Y always equals effect Z, they described an early version of the "doctrine of replication," now a cornerstone of the scientific method and, as we'll see, a concept having an enormous effect on our world view. The appearance of this idea in a school which imagined successive but nearly identical *time lines* is most significant.

A group of Hellenistic Academics, most notably Carneades and Philo, took it upon themselves to critique schools of thought rather than create another one. In a somewhat more dogma-inclined version of the Socratic method, they sought a "suspension of judgment" regarding belief in any school, yet definitely tended to take sides. To root out the best of the Stoics, the Academics set about dismantling the Stoics' three arguments for determinism.

Carneades, for example, denied that the causes *leading* to fated events were foreseeable; in other words, it might be an eternal fact that Lincoln died in 1865, but even the gods couldn't foresee this or say how it would occur. In effect, the Academics just seconded the Stoics' "principle cause" idea, saying that the eternal truth of actions lies not in an ancient causal sequence but in your "nature." Carneades was keen on the idea of volition, which is defined as "causes emerging from the stimulus of other causes on an independent self," believing that one's intrinsic nature is a cause compared to which other causes are merely "contingent." Obviously, this does not satisfactorily deal with a more reductivist theory of "intrinsic nature." However, this idea has important implications for the question of form vs. content.

The Stoics' chief rivals were Epicurus and his followers, particularly Lucretius. Epicurus expanded on Democritus's Atomism while abandoning the belief in any kind of predestinatory determinism. Like most philosophical attempts to prove free will while accepting the impossibility of uncaused events, his arguments were pretty lame; as it happens, though, his arguments, like those of the Stoics, are still the most common.

First, he appealed to *common sense*, or rather to his opponents' fear of looking silly; if they were trying to win an argument, he pointed out, then they must believe that the winner isn't yet determined, whereas their argument implied that the whole course of the argument was fated and inevitable. While Epicurus no doubt embarrassed his opponents with this observation, it's still no argument against the possible reality of—as opposed to belief in—strict reductivist causality. Next, he said causal determinism allows for *options* in most cases, the existence of which proves we have the ability to make free *choices*. In choosing between options open to physical law, man is exercising *reason,* and according to Epicurus's follower Lucretius, reason is a realm untouched by material necessity. In an argument similar to Spinoza's mind/body synchronism, Lucretius believed that Mind, in instructing the body how to act and react, possesses its own "volition" (an idea, as mentioned, later appropriated by Carneades). But again, the volition argument is vulnerable to reductivist disproof.

Though it may seem hard to distinguish between Lucretius the Epicurean and his rivals the Stoics, the point is that both desired to find an autonomous willful component in the barren determinism of their shared predecessor Democritus. But whereas the Stoics believed in absolutely predetermined material activity, which took on a more autonomous form when expressed within human activity, Lucretius argued that there exists a degree of "choice" or indeterminism in even purely mechanical interactions.

This idea derived from Epicurus's extraordinary cosmological model. Building on Democritus's Atomism, Epicurus taught that these atoms form "compounds" while "falling" through empty space; though the atoms generally fall in straight lines parallel to one another, occasionally a random "swerve" occurs in their path, which brings them together and ultimately builds "compounds." Inferences from Cicero's description of Epicurus's lost works suggest that the Epicureans believed that this swerve also played a part in the "development" of the soul, which, of course, was made out of soul-atoms. As random swerves in the atoms of the soul accumulated, a person underwent an indeterminate "development"; according to Epicurus, "That which we develop is at first absolutely up to us." In a sense, Epicurus took the "principle cause" idea out of the Stoics' definition of an object's "intrinsic nature"; he agreed that freedom is implicit in conscious being, but he didn't restrict the scope of this freedom by defining it as the exception to the rule (or a special case) of determinism.

In his "swerve" concept, Epicurus came dangerously close to breaking the Great Taboo—thou shalt not suggest that there exists uncaused actions—and Cicero later took him to task for it: "If we don't all want to incur the wrath of the natural philosophers for saying that something happens without a cause, we must . . . [say] that it is the atom's own nature to move as the result of weight and heaviness . . ." Once again, the formula is: auxiliary cause (material weight and heaviness) and principle cause (the atom's own "nature"); like politics-minded rationalists ever since, Cicero and his establishment peers insisted upon the responsibility of personal "nature" in the face of the deterministic vicissitudes of material "nurture." (It seems that the Stoics and their apologists were probably more in favor with the ruling class than were the somewhat more liberal Epicureans—perhaps this is why history has twisted the legacy of Epicurus into the hedonism implied by the word *epicurean*, even though Epicurus's philosophy and ethics were based on moderation and the "simple pleasures.")

Epicurus certainly anticipated Cicero's argument (for the record, Cicero lived two centuries after Epicurus). In defending the apparently heretical concept of an uncaused "swerve," he tried to define a situation in which an apparently uncaused action can be understood as deriving from an unknown quasi-causal principle; he suggested that a complexly unified material system can somehow manifest non-material properties, which themselves initiate *entirely new* causal chains. This idea is a variety of Holism (and is an example of why Epicurus is far and away my favorite philosopher!); however, the system described is by definition anomalous, and thus outside the range of respectable scientific consideration . . . and thus denied validity as a conceptual model of reality (we'll return to *that*).

## The Dialectic of Time

In narrowing my focus to just the earliest known formulations of only the Free Will debate as such, I must put aside not only later variations on the debate but also the larger "existential" context in which, more recently, they've been situated. I genuinely believe that the problems posed by astrology—if not approached in too parochial, trendy, or simplistic a manner—inspire astrologers to make significant contributions to philosophy; therefore, I do wish astrologers would assimilate, or at least notice, the post-Hegelian discussions on the nature of Being and on the bizarrely unique experience we as humans have of Being. Perhaps by inference, if nothing else, the reader can find such themes in this chapter.

In outlining the Free Will argument, I hope to impress upon the reader the unshakeable assumption which informs it in both the most and least formal discussions: Everything is caused by something else; there is no uncaused action or form. Aside from Epicurus's near-deviation from this rule (which, according to the 20th-century philosopher Yves Simon, is the single example of such deviation in the whole of the relevant literature), no "legitimate" philosopher has attempted to tackle the free will question (as such) from a different initial perspective. To describe the implications of this fact—and, indeed, to suggest a way out of the dilemma—I'd like to move from general philosophy to the consideration of a very specific element of the scientific method: *the doctrine of replication*.

The extraordinary success of the scientific revolution ultimately rendered much philosophical speculation moot. When Hamlet says to Horatio in a play written circa

1600, "There's more to heaven and earth than is dreamt of in your philosophy," by "philosophy" he's also referring to science. Once science really came into its own, though, it ceased to be a branch of philosophy because concrete proof (rather than speculation and abstract logic) now became the most reasonable and satisfying goal. So in terms of its impact on the prevailing world view, any newer philosophical speculation regarding free will and determinism tends to be quite irrelevant; the scientific method has proven its practical validity again and again, so its metaphysical implications seem to have become the standard by which all other metaphysics are judged.

The doctrine of replication is simply that, given a rigorously controlled set of conditions, *any valid experiment will upon repetition invariably produce the same results.* So long as the materials and procedures of the experiment are precisely the same, it doesn't matter whether the experiment is done today, next week or a thousand years from now—its results will always be the same. The key to this is, of course, the rigorously precise repetition of the experiment—all relevant factors must be, either literally or proportionately, replicated to the smallest detail. However, a simple fact of reality unavoidably intrudes (and must, therefore, be taken for granted): To repeat something is to do it at two different *times*. Everything is the same except the factor of "when"! As a strictly practical measure, the factor of "when" must be seen as neutral, empty, and insignificant, which indeed it is in terms of the mechanistic interactions measured by science; what has happened, though, is that the notion of neutral, empty, equivalent moments has invaded the general world view of the modern era. Even though it's merely a practical postulate within the narrow reality of the scientific method, it has grown to the stature of a dominant assumption in all "common-sense" models of reality—just as Democritus's "atoms" did in the Roman Empire two millenia ago.

In combination with older assumptions about causality and the nature of time, the trivialization of the factor of "when" has led to a vision of reality in which time is relegated to the role of a neutral, empty, linear frame of reference, which is "filled" by the events of the past and present; the future is an empty "space" waiting to be "filled" by events emerging from the past. What's missing from this picture? Oh, not much—just the ever-present NOW. In creating a practical (as opposed to true) model of Time, based exclusively on that which can be utilized by science, physics, and mathematics, we've arbitrarily restricted the definition of Time by excluding the possibility of a unique NOW; again, a practical necessity has become a philosophical absolute.

The ultimate results of the scientifically restricted definition of Time, in which Time is simply the $t$ in various equations, are the paradoxes of Relativity; the fact that the entire course of science led to these paradoxes is deeply significant. Time as it is *experienced* does not slow down and speed up; Time as it is *experienced* is a moment common to all creation, regardless of perceptual non-simultaneity. But the restricted time of science, the $t$ in the equation, behaves differently. As an object approaches the speed of light, its "time" slows down relative to the "time" of a less swiftly moving object; in fact, because everything is in motion (i.e., because there's no objectively still frame of reference), everything is operating within a different "now" relative to everything else. Though the distinctions are minute, you and a person across the room are living within different time frames because, for example, one of you is a bit closer to the equator and thus traveling on Earth a bit more quickly; in fact, your feet are in a different time frame than your head because your feet are closer to the center of the Earth and thus moving more quickly around it. There is literally no such thing as strict simultaneity—the concept of the present moment, of the NOW, has been completely obliterated! That is, *if* we accept only the restricted definition of Time necessary for the operations of science, physics, and mathematics, a thoroughly artificial and arbitrary delimitation.

Let's look at this from a different perspective. Suppose you're on Earth and your friend is traveling in a spaceship so that her speed causes her to age only half as quickly as you do. We might depict it as in Figure 1.

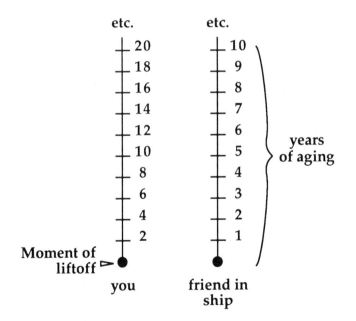

Figure 1

Isn't it possible, though, that in some way (too subtle for quantitative models to describe) you and your friend continue to live within the same "moments"? This is hard to depict in a diagram, but here's an approximation in Figure 2.

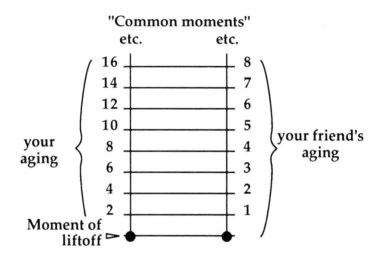

**Figure 2**

Here the horizontal lines are a few of the common "moments" you and your friend share.

According to Relativity, even in everyday reality everything exists within its own time frame, if only infinitesimally different from that of all others. Still, is it only a *perceptual illusion* that there exists a common moment shared by you and your immediate surroundings (such as the rest of your body)? According to the restricted definition of

Time invented for the benefit of science, the answer is yes; we don't need Augustine's (or Lao-tse's) philosophical concept that the present moment is an illusion—now physics has supposedly settled the question! There is no NOW!

Because the relativity of Time—the obliteration of the reality of NOW—is predicated on a restricted definition of Time in which NOW has already been rendered qualitatively neutral, I reject its absolute application, and I suggest that we are correct in our intuitive assumption that the definition of Time has been artificially restricted. There *is* such a thing as simultaneity, there *is* a shared moment, there *is* a NOW; in fact, in terms of reality as it's lived, *that's all there is*.

Time is *experienced* exclusively in the NOW but *observed* as a function of the material developments of the immediate and distant past. We've imposed our framework of observation upon our "objective" models of Time's function, meanwhile increasingly ignoring the attributes of Time as it is unceasingly experienced. This is rationalized as being a necessary deletion of subjectivity in our attempts to positively and objectively understand nature—first, because of the doctrine of reproducible results; second, because there are (presumably!) aeons in which there's no consciousness around to "experience" Time and the ever-present moment, so the experienced qualities of Time are not essential to its nature. While this is a perfectly valid model for a certain range of application of the scientific method, it has no *a priori* validity as *the* model for an understanding of Time; the fact that we experience the present is not proof that the present is exclusively an experiential projection, that the concept of NOW is strictly a perceptual illusion. Why not allow NOW to continue to exist and to have characteristics, regardless of whether any "consciousness" is around experiencing it? Why not, in fact, allow NOW to exist regardless of the existence of "space/time" (as we understand space/time up to but not including a trillionth of a second after the Big Bang)?

The point is that we *can* base our conceptual model of Time on the priority of the ever-present NOW. In this sense, not only do we come to "fill" the moment, *the moment meets and surrounds us.*

I propose that we work with a **Dialectical Model of Time**. On the one hand, there's the linear, empty, neutral characteristic of Time, which in the largest sense behaves the way Einstein suggested, but generally is understood as a conceptual frame of reference for material development; on the other hand is the function of the *moment*, the ever-present NOW. Relativity is the synthesis of the two; the former waxes to prominence in materialistic analysis, the latter in what is commonly termed "mystical" insight (though the list of parallels to this dichotomous paradigm is just about endless). I further suggest that astrologers—having years of experience watching astrology work—have a role to play in synthesizing this dialectic because astrology is the one and only "mystical" study whose components are objective, constant, determinable, measurable, and common.

To get a sense of what the function of the moment is, first understand what it is not: It's not just the present state of age-old causal chains and previously determined material interactions. That would make it simply a newly "filled" extension of the past, part of the same old linear model. It's also not a material "synergy" because in a reductivist sense that also derives exclusively from the linear model. If we are to wrench the reality of the moment out of the neutral time-line model, we must allow it to have a character *independent* of the status or sum of past moments—anything less negates the attempt at dialectic, resulting through appropriation and assimilation in merely a univalent extension of the linear model. The moment is either an independent, qualitative, indeterminate *actor* in material reality, already "full" regardless of which events have come to "fill" it, or else it is, quite literally, nothing at all—simply the *t* in equations that tells us our feet and shoulders exist in different time frames, our sense of shared moments and simultaneity is an illusion, and our lives are predetermined.

The outstanding attribute of the moment must, therefore, be that it is *content-independent*. Again, we're dealing with an analytic description of one half of a dialectic, so I emphasize that by content-independent I'm referring to the moment's ideal extreme nature; if this seems intellectually arbitrary, keep in mind that strict causality is itself an ideal extreme, albeit one disguised as a common-sense middle ground. To examine this, and to incorporate the spirit of the Free Will debate's various quasi-solutions, we need to take another look at the debate itself.

### Linearity and Content; The Moment and Form

A profound clue to the wrong turn taken by rationalism is provided by the intellectual context in which the Free Will debate first flourished, the period dominated by Democritus's Atomism. Clearly, the driving force behind the causalist assumption is that of *reductionism*, and this reductionism is overwhelmingly, exclusively *content-oriented*. The past is seen as a field of myriad, innumerable bits of content—causes, effects, materials—proceeding in linear time to the present, where the content merely continues to multiply and fragment in ever more complex causal chains. All "holistic" interaction is reducible to the conglomeration of past causes and materials, and any "new" attributes of a given whole are nothing more than materialistic results of its parts.

Now look at some of the attempts to find free will

within this materialistic determinism: the "principle causes" of the Stoics; the "active causes" of Chrysippus; the "intrinsic nature" of Carneades; the "volition" of Lucretius; the "compound-building swerve" and "complexly unified system" of Epicurus; the "transcendent Mind" of Descartes; the "monad's appetition" of Leibniz. All of these are attempts to discover a principle in which some sort of formal (form-al) interaction supersedes the determinism of reductive content analysis. With the exception of Epicurus's much-maligned "swerve" and "non-material properties," all are hoist by their own petard in that the causalist framework in which they're placed necessarily entails a reductivist contradiction of independent "forms." Philosophers have intuitively recognized *formal* principles as the only escape hatch from causal determinism; but these principles must be sought outside the realm of linear, content-oriented, material interaction, or else they're invariably subject to reductivist negation. Form is the realm of indeterminism, but only if it is understood as being *independent of*—as opposed to a function of—content, which is the realm of determinism.

In all of the above formal principles (principle cause, volition, monad, etc.) the function of form is imposed upon, or found within, already operative material complexes of integrated content. I suggest that we transfer this concept from the realm of *matter* to the realm of *Time*, specifically to the attributes of Time involved in the "moment" half of its dialectic—the NOW. Recognizing the priority of the omnipresent NOW, we can go ahead and allow this NOW to have its own character. Unfortunately, most attempts to reach this idea of the priority of the present tend to do themselves in; they take the valid notion of attributes inherent in the NOW and decide that since NOW is ever present these attributes are therefore "eternal." Pythagoras's "numbers as architects of reality," Plato's "ideal forms in heaven," Leibniz's "divine harmony," Jung's "archetypes as the fabric of collective unconscious"—all are reified versions of attributes perceived cumulatively in the present. The important point is to recognize the structural attributes inherent in the NOW, not to posit these principles as ontologically valorized prototypes. We can experience "Zeus" (Homer), the "5 principle" (Pythagoras), "ideal beauty" (Plato), or "the Old Man" (Jung), recognizing that they are functions of the NOW but not of the observed model of linear time, without stating that they are "beyond time" or "pre-existent." They are part of time and not beyond it, but they're also part of time as it's experienced in the present, Time as eternally indeterminate structural principle.While the materialists have denied the priority (or even existence) of NOW, more mystical types have unnecessarily extracted that priority and defined it as "time-less"; both give undeserved credence to the materialistic, observational, neutral timeline model.

We might imagine linear causality as the "horizontal" component of Time with each moment in the NOW as a new vertical component. Strict causality might be depicted as in Figure 3.

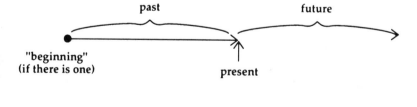

Figure 3

The function of the present moment might be seen as in Figure 4.

**present
moment**

**Figure 4**

The structural indeterminism of the present moment suggests the beginning of a *new* time line (which makes this model similar to Epicurus's), whose "first cause" is the present moment (see Figure 5).

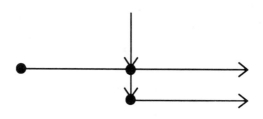

**Figure 5**

Here the top line is the continuation of old cause-effect chains; the vertical line, the structural indeterminism of a given moment; and the lower line, a new cause-effect time line.

However, this has happened at *every moment*; Figure 6 is a simplified diagram of four such moments.

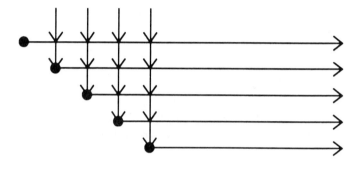

**Figure 6**

The complete extension of this picture would give us a diagram of Time shaped something like the state of Nevada. The point is to understand the *dialectic of Time*: old cause-effect sequences continue, but each moment introduces a new, *indeterminate* formal principle, which itself sets the pattern for a new *deterministic* time line; since this happens at every moment, there's a factor of *constant creation* at work. Finally, it's perhaps misleading to depict each new time line as separate from the others. A better (but unportrayable) model would show the overlapping and superimposition of each new time line.

In contemplating such a model, it's essential to remember that any attempt to attribute character to the NOW must conceive this character as being entirely content-independent. The moment is independent of all past and future moments and of all events and materials "occupying" it; it does not exist as "potential" before it arrives because it *does not exist at all* before it arrives; it is completely indeterminate. We are thus presented with an image of constant change on a level much more profound than that of prosaic material "constant change." In fact, if you look around you as you read this, it's probable that not much observable "change" is occurring—the walls (at least on the "macro" scale) are still where they used to be, and so on. But if each succeeding moment has its own character, experienced fleetingly but cumulatively in the NOW, the concept of constant change is brought to its most ideal, abstract level—a reality model not unlike that presented in the I Ching or Taoism.

So the moment is seen in two ways: as a neutral, empty extension of past causal sequences *and* as an indeterminate structural principle assuming the role of "first cause" in a *new* causal sequence, a sequence whose development is necessarily "programmed" by the structural qualities of the moment initiating it. (Am I going to say that the birth chart permanently "programs" a person? Far from it!) The problem now becomes: How do we describe the qualities of the moment? And how do we relate a moment in a given causal chain to the moment(s) which initiated that causal chain? In other words, how can content-independent, pure form be described?

To answer this, consider the word *four*. We can't conceive of "four" or any number in and of itself; we can think only of four *things*. We can intellectually comprehend the position of "four" in the sequence of the integers, but of itself "four" means nothing without some assumption of content. Numbers are purely formal principles. Now consider a four-part structure. Again, we need a content-specific illustration of this to conceive of it: a circle inscribed with a cross; winter, spring, summer, fall; Fire, Earth, Air, Water; new yang, old yang, new yin, old yin; etc.

However, we *can* extract a sense of the "nature of four" by considering the holistic interactions of each of a number of structures conceived as having four parts. This I'd like to call **The Principle of Metonymy**. Metonymy, simply understood, is a counterpart to metaphor; as I understand it, it also has the function of *extended* metaphor, particularly when the extended metaphor is well (or perfectly) conceived. Metonymy, as I'm defining it, relates to *parallelism of structure*. When we extract the (approximate) structural paradigm underlying a variety of paralleled structures, the components of this paradigm become what may be termed a "meta-language" for various real-content structures: a language of form.

As we perceive it, form is necessarily a projection of our own human intellectual limits, a function of our level of ability to understand holistic interaction; this fact, though, means only that our characterization of form is an *approximation*, not (as some might suggest) an illusion. A given system—say, the activities of the Federal Reserve relative to the U.S. economy—might in fact be a structure with a million parts (and some economic equations with exorbitant "degrees of freedom" certainly convey this impression), but as humans (writing economics textbooks or letters to the editor) we're incapable of conceiving million-part structures; the contents of the structure must be arranged and condensed so that our conceptual model is within our range of comprehension.

Once a satisfactory approximation has been developed, the number of dynamic parts which we've conceived the structure to have should provide a clue as to how it behaves in terms of its parallels to other systems similarly conceived. Ultimately, we should be able to approximate a language of form applicable (with due caution) to any holistic interaction or system. Any description of "the nature of the moment" would necessarily be in terms of such a "meta-language." So . . . is there any way to begin to sufficiently "define" the moment such that it may be understood structurally and thus be susceptible to description via a formal meta-language?

First, what uniquely defines a moment? Relative to this galaxy, I suppose it's defined by the changing state of the Doppler effect from various quasars or something along those lines, but in terms of common human experience here on Earth, *one and only one* context uniquely defines a moment: the positions of the Sun, Moon, and planets—plus, if we mean a moment relative to a given spot on Earth, the celestial sphere's orientation to the local horizon and meridian. There is no other commonly experienced (and distinctly measurable) frame of reference that uniquely defines a given moment. Only the most basic words in the language of astrology will do.

Given, then, that the referents of the language of astrology themselves form various holistic systems (the solar system, the harmonic divisions of a circle, the four-sector diurnal sphere, the rounded-to-twelve soli-lunar division of the ecliptic, etc.), the temporal relations of these systems can be seen as the only such relations uniquely and equivalently predicated on the selection of a given moment; they are thus the only candidates for a consistent, easily cross-referenced meta-language describing the formal characteristics of a moment and the relation(s) of one moment to any other(s). Any holistic system that is subject to linear, causal development may thus be described in its "initial" formal structure in terms of the language of astrology, and its developments may be described in terms of astrological developments relative to the astrological language formally describing its structural character. The tricky part is that *both* the holistically contingent meta-language of astrology *and* the basic structural nature of whatever's being described must be accurately understood, or else the metonymic parallel between the two will be even more faulty than this already approximate system of signification necessarily entails. Further, because the entire system of parallels is based upon the *uniqueness* of a given moment and a given structure (though the language describing both is necessarily generic), every case will be to some degree anomalous.

Sophistry, right? Wrong. The charge of sophistry implies that a given systematic approach is entirely fallacious and that every instance of its "accuracy" can be attributed to other factors; if this is not the case, then the charge of sophistry can apply only to the *misapplication* of a given system, not the the system itself. Michel and Francoise Gauquelin have proven, beyond any doubt, that at least some of the age-old metonymic parallels between astrology and personality are accurate (in this case, given a large sample, the parallel between certain planets' placements in the diurnal sphere at birth and the eventual profession and characteristics of the person born *if* the person's expression of these characteristics is so "pure" that s/he has become unusually successful in their professional application); every attempt to attribute this accurate parallelism to non-astrological factors has failed. While I don't have the space to give a detailed account of the Gauquelins' research (I refer the reader to Michel Gauquelin's book *Birthtimes: A Scientific Investigation of the Secrets of Astrology*), the point is that their findings (however limited) have utterly destroyed all *a priori* arguments against astrology. Now, if astrology or any of its techniques are to be deemed ridiculous, this must be on the basis of something other than the "common-sense" critique that "it just isn't possible—there's no conceivable causal mechanism to account for it."

One final note. Because the theory of Time upon which astrology is based is dialectical, it should be understood that this dialectic operates *throughout* a person's life; certain structural principles rooted in certain salient moments (above all, apparently, the nature of the moment of birth) will dominate in terms of deterministic development—but throughout life, if one is not stuck in a hellish environment, there are moments of greater or lesser "rebirth" as the individual (or whatever whole is developing) participates in the constant creation of the NOW. A swerve of the soul-atoms indeed!

The other chapters in this book will address a number of issues related to practical application techniques in Mundane Astrology; I have stressed philosophic considerations because I believe that without them the practical issues are on much shakier ground. However, as you've probably noticed, nothing in this chapter has had specific reference to *Mundane* Astrology. Because this astrology involves "national charts" and other tools not specifically connected with the moment of birth of human beings, it seems all the more far-fetched; even a skeptic might grant a little intuitive benefit of the doubt to the meaning of astrological patterns operative at someone's birth, but the notion of a nation (or treaty, organization, event, etc.) having a "birth chart" seems, at best, overcredulous. After all, the conception, gestation and birth of a person seems to some extent to be in the "hands of fate," whereas a non-biological entity can be planned for months or years and then officially mandated at whim; the former seems organic and natural, whereas the latter seems calculated and artificial.

I've attempted to show how the factor of "when" is relevant to *all* "creations." You can't escape the fact that everything, even that which is planned and executed by self-interested human beings, has to take place at some time; any truly significant "beginning," no matter how artificial, is thus as susceptible (within its own context) to formal and developmental description in the language of astrology as is even the most natural event.

## "National" or Foundational Charts

Every moment at every spot on Earth is a "chart"; clearly, though, a collection of charts for every half-second at every geographical coordinate would be too much information with too ambiguous a referent. Just as the most complex system must be organized and condensed in order for its dynamics to be comprehensible to the human mind, so too must the material developments occurring in time be related to specific or "radical" moments. A chart for a moment/place has meaning only if something has begun, reached a critical point, or ended at that moment/ place; the subject could be abstract or concrete, but in any case there must be a subject. Further, the subject should be conceivable as having a "life span"; the chart for the first shot of World War I certainly has relevance, but eventually other moments become more significant in the predominant structural developments of society. On the other hand, had the South seceded successfully, the chart of the first shot of the American Civil War would perhaps still be among the most salient structural referents for American society.

However, every moment is not only a "chart" but is also a point of development relative to an earlier "radical" moment. Remember, a moment is dialectical: 1) it's a holistic singularity—a "chart"—relevant as a new whole only if something has begun or reached a particularly salient crisis at that moment, in which case the moment becomes the structural point of reference for a new "time line"; and 2) it's another link in the developmental process emerging out of each previous "time line," in which case some method must be employed to translate its structural information in order to determine what (if any) relevance the moment has to which (if any) known time lines.

Before a nation exists, a variety of other sociological factors have contributed to its genesis. These factors are rooted in various moments, all of which have their own developmental relationship to the period of a nation's inception; this period may thus be seen as a combined function of the second half of the dialectic described in the above paragraph. But the dynamic interaction of these sociological developments (which, of course, are activities and experiences in the lives of men and women) eventually produces something new, something which itself becomes a structural referent; at this point, the moment ceases to be merely a developmental link in numerous older cause-effect sequences and becomes a truly "significant" holistic singularity. Many sociological complexes led to the existence of the USA, but at some point the USA itself became a sociological complex, and that point is more relevant to its own development than are the roots of its antecedents.

Whereas the moment of birth is the likeliest salient moment for the "beginning" of a life, and other moments (such as the time one's parents met, one's conception, etc.) are in some way subsumed by it, for a nation the "meeting of its parents," its "conception," and even its "midlife crisis" could themselves be relevant moments for particular structural realms of development. The USA, for example, was truly "reborn" at the time of the 13th, 14th , and 15th Amendments to the Constitution, the first year of the FDR Administration, and again at the implementation of the

National Security Act in 1947. Are we to regard these periods as truly radical holistic singularities, or just as especially significant phases of development out of more encompassing structural paradigms? That's a matter for debate and research.

But which moment or date marks the truest "beginning" of the USA? That of the Declaration of War on Great Britain? Of the Declaration of Independence? Of the Constitution? Of the Inauguration of George Washington? It's likely that *all* these moments are structurally foundational, significant, holistic singularities; one or another, however, may prove to be most applicable to the developments of the USA, and certainly at least one is especially radical. The point to understand, though, is that the USA, as well as any other nation, is rooted in one or more moments in time, is circumstantially associated with a specific example of the factor of "when," and is quite as significantly defined by this factor as would be anything else which has come to exist and which participates in developmental processes rooted in time. Nations may thus be described, both formally and developmentally, in the language of astrology.

## The Planets

As stated, the tricky part of astrology is understanding both the holistic paradigms of its component systems *and* the structural principles of whatever the astrological language is used to describe. Because astrology is a metalanguage, it has no meaning without context, but the content filling the structural functions described in astrology is *relativistic*. For example, all human beings have a Saturn return around the age of 29; but to be 29 years old in Mesopotamia in 40,000 B.C. means something different than to be 29 in Europe in 1400. Even relative to 1990, to be 29 in Sweden (where the average life span is almost 80 years) means something different than to be 29 in Afghanistan (where longevity averages 42 years). So although the structural function of Saturn is the same, the holistic context in which this function is defined is different, and hence *Saturn means something different in each case* because the content "filling" the Saturn function is dependent on different contexts.

"Saturn" of itself is a purely formal term. Saturn in a national chart, Saturn in one's birth chart, Saturn in a lunation chart, Saturn in the 20-year Jupiter/Saturn cycle—each of these Saturns has meaning, and each meaning is different, but all are related to the Saturn function in the astrological meta-language of form. One factor defining a given context is its *life span*. A chart of this week's Quarter Moon, theoretically at least, has relevance for only seven days; your last solar return has relevance for a year; the chart of the last Uranus/Pluto conjunction, for 140 years; and the chart for the crowning of William the Conqueror, for perhaps a millenium or more (at least in the context of English history). In each case, the content assumed by a given planet has greater or lesser depth; the interrelationship of content in this week's lunation is certainly much less profound than that in the chart of the Magna Carta.

Ideally, one should approach this problem with a combination of theory and empirical research; the Neptune-Pluto trine in the mid-1770s charts of the USA can be understood through both meditating upon the words "Neptune-Pluto trine" relative to one's theory of these words *and* noting transits, progressions, etc., to the positions of Neptune and Pluto in these charts, searching for patterns among the events accompanying these directions. At any rate, certainly Neptune and Pluto mean something much more complex in the USA's foundational chart than they do in, say, the chart of the Fillmore Administration.

## The Ecliptic and Transits

The only reasonable basis upon which to conceive a theory of a zodiac is that *where* a celestial event occurs may be significant; the signs are always in the same order and always the same size, so this is one holistic system that is especially abstract or artificial. However, as noted, the "birth" of anything involves a complex historical process and the interaction of a variety of already existent forms; it's with this in mind that ecliptically based analysis in Mundane Astrology should be approached.

A simple way to understand the Dialectic of Time is to realize that *all "charts" are also transits to past "charts."* This statement sums up (simplistically) both halves of the dialectic. Where do we draw the line in theoretical reduction of charts to their component status as transits to past charts? Even a mere thousand years in history represents several complete transformations in the structure of society, so any especially significant event is already overburdened with structural antecedents.

For example, on July 4, 1776, Uranus was in the 18th degree of sidereal Taurus (though I personally use tropical signs, I here refer to sidereal to avoid confusions resulting from long-term precession in the timing of transits); perhaps the 18th degree of sidereal Taurus was a significant point in any or all of the following charted moments: Columbus's landing in the New World; the invention of the printing press; the landing of the first American colony; the first day the Greeks experimented with republican democracy; or God knows what else. The point is, in the past several millenia there have probably been a thousand extremely relevant moments leading to the Declaration of Independence, all or some of which may have had this degree of the ecliptic emphasized. We don't know; what we *do* know is that 18° sidereal Taurus was occupied by Uranus on July 4, 1776, and to whatever extent that date is "radical" for the USA—and thus represents the culmination and crisis of many interweaving historical sequences—any future transit to that degree is a transit not only to the Declaration chart but also to all the relevant charts Uranus was itself transiting on July 4, 1776. Thus, whatever extent a national chart represents a truly meaningful moment, all transits to it are also transits to the factors the chart itself was transiting.

With this in mind, the ecliptic may be conceived as a "reservoir of history"—a reservoir of the innumerable formative moments and causal sequences that have preceded any given moment and, in particular, any given "new beginning."

## Planetary Cycles

The role of the ecliptic as the reservoir of history is especially significant in terms of planetary cycles; for example, every 20 years Jupiter and Saturn conjoin, but each time the conjunction occurs in a different *degree* (with its own harmonic relationships). This is one of several factors that give each Jupiter/Saturn cycle its own unique quality; each time it has a unique cycle relationship to innumerable past events which are still unfolding.

Of course, the Jupiter/Saturn cycle is not simply defined by its conjunction; all planetary cycles are ongoing. However, if we are to understand a cycle of any sort, we have to define some point of reference. Once some point in the cycle is conceived as its beginning (and therefore its end), the rest of the cycle may be understood *structurally* as an edifice built upon this point of reference; then, conceived as a structure, the cycle is susceptible to metonymic correspondence with other wholes similarly conceived. The most appropriate point of reference in a planetary cycle is the conjunction (though conceivably the opposition might also be an interesting foundation); applying numerical division (numbers being perhaps the most ideal language of form), the cycle is (most comprehensibly) divided by twos and threes: 2, 2×2, 2×2×2, 3, 2×3, 2× 2×3. Divisions not based on these numbers are generally close enough to one or another of them to be arranged and condensed within the simpler divisions, particularly regarding all but the three longest cycles since in terms of time the difference between, say, a Saturn/Neptune septile and a Saturn/Neptune semi-square is too little to be structurally comprehensible; given this, the semi-square is preferable to the septile as a structural principle because the former derives from simpler structures (the opposition and square). Again, the point is to conceive of a structure in order to derive a formal language.

In theory *and* practice, divisions based on two are the most concrete in terms of their meaning. Theoretically, they represent obvious divisions and turning points, midway positions that convey tension because they are no longer part of the past while not yet part of the future (so to speak); they imply concrete manifestation in the "tip of the iceberg" sense—in other words, suddenly visible phenomena hinting at much larger, older presences "under the surface." In practice, the second harmonic and its derivatives ("hard" aspects) are more tangible due to what may be termed "the calculus of society"—the cumulative effect of the developmental stages of all societal factors. Relative to the formal structures to which they're referred (which include all human beings, nations, contracts, organizations, still-unfolding events, etc.), these aspects reinforce almost all other aspects. Put simply, hard cyclic aspects tend much more frequently to involve "double-whammy" transits, or else a combination of ease and tension, but rarely an entirely flowing and easy dynamic.

Another way to understand planetary cycles (noting that the description above tends to refer to the "linear" half of the dialectic of time) involves the meaning of the word *moment*. I've emphasized the importance of the moment in defining a theory of astrology; however, I deliberately left undefined the scope of the word "moment." The moment is centered on the NOW, but conceivably there are billion-year moments, century moments, and nanosecond moments. Because translating the formal language of astrology is difficult enough without allowing this language to be dynamic in arrangements meant to describe initial form, we utilize "birth charts" (or lunations, returns, ingresses, etc.), each of which is understood as a particular, frozen description of a minute or second; further, except in the case of the Astro*Carto*Graphy map (which is truly the most revolutionary development in modern astrology with a language all its own), we pin these minutes or seconds down to a specific location.

However, since a structurally defining "moment" could cover any length of time, and also could have the entire planet as its location, the language of astrology includes long-term cycles, which are in truth an even more abstract language for moments of various lengths. The Jupiter/Saturn cycle is thus the vocabulary of 20-year-long "moments."

Briefly, a few basic points about planetary cycles should be registered: Only one-third of the various two-planet cycles take more than $2^{1}/_{2}$ years from conjunction to conjunction. Only six take more than 35 years. Only three take more than a century: Uranus/Pluto, which alternates between cycles of 115 and 140 years; Uranus/Neptune, about 171 years; and Neptune/Pluto, about 490 years. The latter cycle has bizarre characteristics, particularly the fact that certain angular phases last disproportionately long times; it's operating with a rhythm that may be too subtle for standard astrological analysis. Therefore, for long-term cyclic analysis, by far the most significant pairs are Uranus/Neptune and Uranus/Pluto.

## Research and Experimentation

It is my dogmatic bias that every astrologer should, however tentatively, define *a* philosophy of astrology; one's philosophy could be doubtful, ambiguous, controversial, malleable, incomplete, but, at any rate, one should have some framework within which the various elements and techniques in one's practice cohere more or less intelligibly. Not only is such a framework a profound aid to intuition and mnemonic association, it also provides a testing ground for the overwhelming number of techniques circulating within 20th-century astrology. The field is vast and it explodes more with each decade; without a tentative philosophical framework, there's no way to integrate any new ideas—and, of course, the new ideas should themselves contribute to the development of the philosophy that accepts or rejects them.

However, no philosophy of astrology is meaningful without reference to reality. For example, one could theorize about the Uranus/Pluto cycle, but look what actually *happened* at some recent eighth-harmonic phases in that cycle:

Conjunction (1851): followed several years of intense, widespread revolution, in which virtually every European nation was involved.

Opposition (1902): primary labor organizations formed in Russia; Lenin/Plekhanov split, later forming basis for Bolshevik/Menshevik rivalry.

Waning sesquiquadrate (1917): Russian Revolution.

Waning square (1932-33): Japan "begins" WWII by attacking Shanghai; Hitler becomes Chancellor of Germany; FDR elected U.S. President; first massive Stalinist purges.

Waning semi-square (1949): Chinese Revolution.

Conjunction (1965-66): Chinese Cultural [sic] Revolution.

Waxing semi-square (1986-87): *Perestroika* and *Glasnost* policies announced in USSR, considered the "most revolutionary period" in USSR since Stalin purges; first major democracy rallies in China, largest mass demonstrations since Cultural Revolution.

An unforgivably brief list, but surely we should *know* these dates and epochal events before theorizing about the nature of Uranus, Pluto, and the Uranus/Pluto cycle. In other words, research may proceed without theory or without any idea of what one might find. For example, I've examined the months in which the last 14 recessions began and ended in the USA (1920-present), looking at the tropical positions of Mars and Jupiter, the outer-planet aspects, and the ex-precessed lunar returns for the relevant months relative to the 11 a.m. 7/6/1775 USA chart; some of the consistencies I've found seem to have little connection to standard mundane theory.

Any such research experience provides challenging and expansive observations for one's own philosophy of Mundane Astrology. What's more, in order to research, say, recessions, one must study and comprehend macroeconomic structures. Studying Mundane Astrology enhances one's "mysticism" by deprogramming the rationalist brainwashing to which we're all subject, and studying Mundane Astrology enhances one's "materialism" by necessitating the study of history and economics (the primary components of the societal superstructure Mundane Astrology describes). And that is indeed a revolutionary dialectic.

## Judy Johns

Judy Johns is an internationally known astrologer whose field of expertise is Mundane Astrology—the study of this planet's people and their power structures and struggles.

She began her astrological studies in 1960 and by 1965 she had started her career as counselor, lecturer and teacher. She is very active in a number of astrological associations, having served as VP of Aquarius Workshops, Inc., as well as director of publications for *Aspects* magazine. She is currently Los Angeles coordinator for AFAN.

A popular and respected lecturer, Judy has spoken before many prestigious organizations including SWAC, ASSC, SDAS, NCGR in San Francisco, UAC '86 and, of course, Aquarius Workshops, Inc. Judy has taught and lectured at Immaculate Heart College in Los Angeles, CalState, Northridge, various Los Angeles area schools and professional organizations. She also contributes her services to local drug abuse programs for young people.

An accomplished author, she contributes the Mundane column for *Aspects* and has written for Llewellyn's "Astrological Guide" series. She is presently completing a book on political astrology soon to be published by ACS.

# THE INGRESS CHART

The Ingress chart was the oldest form of astrology used in ancient times. Mundane, or political, astrology was based on a long series of observations. The beginning of this astrological tool is lost in the mists of time. But we do know that it was used by Babylonians, Assyrians, Chaldeans, Greeks and Romans throughout history.

The Ingress chart was used to forecast the fate of kings, to warn of attacks from hostile nations and to predict the quality of the harvest of crops in the field. The ancient astrologers warned of wars, changes in governments, famines, plagues and the rise and fall of empires. These astrologers used simple means to foretell the future—the transits in the ever-changing sky. The destiny of the nation was based on the analysis of the effect of equinoxes, solstices, New and Full Moons, eclipses and planetary conjunctions.

Today's Mundane Astrology is rather similar to that of those early astrologers. The same set of observations is used in modern-day analysis to predict many of the same types of events. History tends to repeat itself because humans remain human. We still have terrible wars (although not too many kings these days), and we still need to predict the future of our food supplies. Civilizations continue to rise and fall, along with the political and economic conditions that set these changes into motion.

The Ingress chart is cast for the moment the Sun enters 0 degrees of each Cardinal sign. The first chart of the year is cast at the beginning of the astrological new year on or about March 21, the Spring Equinox, when the Sun enters Aries. The Summer Solstice chart delineates when the Sun enters Cancer, and the Sun enters Libra at the Autumn Equinox. The last Ingress chart depicts when the Sun enters Capricorn, the Winter Solstice.

An Ingress chart is set up for the capital city of any nation you would like to explore. Ephemerides give the date and time of the Sun's entrance into each Cardinal sign. The chart is cast using the longitude and latitude of the capital or any city you wish. If you are calculating the chart by hand rather than by computer and the location is in South Latitude, remember to add 12 hours to the sidereal time and reverse the house cusps.

The planetary pattern will remain the same for the entire world because the chart is cast for a specific moment in time. However, because of the differences in longitude and latitude of the various world capitals, the house positions will alter. Mars may be found rising in one capital and may be conjunct the Midheaven in another. A T-square may be in the 2nd-5th-8th Houses of the chart in one country and in the 1st-4th-7th in another.

I cast all four quarters of a year at a time and copy them on the same page in order to have an overview of the entire year. The charts interlock as one event leads to another and so on. I think you get a better feel of the flow of the year this way. Your judgment of the chart patterns is usually more conclusive when you are able to look at the whole orange rather than just one of its quarters.

*The Ingress chart is my primary tool* for political astrology. The Ingress occurs at a specific and unarguable time. The second tool for me is the *natal chart of the nation*. In most cases, the problem with the natal charts, however, is that the exact time of the foundation of the nation is generally unknown, and in many cases even the date is questionable. The third chart I work with is the *chart of the leader of the country*. The old saying "As goes the King goes the country" is still quite applicable. If an accurately timed chart is not available, I use a solar equilibrium chart, placing the Sun on the Ascendant as if it were a sunrise birth. If a major political event is about to occur, it will echo from the Ingress chart through the national chart and will also be shown by stress aspects in the chart of the leader.

Mundane, or political, astrology is just as demanding as humanistic astrology. It requires practice, an interest in history and/or a passion for current events. Just like any other astrological study, the art of interpretation comes from setting up multitudes of charts and reading them, again and again, against the history books or the happenings in today's news.

In spite of the importance of the mundane field, there are only a handful of books on the subject although books on personal horoscopes run into hundreds of volumes. This is probably quite a normal consequence of every individual's love of self. Every person is interested in his/her own personal destiny, opportunities and happiness. Yet in these days when the world is attempting to shake off the remnants of a Stone Age individualism in preparation for New Age cooperation, it is this non-self, the circumstances around us, that is more important than the self. Mundane Astrology defines the major cyclic trends that influence all our lives and applies these trends to the individual. When asked about the great stock market crash of 1929, one fellow said, "That didn't affect me; I don't have no stocks." The other fellow replied, "But, the stock market crash is the reason why you are standing in this bread line."

A complete how-to-do-it is beyond the scope of a chapter, but here are a few important steps to follow.

## The Planets in Brief

**The Sun** rules the head of the nation and the government.

**The Moon** rules the masses, crops, popular opinion.

**Mercury** rules trade, the media, commerce, advertising.

**Venus** rules art, fashion, recreation.

**Mars** rules the armed forces, war, violence, machinery.

**Jupiter** rules banking, courts, judges, churches, the clergy.

**Saturn** rules loss, depression, labor, farmlands, big business.

**Uranus** rules change, disruption, strikes, radio, air travel.

**Neptune** rules minorities, the oppressed, hospitals, fraud, oil.

**Pluto** rules atomic energy, fanaticism, crime, dictatorships.

## The Houses in Brief

**1st House:** General conditions of prosperity and health of the people of the nation.

**2nd House:** Currency and its circulation, the government treasury, taxation, and the national income.

**3rd House:** Transportation, communication, trade relations with adjacent countries.

**4th House:** Real estate, crops, mining, the weather, the party out of power.

**5th House:** The Senate, ambassadors, amusement and entertainment, children, speculative activity.

**6th House:** Public health, civil service, police and armed forces, labor conditions.

**7th House:** International relations, treaties, threats of war, foreign trade.

**8th House:** Foreign debt, financial results of treaties, the cabinet of the government, the death rate.

**9th House:** The courts, legal and religious developments, foreign trade and shipping, insurance.

**10th House:** The president or ruler, the party in power, influential business leaders.

**11th House:** The Congress, legislation affecting business and government, international friendships.

**12th House:** Hospitals, jails, secrets of the country, conditions of exile, terrorism, covert aggression.

Once you have set up the Ingress chart for a nation you are interested in, check to see if there is a *major conjunction* operating. The rare conjunctions of the outer planets have long-range political and sociological implications. They are in place long enough to set into motion major events. Note which house they fall into and what houses they rule. For example, in 1989 Saturn conjoined Neptune in Capricorn. This conjunction fell in the 7th House for Washington, D.C., for three of the four quarters of the year, highlighting international friendships, war and foreign affairs. In the Libra Ingress, the combination fell in the 8th House, accentuating financial relations with others. All major conjunction degrees remain sensitive to transits, New and Full Moons and eclipses until the next conjunction of the same planetary pair.

Next, *determine the aspect patterns* within the Ingress chart, noting the houses that these planets rule. Planets placed at the angles are the strongest and usually produce events that occur quickly and are easily seen. Planets in Fixed houses are resistant to change, providing rigid conflicts if indicated by the aspects. Planets in Mutable houses usually foretell rumors or some behind-the-scenes plan not yet ready to surface.

Hard series aspects are the most important in the Ingress chart. Their order of importance is: conjunction, square, opposition, quincunx. Hard aspects usually produce newsworthy events. The soft aspects, trine and sextile, aid in negotiation and imply the use of reason. Important political activity is a product of stress aspects.

Pay special attention to the *rulers of the Ascendant and the Midheaven*. The 1st House governs conditions of the general public, and the 10th determines the leadership of the country and its status before the world. Aspects to the Ascendant generally bring events that impact nearly all of John Q. Public, while the effects of aspects to the Midheaven and the 10th House can be expanded to include influential business leaders and popular public figures.

Make a list of the dates when *transiting Mars* makes new aspects during the three-month duration of the Ingress chart; transit Mars frequently travels through as many as three different houses. Mars is like a fuse, sparking and setting off activity. A very reliable timer, if Mars triggers the chart, you can be sure you will hear about it on the 6 o'clock news.

The *New and Full Moon positions* will also trigger the Ingress chart. List when they occur, in which house, and what aspects are formed. A chart cast for the moment of the New and/or Full Moon for the capital will give you the political picture for a two-week period. Take the time to do them when a current crisis is brewing. The Ingress chart will give the "Big Picture," but sometimes it is fun to peek behind the curtains. The New Moons tend to give birth to political events; the Full Moons tend to launch them into action.

If the New/Full Moons happen to be eclipses, note where they fall in the natal chart of the country as well as the chart of the leader. The influence of these eclipse charts last for a longer period of time than the lunation charts. In the case of a Total Solar Eclipse, the influence can be sensitive for years. The Lunar Eclipse can operate for months. The effect of an eclipse is always the strongest for an area where the eclipse is visible.

Finally, list the *stations of the planets*, either direct or retrograde, during the Ingress. Major political events tend to change direction during these stations. Within a few days of these retrograde/direct periods, significant action is often noted. Treaties or agreements made prior to a change in direction by one of the planets usually have to be rewritten, reworked or altered in some way. In extreme cases, I have seen the course of events turn 180 degrees.

## The 1941 Libra Ingress

History is always a good teacher because hindsight is always 20-20. The period of World War II has been a passion of mine for many years. Perhaps a look at one of the events of the war will show an example of how the Ingress chart works. This is an astrological study of Pearl Harbor, the events that led up to the attack, and the eventual outcome of these events.

A complete study would include the entire year. But in this case, I will be using the Libra Ingress chart alone for both the United States and Japan. Just as one swallow does not make a summer, one quarter of the year does not tell the whole story. The year 1941 was so rich with history it is difficult to isolate one event. Please remember that simultaneously both of these countries had complicated dealings with other nations as well as with each other. For the sake of simplicity, this delineation tries to isolate events that pertain to "The Day of Infamy."

The Japanese air strike at the United States Pacific Fleet at Pearl Harbor on the Sunday morning of December

7, 1941 combined the wars in Europe and Asia into one gigantic global struggle. Ever since 1939, the United States had moved closer and closer to war without actually getting involved in it.

Let's look back into history to the Libra Ingress charts of 1941. (All charts are calculated using Koch houses.) Europe was already in the throes of a terrible war. The United States had not yet joined the conflict overseas but was embroiled in a trade dispute with Japan. As Japan became more overtly expansionistic, the United States became more overtly disapproving. The Japanese had invaded China in 1937, but were now casting an eye at Southeast Asia and the East Indies.

Early in 1940, the 1911 trade treaty between the United States and Japan had lapsed. The American government refused to renew it and said that the U.S. would only trade with Japan on a day-to-day basis. The next month both sides took what was for each a final stand.

Japan's ambassador to Washington, tall, one-eyed Admiral Nomura, called on President Roosevelt to discuss the "thorough settlement" of Japan's differences with the U.S. He proposed that the U.S. unfreeze Japanese assets ($131,000,000), re-open trade, and then they'd divide the East Indies between them. U.S. Secretary of State Cordell Hull countered with the suggestion the Japanese get out of China and Indochina and recognize the Nationalist Chinese government. Only then would the U.S. sign a trade agreement. For all practical purposes, negotiations had collapsed by late November.

The major conjunction of Saturn/Uranus was approaching completion in late degrees of Taurus in September of 1941. Crisis is the usual outcome of this planetary combination. Saturn is generally an index of misfortune, and when coupled with Uranus, their energies sharply conflict. This conjunction fell in the 9th House for Washington, D.C., indicating problems with foreign trade or international diplomacy.

The Saturn/Uranus conjunction is found in the 1st House for Tokyo, influencing the general conditions of prosperity and wealth for the Japanese people, who were heavily dependent on American industrial imports. The New Moon in November opposed this Saturn/Uranus conjunction. Negotiations halted, the Japanese began intense preparations for the air strike on Pearl Harbor.

Mercury opposed Mars in the Libra Ingress chart. This aspect can bring conflicts, both verbal (Mercury) and physical (Mars). In Washington the opposition was from the 1st House to the 7th. An angular Mars can bring threats, if not the actual outbreak, of war.

In the Tokyo Ingress, the Mercury/Mars opposition fell on the 6th/12th House axis. The 6th House relates to the use of military force, and the 12th speaks of covert action or terroristic activity. Washington was talking tough, and Tokyo was planning Pearl Harbor.

In the Washington Ingress, Mars ruled the 8th House, and Mercury, the Ascendant and the Midheaven. This accounts for the heavy loss of life at Pearl Harbor. The ruler of the 8th in the 7th opposed to the ruler of both angles reflects the danger of open warfare with heavy casualties. Because Mercury ruled both the Ascendant and the Midheaven, the country reacted quickly. When the people of a nation are impacted, the Ascendant of an Ingress chart is activated. The Midheaven reflects the nation's standing before the world.

The Sun in the Ingress represents the executive head of the nation. In September of 1941 the Sun was conjunct Neptune. It was a difficult year for all heads of state around the world. Because of the slow motion of Neptune, each Ingress chart had the Sun opposed, square, conjunct and square again to Neptune.

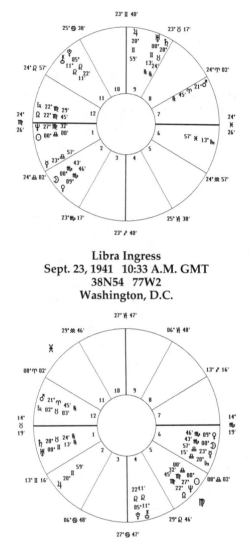

**Libra Ingress**
**Sept. 23, 1941   10:33 A.M. GMT**
**38N54   77W2**
**Washington, D.C.**

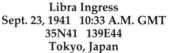

**Libra Ingress**
**Sept. 23, 1941   10:33 A.M. GMT**
**35N41   139E44**
**Tokyo, Japan**

The Sun/Neptune conjunction for Washington was in the 1st House. So far Roosevelt had kept the American people directly out of the conflict. But the Sun was ruler of the 12th House and Neptune was the ruler of the 7th. This combination indicates covert activity planned by a foreign power that could involve the people of the United States. (Saturn/Uranus in Japan's 1st House.)

This Sun/Neptune conjunction in the Tokyo Ingress was found in the 5th House, and the Sun was ruler of the 5th. Neptune-ruled Pisces was intercepted in the 11th. The 5th House rules ambassadors and diplomats. Japan's diplomatic activity was intended to dramatically change Washington's policies or rules.

Venus, the ruler of the Tokyo Ingress Ascendant, opposed the Ascendant and squared Pluto in the 4th House. The financial implications of frozen assets and Washington's stubborn refusal to negotiate underscored the possibility of the use of force as an option. Venus is usually a soft influence in an Ingress, but it also relates to money supply and currency—in this case, cold hard cash!

The Ingress Moon at 0 degrees of Scorpio was quincunx Saturn/Uranus from Washington's 2nd House to the 9th House and square Pluto in the 11th. The Moon is an index of the needs of the general public, the 2nd House is the economy, and the 9th rules foreign involvement.

For Washington, the Moon ruled the 11th House, Saturn was ruler of the 5th House, and Uranus ruled the 6th House; Pluto was ruler of the 3rd House. Whew! These rulerships indicated some legislature (11th) in connection with the economy (2nd) involving foreign trade policy (9th). The economic sanctions were a power play message (Pluto/3rd) intended to curb Japanese expansionism.

The Ingress Moon at 0° Scorpio was quincunx the Saturn/Uranus conjunction from Tokyo's 6th House to the 1st and square Pluto in the 4th House. The Moon was the ruler of the 4th, Saturn ruled the Midheaven, Uranus ruled the 11th, and Pluto, the 7th. This promised the use of the military (6th) to force an issue (Saturn/Uranus) relating to nationalism (4th) directed toward a foreign power (7th) to gain an advantage for the population.

In September of 1941 Japan reaffirmed her relations with Germany and Italy. The three nations signed a pact which pledged full support should any one of the three become involved with a country not yet at war. The Germans thought that it applied to Russia; the Japanese thought it applied to the United States. Pluto ruled the 7th House of warlike conditions, and the Moon, ruler of the 3rd House (governing treaties), squared Pluto.

Jupiter was conjunct the Midheaven in the Ingress chart for Washington. The U.S. position was based on moralistic issues. Washington viewed the Chinese as the "good guys" and the Japanese as the "bad guys." The square of Jupiter from the 9th/MC to Neptune in the 1st tends to indicate distortion in such a viewpoint. Clearly, leaders in Washington never imagined the possibility of Japanese aggression.

Jupiter in Japan's Ingress chart was in the 2nd House square to Neptune in the 5th House, giving Japan confidence. Great expectation is a quality associated with Jupiter. The Japanese military strategists said they had all the oil (Neptune) they needed. These strategic leaders thought they could overrun the Pacific region in no less than six months.

Neptune was conjunct the United States' Ingress Ascendant, and the Mars quincunx from the 7th House (opposing Mercury) threatened a secret attack from a foreign power. In the Tokyo Ingress, Mars was in the 12th House quincunx Neptune in the 5th House (indicating the snarl in diplomacy) and opposing Mercury in the 6th. Neptune rules the Navy as well as the sea, and Pearl Harbor was the home base of the entire Pacific Fleet.

Mercury stationed retrograde on October 15 at 12 Scorpio 09 in the 2nd House for Washington. The U.S. lost the illusion that it was not engaged in a shooting war. The *U.S.S. Kearny,* a crack destroyer barely a year in service, was torpedoed by a German U-Boat off the coast of Iceland. On October 17, 1941 the first U.S. casualty list of World War II was posted. Eleven crewmen were killed; ten were injured.

In Japan, on October 5, Lieutenant Yoshio Shiga and about 100 other pilots were informed of the secret plan to attack Pearl Harbor and were sworn to secrecy. These pilots began practicing the low, short torpedo runs that needed to be mastered. Mercury was retrograde in the Tokyo Ingress chart, 6th House ruling the military.

Jupiter turned retrograde on October 10 at 21 Gemini 26 sextile Mars in the U.S. Ingress chart. This seemed to activate hostile intentions (Mars) from one or more foreign powers (9th). The Japanese had been plotting the possibility of such a strike force as early as August, but now these plans were becoming a reality.

In October, as the New Moon at 26 Libra 48 squared the Tokyo Ingress chart Midheaven, General Hideki Tojo replaced Prince Konoye as Prime Minister of Japan. This was an indication that Japan was firmly committed to its policy of aggression. (Suguru Suzuki, the youngest lieutenant commander in Japanese military service, was in Honolulu, taking many pictures of Pearl Harbor from a private plane that served sightseers. It was easy; anybody could do it.) This New Moon was also conjunct Mercury and opposed to Mars, and the rattling of sabers could be heard in many nations, for the aspects formed at Ingress are global. They are specific to location by house position.

In Washington, the Libra New Moon fell in the 2nd House, conjunct 1st House Mercury and opposed to 7th

House Mars. Further economic sanctions were implemented to increase pressure. Meanwhile, Tokyo was installing air raid shelters in the Imperial Palace.

The November 4 Full Moon was in the 12th House for Tokyo and conjunct the Ascendant, triggering the ASC/ Venus/Pluto T-square. The United States had hit a sore spot, strangling Japanese trade with the U.S. In Washington, the Full Moon fell in the 8th House, making a T-square by opposing Venus in the 2nd, both square Pluto in the 11th. The use of economic leverage (8th House) would not quite work out the way it had been planned.

The mid-November New Moon at 26 Scorpio 16 caused the formation of a Yod in the Ingress charts. In Washington, the 3rd House New Moon quincunxed Mars in the 7th and Jupiter at the Midheaven. This triggered the Saturn/Uranus conjunction by opposition, and negotiations had completely broken down. The lines of communication were not open as these two nations truly did not speak the same language, in more ways than one.

In the Tokyo Ingress, the New Moon formed the Yod from the 7th quincunx the 12th House Mars and the 2nd House Jupiter. The 7th House rules active aggression, the 12th, covert activity, and the 2nd, the economy. The New Moon formed an opposition to the 1st House Saturn/ Uranus. These triggers to the major conjunction were, in part, what helped propel the two nations headlong into conflict.

Mercury turned direct on November 4 at 26 Libra 22, squaring the Tokyo Ingress MC. Two days later, Pluto stationed retrograde. By now things were moving pretty fast in Tokyo. November 3 brought Admiral Nagano's final blessing to the plan, on November 5 the official Top Secret Order was received, and on November 7 Admiral Nagumo was officially named Commander of the Pearl Harbor Striking Force.

Mars turned direct on November 10 at 11 Aries 04. All this time Mars was transiting the Tokyo Ingress 12th House and transiting Washington's 7th House. A few more Japanese people were let in on the secret as Admiral Nagumo proceeded. Supply officer Shin-Ichi Shimizu piled winter gear onto the freighter *Hoko Maru* about November 15 and chugged off for Tankan Bay—the rendezvous point for the strike force. The Admiral followed two days later on his flagship, the carrier *Akagi*. Soon all 32 ships were waiting in place, packed together in the cold, gray harbor in the Kuriles. They received word by radio to attack on December 2. The message read "Climb Mount Niitaka," the code to proceed with the offensive.

On December 3, the Full Moon at 11 Gemini 19 fell across the 9th/3rd axis of the Washington Ingress. The Americans knew something was going to happen. They had broken several of the Japanese codes and were aware that Admiral Nomura in Washington had been instructed to burn his code books (Mercury/Mars) and present a "note" to the U.S. government at precisely 1:00 p.m. on the 7th. They even knew what the message contained, as well as the fact that it was 7:30 a.m. in Hawaii. But this information was not especially noted as significant. The December Full Moon fell across the 1st/7th House axis of the Tokyo Ingress. The Japanese code "Tora! Tora! Tora!" signaled at 7:53 a.m. had written a new chapter in history, and catapulted the U.S. into World War II.

## The Natal Charts of the U.S. and Japan

Pursuing our journey through history, let us direct our attention to the natal charts of the United States and Japan. There are many ideas as to the "correct" chart of the U.S. This is the one I have chosen. The natal chart of Japan for this period in history is drawn for the first constitution of the country. Feel free to apply these same principles to the charts that you believe to be the "correct" ones.

When you place the planets of the Ingress chart around the chart of the nation, it is like reading transits to a natal chart. Remember, the chart of the nation, if available, is the second tool in prediction. If an event is of sufficient importance, it will echo through the natal chart of the country and the country's leader.

In the United States' natal chart, the conjunction of Saturn/Uranus was in the 12th House of covert activity trine natal Pluto in the 9th of foreign involvement. At first glance, it doesn't seem to be so malefic. But what does Pluto do in the chart? The U.S. natal Pluto rules the 6th House of the military, is found in the 9th (we frequently use our military in foreign lands), and opposes Mercury in the 3rd. Pluto/Mercury across the 3rd/9th axis can indicate the use of verbal force or powerful negotiations with regard to foreign powers. The 3rd/9th axis also governs import/export conditions, and trade wars are not new to the United States.

The major conjunction of Saturn/Uranus occurs with 45-year regularity. Since the combination is rare, the situations connected with it are usually significant. The 12th House is associated with behind-the-scenes activity. In 1941, the conjunction brought the secret attack that meant the United States could not remain on the sidelines of war and was forced to enter the conflict.

In Japan's natal chart, the Saturn/Uranus combination fell on the 2nd House cusp conjunct natal Pluto and natal Neptune. Of course, economic survival was the whole point of the argument. In the days before 1853, when Admiral Perry forcibly awoke Japan from her long sleep of isolation, she was self-supporting. In the process of Westernization, Japan rapidly became industrialized, and just as swiftly became aware of her basic lack of economic resources. Ingress Saturn/Uranus squared natal

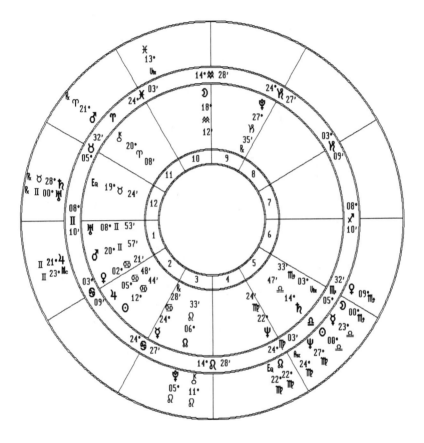

United States of America
July 4, 1776   2:17 A.M. LMT
39N57   75W10
Philadelphia, PA
Outer Ring—Libra Ingress of Sept. 23, 1941

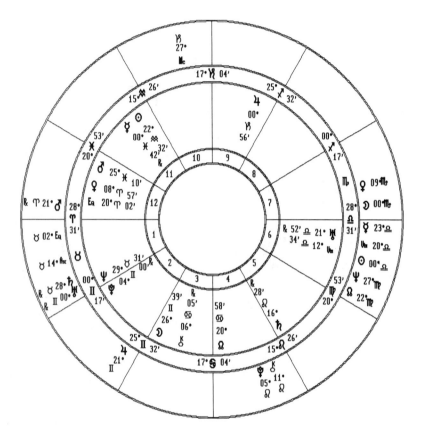

**First Constitution**
**Feb. 11, 1889   10:30 A.M. LMT**
**35N41   139E44**
**Tokyo, Japan**
**Outer Ring—Libra Ingress of Sept. 23, 1941**

Mercury in the 11th and quincunxed Jupiter in the 9th House. The overwhelming line-up of malefics to Mercury quelled the use of reason and certainly clouded the judgment (Jupiter) of the leadership.

In the U.S. chart, Ingress Mars squared natal Mercury and quincunxed 4th House Neptune. This can suggest violence (Mars) over negotiations (Mercury) related to unusual conditions (Neptune) over native soil (4th House). U.S. natal Neptune is square to natal Mars. This trigger of transit Mars not only vibrates the natal Mercury/Pluto opposition but also sets the Mars square Neptune into motion. The Japanese government goaded the United States into action by the attack on Pearl Harbor. The overriding emotion that surged through the nation was cold fury. In 1941, Americans expected an enemy to announce its intentions before it fought. Japan's move, made while her envoys were negotiating in Washington, outraged the American public.

When military men (Mars in the 1st) were killed in the attack on U.S. soil (Neptune in the 4th), massive waves of patriotism swept the general populace. For good measure, Ingress Jupiter, ruler of the 7th (war), was also conjunct natal Mars, square natal Neptune. It is difficult to avoid all inequities in the democratic process in time of war, but the United States had little excuse for the treatment of its citizens of Japanese ancestry. President Roosevelt, on the urging of the War department (Mars), authorized moving 112,000 Japanese Americans to relocation camps. These centers were, in fact, prison camps complete with barbed wire and armed guards (Neptune in the 4th).

For Japan, Ingress Jupiter at 21° Gemini in the 2nd House squared natal Mars in the 12th. Military expansion in a covert manner may have seemed a likely outlet for the frustration of stalled negotiations. Japan now considered that she was faced with either war or economic ruin. Mars in the Japanese natal chart squares the Moon in the 3rd and quincunxes Uranus in the 6th House. The use of aggression by this global power strongly affected masses of population (Moon). The Moon trine the Sun indicates the willingness of the nation to follow the lead of the current administration (Emperor Hirohito) without question.

Jupiter can tend to the expression of religious fanaticism. Ingress Jupiter at 21° Gemini square natal Mars (quincunx natal Uranus and square the Moon) may indicate the suicide attacks which were common among the Japanese warriors. This East/West dichotomy in thinking was an unusual factor in the ensuing battles. The fact that the Japanese solider was so willing to die made him a formidable adversary. This is backed up in the Yod formed by Ingress Pluto to natal Mercury and Jupiter. Military honor was tied to loss of face for the Samurai-like soldier (Mercury, ruler of the 2nd House of self worth, the 3rd House of communication, and the 6th House of the military).

When the Midheaven is part of the pattern, the standing and honor of the nation is involved. The Midheaven of the Washington Ingress at 23° Gemini also triggered natal Mars square Neptune. The announcement of war was swift. On December 8, 1941 at 4:10 p.m., President Roosevelt announced that "December 7th is a date that will live in infamy." The Senate voted 82-0 for declaring war. FDR took only six minutes to inform an astonished America of the attack. After 22 years and 25 days of peace, the United States was at war.

The Ingress MC at 27° Capricorn fell in the 10th House for Tokyo, square the natal 6th House Uranus. The world would be shocked by the military advances of the tiny island nation. In the short term, Japan enjoyed certain advantages. Although she was taking on the world's two greatest maritime and industrial powers (Britain and the U.S.), their homelands were virtually beyond her reach, but many of their possessions were extremely vulnerable. Japan's early successes were due in large part to her superiority at sea and in the air.

When the Ascendant is part of the Ingress pattern, all of the general population is affected. For Washington, the Ingress Ascendant at 24° Virgo conjuncted natal Neptune in the 4th on the 5th House cusp, which is square Mars. In the U.S., droves of men lined up to volunteer to go to war. In one case, a man undergoing a medical examination prior to enlistment was refused duty. Asked to take his clothes off during the exam, doctors determined that he was wearing a wooden leg!

In Japan's natal chart, the Ingress Ascendant at 14° Taurus squared Saturn from the 1st House to the 5th. To a nation dependent on importation of basic goods, the economic sanctions placed on the country were intolerable. By the spring of 1941, American embargoes had cut imports of gasoline, copper, scrap iron and other strategic commodities. Peaceful negotiations had failed through regular diplomatic means, forcing alternative solutions.

Ingress Node and Neptune quincunx the natal Sun from the 6th may speak of an Emperor bowing to the demands of his military council. The square to the natal Moon highlighted the extreme needs of the populace that were not being met, thus the use of war as an option. At the same time, Node/Neptune was quincunx the Japanese Ascendant. Decisions were being made that would ultimately alter the entire nation.

The Ingress Sun square 9th House Jupiter points to the overly optimistic feeling among military leaders that this ploy (the attack on Pearl Harbor) would succeed.

In the U.S. natal chart, Ingress Pluto conjoined the natal North Node in the 3rd House. Great masses of lives were about to be embroiled in the lengthy conflict, during which thousands would die. This North Node sextiles Uranus in the U.S. chart. An interesting fact about the attack was that the Japanese air strike neither damaged nor sank a single carrier because they were out on exercises at the time of the air raid. It was to be these carriers, not the familiar battleships, that would be vital to war in the Pacific. Deprived of their battleships, Americans, out of necessity, fought a new kind of war.

In the U.S. chart, the Ingress North Node at 22° Virgo conjunct natal Neptune seems to be an indication of the ease of the attack. The U.S. military personnel had no warning of the raid that would change the course of history. Outraged at this lack of warning, President Roosevelt removed the commanders of the Army, Navy and the Air Force in Hawaii on December 17, and named U.S. Admiral Chester Nimitz commander of the Pacific Fleet.

In the U.S. chart, Ingress Mercury at 23° Libra in the 5th (diplomatic) House square natal Mercury, which opposes Pluto, hauntingly points to the snafu in negotiations that played so large a part in the events that would follow.

Ingress Moon in the 5th square natal Pluto in the 9th (opposing Mercury in the 3rd) indicates the sacrifices wives and mothers made in the service of their country during this stressful period. The war would alter the family unit in unimaginable ways. Ingress Venus quincunxed the natal Ascendant and Uranus. Because of the ravages of the war, many impending marriages were delayed, canceled or destroyed by the events that would follow. Women began work in factories, doing the jobs left behind by men now at war.

In Japan's natal chart, the Ingress Moon in the 7th House of war is almost redundant; the fact that it quincunxed the Neptune/Pluto conjunction (which quincunxes Jupiter in the 9th) underscores the commitment of the public to the wishes of the Emperor, "The Son of Heaven." He was also their God, which was the accepted belief at the time. During this period of history, no Japanese commoner had even seen the face of the Emperor as it was considered bad form to do so.

### Franklin Delano Roosevelt

The next chart to examine is the natal horoscope of the leader of the country. Franklin Delano Roosevelt was starting an unprecedented third term in the White House. He began to lead the U.S. away from its traditional isolationism and to align the nation more and more on the side of Great Britain and Russia in the war against Germany.

In President Roosevelt's chart, the Ingress Saturn/Uranus combination fell in the 9th House conjunct his natal Pluto, which in turn squares his natal Mercury. International events requiring great statesmanship would be thrown upon his shoulders. We can be sure he gave these events much thought. Engaged in a war of nerves, he could not order an attack on Germany without the declaration of war passing the Senate. He was also well aware that such an attack might bring Japan into the conflict.

Ingress Jupiter and Midheaven fell on his MC, square his natal Ascendant. The future of the nation was suddenly thrust into his hands, and there was no choice. Both the Ingress Jupiter and Midheaven triggered his 10th House natal Mars, forcing him into military retaliation.

Ingress Pluto in his 11th House formed a T-square with his natal Saturn/Venus square. Well aware of the consequences, his only choice was to declare war and enter the U.S. into the global conflict. Notice how the angles of the Ingress chart echo his own. This definitely ties the leader to the events of this quarter of the year and underscores the nation and the leader's role in global events.

Not only does the Ingress MC/Jupiter trigger his

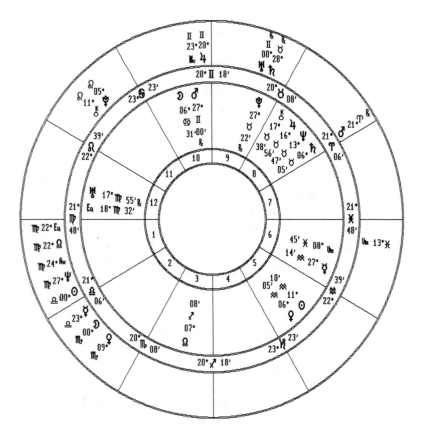

Franklin Delano Roosevelt
Jan. 30, 1882   8:37 P.M. LMT
42N42   83W55
Hyde Park, NY
Outer Ring—Libra Ingress of Sept. 23, 1941

Mars (use of force or military) but so does the Ingress Node/ASC/Neptune by their square to natal Mars. I am fascinated by the synchronicity of world events and the people who live in the times of these events.

Venus is usually a soft influence in the chart, but in this case it sets up a Grand Cross working in tandem with Ingress Pluto. The 2nd, 5th, 8th and 11th Houses are drawn into rigid conflict with heavy consequences. It was clearly a very difficult time for FDR.

Ingress Mars in the natal 8th House quincunxed his Ascendant, forming a Yod involving natal Mercury in the 6th. This Yod dumps out in the 7th, a Neptune-ruled house. This forced him to respond to a hostile, covert attack with a declaration of war.

### Emperor Hirohito

Hirohito, the Imperial Son of Heaven, was a shy and ineffectual-looking man. He was more interested in marine biology than in politics and war. The Emperor's position in the constitution was not powerful. He presided over all cabinet meetings but, according to tradition, never joined in the discussions. He was not associated with any political party or group, and his ministers would never have asked his opinion on anything because that would be embarrassing. The Japanese people loved their Emperor and he was respected as a deity. Once the war had begun, they felt they were fighting the war for him and would gladly die for him.

Japanese Emperor Hirohito had the Ingress Saturn/ Uranus in his 6th House squaring natal Mars. *Both* leaders had this major conjunction in aspect to a planet of power in their natal charts. FDR had it conjunct his natal Pluto. One is tempted to say that they each were earmarked to play a major part in history.

The Japanese leader had Ingress Jupiter in the 7th

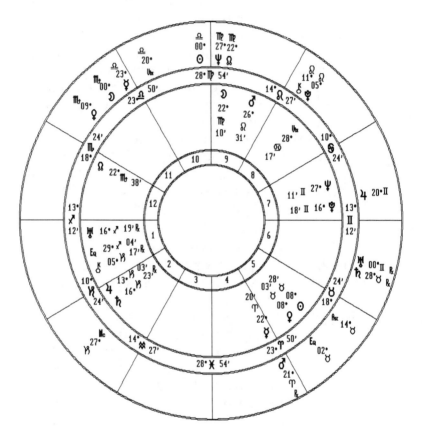

**Emperor Hirohito**
April 29, 1901   10:10 P.M. LMT
35N41   139E44
Tokyo, Japan
Outer Ring—Libra Ingress of Sept. 23, 1941

(war) conjunct natal Pluto, opposing natal Uranus (often the planet of surprise). This triggered the ominous T-square in Hirohito's natal chart. Ingress Node/Neptune conjunct this Moon/Neptune/Uranus T-square only serves to underscore this statement. With chilling 20-20 vision after the fact, we see that this T-square dumps out in the 4th House. The U.S. war with Japan ended only after Hiroshima and Nagasaki were destroyed by the new U.S. atom bomb.

Ingress Pluto in the 8th square natal Venus may have indicated the failed diplomatic negotiations as well as the heavy loss of life of the youth of his country. Pluto's square to his natal Sun reflects the great stress he felt during this period. Pluto/Sun aspects are always associated with ultimate tests in one's life. It was no less difficult for Hirohito than for FDR.

Since Ingress Venus opposed natal Venus, ruler of his 11th and 6th Houses, I am not totally convinced that this aggression was favored by the Emperor. One of the more marked qualities of his chart is the T-square, but it is in Mutable signs. He may have been convinced of the plan by his more aggressive military advisors.

The Ingress Midheaven in his 2nd quincunx natal Neptune in the 7th House painted Hirohito in a very black light. His country's aggression would set events into motion that would alter the balance of power in the international arena.

On December 8, 1941, the formal declarations of war between the two countries were announced. The transiting Sun had reached 16 Sagittarius 01 in the sky. This degree conjuncted Hirohito's 1st House Uranus and squared FDR's 12th House Uranus.

Thus ends this story of two men, two nations and the world events that were set into motion during a three-month period of 1941.

**Jim Lewis**

Jim Lewis is the internationally recognized authority on relocation astrology. He began his professional career in 1969 as a personal service astrologer for *American Astrology* magazine. In 1975, he began work on *Astro\*Carto\*Graphy* and now devotes most of his time to popularizing the concepts of locational astrology.

His work with *Astro\*Carto\*Graphy* earned him the Marc Edmund Jones Award, and since then he has appeared on the faculties of major astrological conferences; he was one of five Americans selected to attend World Conferences in Switzerland in 1981, 1984 and 1990. His lecturing credits include 12 nations and 20 states and provinces. *Astro\*Carto\*Graphy* is available in six languages.

In 1982, he completed work on *Cyclo\*Carto\*Graphy*, an important adjunct to *Astro\*Carto\*Graphy*, for which he was awarded a U.S. patent. In 1987, *Astro\*Carto\*Graphy E\*plained*, a computerized, interpretive service, was completed. As well as contributing frequent articles on many aspects of astrology to the popular press, he annually publishes the *Source Book of Mundane Maps*. *The Astro\* Carto\*Graphy Book of Maps* was published by Llewellyn in 1989. He has been very active in AFAN, an activist organization serving the astrological community, since 1982.

# ASTRO*CARTO*GRAPHY:
®

## Bringing Mundane Astrology Down to Earth

In this article, an introduction to the Astro*Carto*
Graphy mapping technique will be followed by a brief
survey of astrological data commonly used to make mundane predictions. Those techniques particularly suited to
Astro*Carto*Graphy will be explored in depth and examples given of how mapping has been effective in analyzing
mundane events in the recent past.

Upon cursory inspection, the concept of Mundane
Astrology would at first seem to be one of astrology's most
tenuous, even though it is historically the oldest. Mundane Astrology (from the Latin *mundus*, "world") asserts
that widespread events which affect large numbers of people can somehow be read in advance from the sky—that
the interrelationships of celestial bodies foreshadow meteorological extremes, wars, famines, stock market activity,
and many other endeavors in which humanity is engaged
collectively. In astrology's early years, rulers of nations
were little interested in abstract psychological concepts or
personal individuation. When humanity had little control
over its environment, there was a pressing need to understand in advance just what that environment was about to
do. The Old Testament describes how Joseph, bought
from his brothers as a slave, was elevated to a position as
confidant to the pharaoh when he demonstrated the capacity to read the future from the ruler's dreams, where-

upon the ruler's wife began finding him irresistibly attractive. This, perhaps, symbolizes the essentiality of foresight and communication with the unconscious for successful kingship in those days before weather satellites.

In our present age of waning fundamentalist scientism, however, a capacity to read dreams and omens is hardly considered seriously. Respectable arguments may be made (as the Gauquelins have done) that there is some correlation between birth moment and personality, and such assertions imply that eventually some causal mechanism may be found. To the arrogant solipsism of Western science, however, it borders on lunacy to suggest that plagues, famines, and stock market gyrations are related to planetary cycles, notwithstanding the fact that numerous historians have tenuously succeeded in relating such cycles to recurring patterns in human affairs.

While this is not the place for detailed theoretical discussion as to why Mundane Astrology should work, those inclined to such speculations might look to the concepts of natural adaptation in a constantly changing environment as a starting point for such inquiry. If, as various astronomers have asserted, planetary angles precipitate solar disturbance, which in turn alters climate and conditions on Earth, it would obviously be advantageous to a species to incorporate endogenous and exogenous responsiveness to such rhythms into their genetic programming. Perception of these rhythms would facilitate anticipation and adaptation to such changes, which adjustments would then seem to be coincident with planetary angles.

Society has changed greatly from the time of Joseph, the pharaoh, and early astrologers. Along with an increased awareness of the world, technology and science have transformed the role an individual will play in the unfolding of destiny. Hitherto, only the king needed an astrologer since only he had the power to make decisions that would act themselves out on a global scale. In modern times, electronic communication has all but created a world consciousness in which every individual, acting on his or her own behalf, creates a general direction to which the "leaders" try to respond. Mundane Astrology was formerly of interest to ordinary people only insofar as crops and livestock were concerned (and even if you knew a famine was coming, there was little to be done about it). Now, travel, investment, relocation, and conscious choice in life directions are all accessible to increasing numbers of inhabitants of the First World, and many decisions that affect the whole planet are the result of the pooling of their individual directions.

Astrology, as it was originated in the Middle East in the second millenium B.C., was a local affair. Societies in that era had little commerce with areas distant from their own and, in fact, astrology's provincialism reflects the primitive state of humanity's concept of its world at that time. The horoscope form inherited from our Greek and Chaldean forebears puts the observer in the center of the universe and, by this structure, assumes that s/he doesn't ever move very far from home. Since modern, natal astrology is mostly applied to an individual, continued use of this localized form is not entirely inappropriate as it may be assumed that an individual carries with him/her a set of beliefs, assumptions, reactions, and processes learned at the home site, even when traveling to other places.

Still, in a world in which privileged members of professional society will travel around the world several times in their lifetime and in which residence thousands of miles from the natal place is common, the local, "matricentric" horoscope may not be entirely adequate. In Mundane Astrology, where the aspects and relationships of planets are sought to be ascribed to various places on Earth, such a wheel-form horoscope with the perceiver located at its center seems woefully limited in an era when resources and ideas are electronically transmitted around the world in nanoseconds.

It is probably for this reason that Astro*Carto* Graphy[1] has achieved such acceptance among astrologers; the wheel-shaped horoscope remains appropriate for the interpretation of personality and individuality, both products of one's unique inheritance, including one's place of birth. But as for understanding one's role in the world, and particularly where mundane considerations are at stake, a larger context seems necessary.

Following this introduction, the origin, interpretation, and reading of Astro*Carto*Graphy maps will be briefly described, but these maps may be seen to represent more than just another astrological technique made possible by computers. The Greek wheel-shaped horoscope astrologically described a moment in time as seen by a consciousness rooted in a particular place, and was entirely sufficient during the millenia during which individuals were rooted to particular localities and family structures. The Astro*Carto*Graphy map, on the other hand, shows the same moment in time with the entire planet Earth (conveniently reduced to a map) as its center and is thus more appropriate to those individuals possessed of "planetary consciousness," that is, an awareness of their role as part of a humanity which is global, unified, and operating with conscious direction as a species. In previous ages, crises such as the destruction of the Brazilian rain forest and homelessness in New York City would have been interesting only to people who lived in those places. In the 1990s, they are the critical concern of every human, and for this reason a horoscopal representation which plots the celestial situation with the entire Earth as backdrop will be far more useful in understanding and anticipating future directions.

Obviously in Mundane Astrology, treating as it does the world, the map expression would seem far more useful, particularly for reading concerns that affect the whole world or human race.

### What is Astro*Carto*Graphy?

If it is accepted that some means need be found for projecting the planetary energies of a particular moment onto a representation of the whole planet, certain problems immediately manifest. Since the Earth is a spinning sphere, its surface, projected outward into space, would encompass the whole universe. As Earth is "stopped" during any moment of time, such as a birth, so its various motions can be eliminated if one accepts the basic astrological assumption that whatever is born at a moment of time carries with it the attributes of that moment throughout its existence.

Once the moment of an event is seen to "stop" the rotation, it is a simpler matter to calculate where on the Earth the various planets and stars were directly overhead (at their *zeniths*) at that moment. On the A*C*G map, these zeniths for the ten astrological planets are the little boxes on the Midheaven lines; they can be theorized to be the entry points and centers of manifestation for that planet's symbolic energy at that instant of time.

A line extended from each such zenith through Earth's poles would describe a *meridian* and identify all those places on Earth at which the planet, for example, the Sun, had reached the top of its diurnal arc for that day—in this case, the Sun at its noon point. A line 180 degrees east or west should define the place where the planet appeared on the IC (the midnight point) at that same moment.

A great circle (i.e., one describing the circumference of the Earth) with the zenith point at its *center* would define the points at which the Sun appeared on the *horizon*, where it was about to set or rise, given Earth's rotation, and so would identify all places where the Sun would appear on the astrological Ascendant or Descendant at the moment of the event in question.

To do the same for the ten astrological planets and to plot such circles out onto a flat map for the world would produce an Astro*Carto*Graphy map of the kind now so familiar to astrologers the world over. Its lines would identify all places upon Earth at which any planet appeared on either of two planes—the horizon or the meridian—at the moment of the occurrence.

Of course, classical astrology and moderns as well have long asserted that planets manifest most strongly if they appear on "angles" (i.e., the Ascendant, Descendant, Midheaven, or Imum Coeli). While this statement originally meant on the angles of a nativity confined to the locality of birth, and when it is realized that a map such as the one described above only takes that same moment and identifies angularities all over the world, it is clear that as the individual born at that moment moves to a place at which one such planet was angular, *s/he is moving to a place where that planet's potential was more sharply focused at his/ her birth.*

The origin of the map can be understood more easily if it is realized that even if the Sun was *not* rising at the time and place of your birth, it *was* rising someplace else, such as Madagascar. Should you travel to Madagascar, it is reasonable to assume that the nature of the astrological Sun would become more prominent in your personality, that is, you'd be more theatrical, arrogant, outspoken, and leader-like at this location. There were many places in addition to Madagascar at which the Sun was rising, and these can be represented as a line drawn across a map. Moreover, similar properties of self-expression can be ascribed to places where the Sun was setting, in the Midheaven, or on the IC at your birth. There would be four lines for each of the other planets as well, and these could also be drawn across our map. The 40 lines, curved on the map according to the angles at which the planets lay in relation to Earth, would all be great circles, or "straight" lines on a spherical globe. This resulting Astro*Carto* Graphy map would be valid only for the moment of the beginning of the cycle for which it was created—in this case, an individual's life. Such maps are available for individual nativities and, in fact, it is in the identification and recognition of an individual's potentials in various places that Astro*Carto* Graphy has had its most widespread application.

Notwithstanding the effectiveness of such maps for the understanding and locating of individual potentials, it should be clear that their application is particularly suited to the area of Mundane Astrology. How better might one take the astrological potentials of a moment in time and project them downward onto certain areas of Earth at which they might be expected to manifest?

Before continuing to apply the A*C*G process to Mundane Astrology, the following summarizes some of the techniques observed to be relevant in reading the maps.

**1. Lines are Permanent.** Since the lines represent the planetary potential of a moment in time, they operate in the same place as long as that moment continues to be relevant. Like a birth chart, they are permanent, "genetic" potential.

**2. Lines are Activated by Various Temporary Factors.** While the original set of lines remains permanent, there is no reason why they can't also be advanced in time by progressions and directions commonly used in natal astrology. In the case of national charts and the like, the accession to a leadership role of an individual whose natal chart activates or reiterates such original lines in a longer-lived mundane chart seems a common way of timing the manifestation of latent potentials.

Projecting A*C*G maps through time is an immense field of inquiry, only explored in the most superficial fashion to date. Application of progressions, transits, sidereal quotidians, PSSR measurements, and entirely new techniques made possible by the features of the map medium represent a fertile field of inquiry that should be stimulated by the few, necessarily limited examples of such modifications noted below.

**3. Orbs of Influence.** As is always the case, the smaller, the better. In natal work, however, orbs as large as 10 degrees (700 miles) either side of the actual line have been observed effective. Lines should be seen as the *centers of zones of influence*, rather than as discrete points. Mundane work would reasonably expect far closer orbs.

**4. Zenith Points.** As noted before, they are centers of planetary activity, the "entry point" of influence, and, like crossings (see item 6), seem to exercise influence along the entire line of latitude on which they fall.

**5. Where All the Lines Cross near the North Pole.** There are two such "vortices" on every map, and it may be assumed that with so many energies linked each would be cancelled out, rather like where no lines are evident. Some people have suggested the *longitude* of this "vortex" to be significant, particularly as it is usually the locus of at least several MH and IC lines.

**6. Line Crossings** (paranatellonta or "parans"). Obviously, a place at which two or more lines cross is affected by each of the planet energies indicated. But anywhere in the world along the latitude of that exact crossing is similarly affected, perhaps because the Earth rotates, transferring the effects of the linkage of the planets across the line of latitude at which the crossing occurs. Since this "paran" links two planets through simultaneous angularity, it may be seen as the most pronounced and powerful aspect in astrology. Unlike conventional aspects, however, it is "place-specific," that is, its effects are limited to the place at which the lines cross and that latitude. Crossings are not to be seen as equal with the major lines and in natal work seem to exert influence of about *one-third* the natal lines' power.

**7. Addition of Other Data to the Maps.** If a given moment in time identifies the terrestrial longitudes at which the planets operated, a subsidiary set of points may be derived by ascertaining the positions at which parans are made to those original lines. For example, if Pluto appears in the Midheaven (which appears to be the "prime" angle) on a given map in a specific place, various degrees of the ecliptic would rise or set when Pluto and that Midheaven are directly above. What these degrees are is determined by the semi-arc, or distance between the horizon plane and the meridian plane, itself a function of latitude.

It has been observed that positions on the ecliptic in paran to powerful mundane lines often identify points particularly sensitive to transits as timing mechanisms, or even identify important planets in the nativities of individuals whom the events foreshadowed by the mundane map are going to affect.

**8. Reiteration of Themes.** Clearly, no one chart is going to define the past and future history of the world, unless one can derive the GMT of the Big Bang. Mundane charts should be seen as individual instants in a flux of history with their positions referred to past charts for amplification and understanding. Mark Lerner has identified, for example, a "nuclear axis" by observing that many charts pertinent to the development of atomic power had powerful placements at about 7-10 degrees of Sagittarius and Gemini. 25-27 degrees Leo-Aquarius seems inextricably tied into U.S. presidents' problems with the country of Iran, and Charles Harvey has pointed out how the 1978 Winter Solstice chart ruling 1979 had Uranus in the Midheaven in Iran, its position in Scorpio activating the natal Fixed cross in that nation's nativity.[2]

Consequently, the occurrence of planets at particular positions in the ecliptic on the occasion of important events should be seen as the major identifying principle by which such degree areas are defined. Similarly, the presence of a planet over an area in a cyclic map, particularly if repeated in several such contemporaneous maps, should be taken as indication of the concentrated inflow of that planet's energy into that area during the time period so identified, and can be assumed to presage activity in keeping with the planet's nature, commensurate with the number and duration of such contacts and influences.

Principles 6, 7, and 8 above constitute what seem to be the most important possibilities for the perfection of a reliable mundane forecasting technique. All are amplified by the utilization of the Astro*Carto*Graphy mapping technique.

Since the calculation of simultaneous angularities is mathematically formidable (especially when oblique ascension is taken into account, as it always should be), the A*C*G maps make possible a wider use and recognition of the paran since they are visibly obvious as crossings of any two lines; the line of latitude affected by such a paran may be found by holding a straight edge through the crossing on the map, parallel to the equator, and observing through which areas it passes. In addition to parans between two contemporaneous planets, mundane researchers are urged to look to parans between planets in a key chart and future transits as well as other such contacts made to important planets in nativities of persons affected directly by events foreshadowed.

Abbreviations used on the maps are those that have emerged as standard in other writings on Astro*Carto* Graphy:

**Planets:**

| | | |
|---|---|---|
| Sun SU | Mars MA | Neptune NE |
| Moon MO | Jupiter JU | Pluto PL |
| Mercury ME | Saturn SA | |
| Venus VE | Uranus UR | |

**Angle abbreviations:**

| | |
|---|---|
| Midheaven MH | Imum Coeli IC |
| Ascendant ASC | Descendant DSC |

### Applications of Astro*Carto*Graphy in Mundane Astrology

Ancient and modern astrologers have developed various means of taking a discrete moment in time, interpreting its astrological significance, and applying it to the problem of forecasting the future in general or "mundane" terms. Certain of these techniques are particularly benefited by the Astro*Carto*Graphy mapping technique, and these are enumerated below and illustrated with examples.

### I. Chart of the Nation

Casting and interpreting a horoscope for a collective social entity, such as a nation, is likely an outgrowth of natal astrology, and so may be of relatively recent origin. Obviously, in the absence of ephemerides, ancient astrologers could not figure backward to the "birth" of their nation, state, or city, so they did not have "natal" charts for such collective entities. For Astro*Carto*Graphy to be reliable, an exact birth time is required; thus, only in cases of modern nations for which such times of inception or substantial reorganization are reliably known can the

Astro*Carto*Graphy map be used. In such cases, it has proven itself to be a tremendously potent tool for ascribing to certain areas of the world planetary effects that symbolize the relations the nation can expect.

One should not believe that any one chart could correctly symbolize every aspect of an entire nation and its undertakings. The following example (Chart 1) is the "Declaration of War" chart, propounded by astrologer Helen Boyd as a major contender for the "birth chart" of the USA. It is a chart for the moment at which the Second Continental Congress voted to create a state of war with England. As might be expected, this chart seems to be amazingly appropriate for the military activities of the USA.

Mars is within a couple degrees of the Ascendant, so the MA/ASC line passes through what were to become the major battlefields of the American Revolution as well as those of the Civil War, the two most important military activities of the nation's first century, and those which established the identity and existence of its Martian potential. The same Mars line passes through the border region between Panama and Colombia, recollecting that when Colombia demanded what was seen as too much for rights to build the critical Panama Canal, U.S. political intervention created from its territory the nation of Panama. The same line passes through Cuba, Ecuador, and Peru and touches Chile, all nations inspired by U.S. example (and aided by subtle support) to declare their own independence from Spain.

The MA/MH line passes through Berlin and Rome, perfectly symbolizing the height of American military power in the two world wars. It also passes through Tripoli (recalling the Marine Corps Hymn and Ronald Reagan's bombing raid) and Luanda. Mars's Midheaven would be expected to be the most successful outreach of

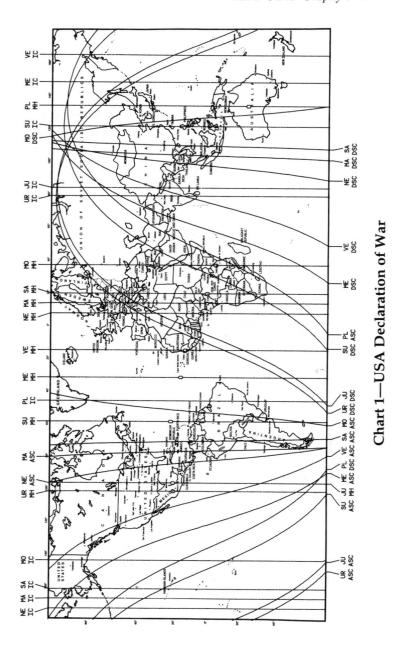

**Chart 1—USA Declaration of War**

military power and seems singularly appropriate to this longitude.

Mars occupied the Descendant in Vietnam, Laos, and Cambodia, a fitting symbol for the decline in military hegemony that Southeast Asia has come to symbolize. Since Mars occupies 27 Virgo 23, it was being transited by Uranus and Pluto between 1967 and 1972, the height of the Vietnam War, aptly exemplifying the responsiveness of natal placements to subsequent transiting activation.

The MA/IC line occupies almost exactly the U.S.-U.S.S.R. border area, following closely the 167th west meridian, a scant two degrees from the actual frontier. As the IC signifies an inner adjustment to the type of energy identified by the planet, this line aptly symbolizes the manner in which having an equal, "superpower" rival has curtailed the hitherto unchallenged U.S. military supremacy symbolized by the MH line through Berlin. Since the U.S. was the sole nation of the Allied Force not devastated by the actual fighting in World War II, it emerged as economic and military victor and held imperial sway over the entire world for those few brief years until the Soviet Union, itself a more subtle victor, arose to challenge U.S. domination. It seems ironically appropriate that the "reverse" of the MA/MH line identifying the Allies' triumph over the Axis powers in Berlin was the standoff between those same Allies and the U.S.S.R.

That secondary progressions work well in A*C*G maps is illustrated memorably by this map as well. As a planet progresses in the context of Astro*Carto*Graphy, it will move eastward across the map (assuming its motion is direct). In this fashion, the all-important Mars lines can be seen to move eastward from initial positions at the rate of about $3/4$ of a degree per year. The accurate calculation brought the progressed MA/MH line to a position over Japan at the time of World War II; thus, two major enemies of that conflict were identified by the natal MA line and its progressed position.

In the natal A*C*G map, PL/MH lies closely over Hiroshima and Nagasaki and there symbolizes the beginning of the Atomic Age which so affected the way the U.S. would subsequently relate to the world. The importance of Pluto in this particular chart is underscored by its position as "handle of the bucket," a position of critical importance. At the time of the dropping of the atomic bombs on the Japanese, the progressed Mars line from this map lay within $1^1/_2$ degrees of conjoining the natal Pluto line exactly over Hiroshima. Moreover, transiting JU/MH lay atop the natal MA/MH at Berlin. If precession is added to the natal values, the progressed MA/Hiroshima contact is exact within four *minutes* of arc.[3]

## II. Charts of Leaders

In their excellent survey of Mundane Astrology, Michael Baigent, Nicholas Campion, and Charles Harvey quote Lynn Thorndike's *A History of Magic and Experimental Science* (Columbia University Press, 1923) as stating that the first known individual horoscope was compiled in 410 B.C.[4] Since that time, the birth chart of the leader of a political entity has been universally regarded as a fundamental source of information that relates to the political entity itself. Even before the emergence of democracy in which, theoretically, the will of the people governed determines who the leader shall be, it was implicitly recognized that the individual identity of the leader was, during his or her tenure or reign, synonymous with the destiny of the country.

This supposition is certainly borne out by perusal of the Astro*Carto* Graphy maps of modern leaders. Nearly every U.S. president for whom there exists a reliable birth time (an essential for A*C*G analysis) initiated or continued some sort of military action under his personal Mars lines, the only exception being Richard Nixon, who "inherited" a war already in progress from his predecessor.

Presented herewith is Harry S Truman's A*C*G map (Chart 2).[5] It illustrates several of the techniques outlined above with singular power.

One of the first, and perhaps the most significant, acts of Truman's Administration was to precipitate Japanese surrender by dropping atomic bombs on Hiroshima and Nagasaki. Truman's PL/ASC line almost exactly crosses Hiroshima, and in so doing, "activates" the PL/MH line already discussed in connection with the 1775 USA chart. This illustrates clearly several of the principles outlined earlier in this essay: the USA natal Pluto "waited" for manifestation until a leader came along whose natal planets "activated" the potential of the national chart. It should be noted that Truman's natal Pluto (0 Gemini 24) makes no traditional aspect to the USA Pluto (25 Capricorn 45). Further confirmation of the efficacy of this technique occurs with the PL/DSC line for the map of the first test detonation of an atomic device in Nevada[6] exactly crossing these other two at Hiroshima. Three Pluto lines—those of the USA, Harry Truman, and the atomic bomb itself—all cross over Hiroshima, eerily recalling that the particular bomb used there was made of plutonium. While these Pluto positions are not aligned in any significant way in the context of zodiacal aspects, a speculum of their (and Mars's) angularities calculated for the latitude of Hiroshima (34°24' North) produces a startling set of correspondences.[7] (See p. 114.)

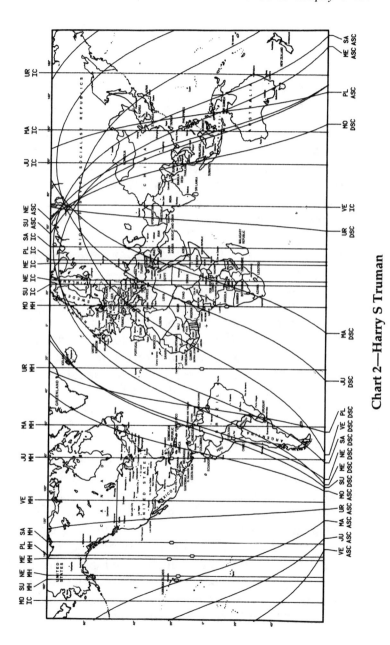

**Chart 2—Harry S Truman**

|                  | Rise     | Midheaven | Set      | IC       |
| ---------------- | -------- | --------- | -------- | -------- |
| Pluto/A-bomb test | 26°06'   | 133°32'   | **240°58'** | 313°32'  |
| Pluto/Truman     | 325°30'  | 60°54'    | **156°18'** | **240°54'** |
| Pluto/USA Boyd   | 225°38'  | 298°16'   | 10°54'   | 118°16'  |
| Mars/A-bomb test | 310°02'  | 53°06'    | **156°10'** | 233°06'  |
| Mars/Truman      | 37°50'   | 140°15'   | **242°41'** | 320°15'  |

For those unfamiliar with the use of such "specula," some explanation may be in order. A planet having latitude, like Pluto, does not exactly occupy an angle when its degree of the zodiac crosses that angle. A trigonometric formula must be employed to determine just when such a planet is actually bodily on the angle in question, and the clearest way to express this relationship of planet to angle is by stating the degree of local sidereal time or right ascension that occupies the Midheaven at that moment when the planet was on the angle. Such correlations are specific to the particular latitude on Earth for which they are calculated. So, the third figure on the first line of the table, 240°58', means that the A-bomb natal Pluto was actually setting when 240°58' of right ascension occupied the Midheaven at the latitude of Hiroshima (equivalent to about 16 hours 4 minutes of sidereal time). Checking the table again, it is obvious that at that identical sidereal time, the Pluto from Harry Truman's chart would be exactly on the IC at Hiroshima's latitude.

Truman's Mars also sets in paran to A-bomb test Pluto and to Truman's own natal Pluto at the latitude of Hiroshima. The relationships of these planets might be more easily grasped by studying the diagram on the following page, which shows a "composite" horoscope erected for the latitude of Hiroshima. It must be remembered that planets on the "Descendant" in this case refers to their actual setting on the Western horizon, not that they occupied whatever degree of the zodiac which was then setting, or were even conjunct one another.

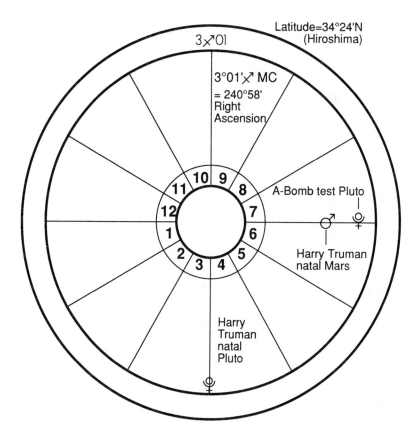

The speculum also reveals a link between Truman's Pluto and A-bomb test Mars. The importance of the Mars/Pluto connection has already been established in the previous discussion of the USA natal chart, which had progressed MA/MH conjunct natal PL/MH above Hiroshima in 1945. The precision of these contacts should amply demonstrate the importance of figuring such aspects in paran as it is only through such contact that Mars and

Pluto placements in these three charts have any connection whatsoever.

While the activation of the potentials symbolized by the USA chart by Truman's Pluto lines could have occurred at any time in his life, the transiting factors in 1945 (i.e., the A-bomb test chart) created links between his Mars and Pluto placements, exactly at the latitude of Hiroshima. These "parans" between planets in these three charts have no established relation to the A*C*G lines' confluence at Hiroshima, this confluence being a product of the clock time of the events. They are an additional and powerfully convincing argument for the importance of latitude and angularity.

Another example of a national chart "waiting" for the "right" leader to come along can be seen in the charts of Margaret Thatcher and the United Kingdom.[8] The MA/MH of the U.K. national chart touches the western end of the Falkland Islands, just like Thatcher's MA/ASC line. Even the choice of angles is identical with that in the Truman/Hiroshima connection.

This phenomenon might be more clearly understood and utilized if planets' positions in relation to Earth are seen as a sort of variation on zodiacal longitude. In the first example, this concept could be summarized by declaring that the USA natal Pluto lay not in "the 4th House and Capricorn" but in "the Midheaven in Japan," and when Truman (who also had Pluto in Japan on the Ascendant, rather than in Gemini) came along, along with the A-bomb itself, a "conjunction" occurred, precipitating the Plutonian potential. Researchers interested in this technique are invited to perform similar calculations in regard to other examples and to correspond with the author.

### III. "Pure" Mundane Astrology

If the first horoscope was erected only in 410 B.C., and astrology existed for at least 1,000 years before that, on what basis did ancient astrologers make their forecasts? It is here that we enter into the realm of what might be called "pure" Mundane Astrology, astrology not directly attached to any birth moment or inception chart.

This is the astrology that the three "wise men" (more correctly translated as "astrologers") probably used to find Bethlehem and about which Babylonian astrologers wrote in the *Enuma Anu Enlil*, astrology's earliest text, somewhere around 1,000 B.C.[9] It might be called "observational astrology" since omens and prognoses for the future are derived simply from a study of the sky. The ancients identified planets as crucially important on the basis of the fact that they moved relative to the "fixed stars" and, from observations of the Sun's equinoctial and solstice points, a framework of reference (the zodiac) was developed against which the motions of the planets could be measured. Attributes were ascribed to certain stars and constellations that would interact with planets passing near or through them.

Such observations indicated the *cyclic nature of celestial phenomena*, and, since the motions of the Sun and Moon through different parts of the sky coincided with seasonal and tidal changes, it was reasonable to assume that their cycles and those of other planets might correspond with more abstract periodicities of human life and experience. For this reason, eclipses, lunations, and the entry of the Sun into the Cardinal signs (solstices and equinoxes) are taken as important cyclical starting points. In the absence of an inceptional chart against which the present planets' positions could be compared, the ancients observed a series of cycles and used their repetitive nature as foundation for predictions. If crops had died the last time Jupiter was in Leo, they might be expected to do so again.

There are numerous types of cycles that modern astrologers use in their attempts to make mundane predictions. Some of the more commonly used are:

1. Precessional great year—the "astrological ages."
2. Transits of planets through signs and their aspects to each other.
3. Transits of planets into north or south declination.
4. Eclipses (the Naros and Saros cycles).
5. Entry of the Sun into signs or constellations (solstice and equinox, or sidereal ingresses).
6. Lunations.
7. Diurnal cycles of momentary local angularity.

Astrologers have long asserted that charts drawn for a particular locality at the moment of such cyclic changes would show the astrological conditions expected to prevail in that locality for the duration of the cycle. Clearly, such cyclic charts would be usefully displayed in the Astro*Carto*Graphy format.

Since 1979, Astro*Carto*Graphy has published the *Source Book of Mundane Maps*,[10] which has included Astro*Carto*Graphy maps for all the lunations, eclipses, and solar ingresses (both tropical and sidereal) for a year. Longer-based cycles, such as declination variations, have not seemed to work well in this context, perhaps because the exact moment of such changes cannot be calculated with sufficient accuracy.

In reading these charts, most of the techniques applied to leaders' and national charts seem also to work reliably, but it has been observed that the Reiteration of Themes factor seems most critical here. Obviously, if Pluto in Scorpio happens to occupy the Midheaven on the occasion of the Full Moon over one's place of residence, one should not necessarily anticipate destruction of the city by invading alien life forms. However, if Pluto occupies the angles in several successive charts over a long period of time, it would become more meaningful.

An example of such recurrent themes was observed in the maps of late 1979 and early 1980. No fewer than 13 occurrences of Pluto occurred on the West Coast of North America; Uranus was angular six times during that period, when, by contrast, Saturn appeared only three times. The period proved to be one of unusual seismic activity throughout California, culminating with the eruption of Mount St. Helens in May 1980, after which there were few occurrences of angular Pluto in the maps.

Among maps for the cycles identified above, *eclipses* seem to be particularly significant and apparently set the tone for the entire six-month period until the next eclipses happen. This was made particularly obvious in 1984. On November 8, 1984, 17:42 GMT, a Lunar Eclipse saw Pluto on the Midheaven near Mexico City and Mars on the Ascendant crossing it nearby. The following eclipse map (Chart 3) for November 22, 1984, 22:56 GMT reiterated those themes, this time with an exact MA/MH over Mexico City and PL/DSC crossing a scant one degree east.[11]

In addition to these exact lines, at Mexico City's equivalent south latitude the zeniths for the eclipse itself and Mars are exact, adding a latitudinal effect to the lines already established there for the eclipse. Mexico City's latitude is 20°26' North. The eclipse occurred at 20°20' South, and Mars at that moment was at 20°25' South. On November 20, 1984, at 5:42 a.m. CST, a gas refinery unthinkingly located in an overpopulated neighborhood exploded, killing dozens, wounding more than a thousand, and making homeless uncounted families of poor Mexican slum dwellers.

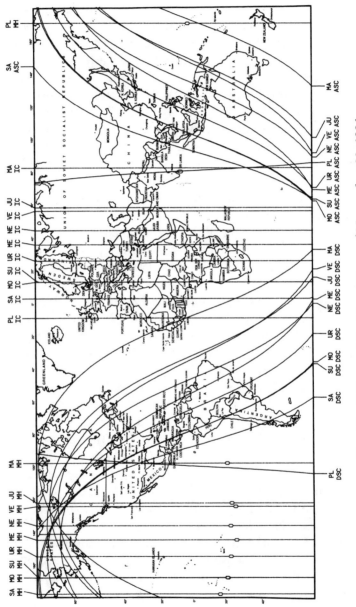

Chart 3—Eclipse of the New Moon of November 22, 1984

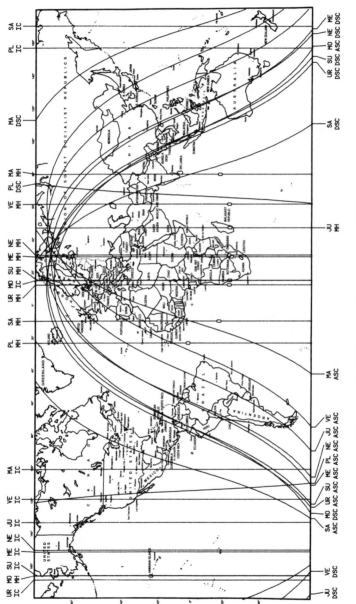

Chart 4—Full Moon of December 8, 1984

The next map (Chart 4) depicts the Full Moon of December 8, 1984, and once again Mars lines, in this case accompanied by Saturn, lie near Mexico City.[12]

At nearly the same latitude (23°16' North) as Mexico City (20°26' North) and almost exactly halfway around the world (176¹/₂° east to be exact) lies the city of Bhopal, India. Early in the morning of December 3, a valve in Union Carbide's chemical plant there was opened to release clouds of methylisocyanate gas upon the sleeping city. The effects gave a new and terrible meaning to the words "industrial accident," leaving thousands dead and tens of thousands permanently disabled in a country with few medical resources and in which most people permanently live on the edge of destitution. Reviewing the three maps discussed in connection with Mexico City for Bhopal, it is seen that the first eclipse (November 8, 1984) had PL/IC about four degrees east; the eclipse of November 22, 1984, saw PL/ASC closely crossing MA/IC; the Full Moon (December 8, 1984) had MA/MH almost exactly overhead. But the zenith's latitudes amplify these indications with striking intensity. On the December 8 Full Moon, declinations of planets were as follows in respect to Bhopal's terrestrial latitude at 23°16' North:

| | |
|---|---|
| Sun | 22°46' South |
| Mercury | 23°38' South |
| Venus | 23°34' South |
| Jupiter | 22°41' South |
| Uranus | 22°29' South |
| Neptune | 22°19' South |

Nor were these eclipses through with Mexico City; six months later it was devastated by a 7+-point earthquake. This unusual line-up of declinations seemed mirrored in the extraordinary series of historic mishaps occurring at almost exactly the corresponding latitude. But only the A\*C\*G maps could have identified the actual locations of the concentrated planetary energies' effects.

Our survey of "pure" Mundane Astrology has shown that (1) eclipses seem particularly potent and affect the areas over which lines lie on their maps for up to six months into the future; (2) reiteration of themes is important, and the more mundane cycle indications that can be amassed for a particular area, the more likely a manifestation is; and (3) declination cycles seem extremely powerful.

Even with these guidelines, if every disaster were as clearly indicated as the example of Mexico/Bhopal, astrologers might be accorded rather more honor than they presently are; however, such is not the case, and it is only fair to admit that these correlations to Mexico/Bhopal were only recognized after the fact. The problem with "pure" Mundane Astrology is that there are so many cycles, the starting points of which can be taken as significant, that even with the simplification afforded by A\*C\*G maps, the volume of all relevant data is still overwhelming. For every overwhelming accumulation of data, a computer program usually gets written, and it may be assumed that at some point patterns will be identified that will simplify the mundane astrologer's task.

## Conclusion

As illustrated above, Astro\*Carto\*Graphy provides a very useful tool for the mundane astrologer. Its most striking successes occur when exact birth times are known—in the cases of leaders' charts particularly—and the ease with which it makes working with parans possible assures greater attention to this critical and neglected measure of planets' relatedness.

As A\*C\*G uses only planets and angles, no reference

to zodiacs, signs, or even the ecliptic is necessary; while some astrologers would see this as a detraction, it eliminates one more set of possibly flawed data. Since aspects to angles must be measured along the ecliptic, and since only rarely do planets actually exist there, the idea of using aspects such as trines and sextiles to a planet's position on an angle is nonsensical. As demonstrated above, the use of interlinked parans between planets' positions at various times more than adequately compensates for the loss of the familiar aspects and eliminates the problem of ascribing evaluative meanings to the different "types" of aspects.

Ecliptic positions are useful, however, in that they furnish a backdrop against which planets' motions may be measured. The mundane astrologer would be wise to note the zodiacal positions occupied by planets at the inception of important political entities or processes and to track not only transits to these positions but parans as well. Yet, in addition to the ecliptic, the Earth itself seems to evince a sort of "memory" for the presence of important planets at certain of its longitudes and latitudes at the times of important historical events, and when these "remembered" positions are activated by subsequent transits or individuals' nativities, important occurrences may come to pass.

Some may see Mundane Astrology as the highest form of astrology. Certainly it will never earn one much money and accrues little of value to those few astrologers who can practice it with occasional accuracy. It does, however, offer a subtler compensation: When an event that is clearly beyond the control of human capacity unfolds in keeping with previously recognized astrological principles, the order and harmony of the universe is manifest, and the astrologer is given evidence that the astrological tools have successfully put him or her in touch with a transcendent direction and purpose.

## Notes
1. Astro*Carto*Graphy and Cyclo*Carto*Graphy are registered service marks owned by Astro*Carto*Graphy.

2. Michael Baigent, Nicholas Campion, and Charles Harvey, *Mundane Astrology*, The Aquarian Press, Wellingborough, Northamptonshire, England, 1984, p. 286. This excellent book gives a thorough exposition (with numerous illustrations) of every technique of Mundane Astrology. It is highly recommended for in-depth reading.

3. I am indebted to Kenneth Irving, editor of *American Astrology* magazine, who originally directed my attention to the Boyd chart and who first noticed the coincidence of its progressed Mars with natal Pluto. The Boyd chart is extensively explored in *The True Horoscope of the U.S.* by Helen Boyd, ASI Publications, Inc., New York, 1978. Chart data: July 6, 1775, 11:00 A.M. LMT, Philadelphia.

4. Baigent, Campion, and Harvey, *op.cit.*, p. 19.

5. Harry S Truman, May 8, 1884, 4 P.M. LMT, Lamar, Missouri. This and other maps presented here are taken from *The ASTRO\*CARTO\*GRAPHY Book of Maps*, Jim Lewis and Ariel Guttman, Llewellyn Publications, St. Paul, Minnesota, 1989.

6. First atomic bomb test, July 16, 1945, 5:29 A.M. MWT, Alamogordo, New Mexico.

7. Thanks are due to Ken Irving for his assistance in calculating the specula on his computer using Astrolabe's *Nova* program.

8. United Kingdom, January 1, 1801, 0 hours GMT, London, England; Margaret Thatcher, October 13, 1925, 9:00 A.M. BST, Grantham, England.

9. Baigent, Campion, and Harvey, *op.cit.*, p. 18.

10. *The ASTRO\*CARTO\*GRAPHY Source Book of Mundane Maps for 1979*, published by Astro*Carto*Graphy, Box 959, El Cerrito, CA 94530, 1979. Similar volumes are available for every year from 1982 to 1990 and are anticipated to be published for future years. A particular edition is usually available in March of the year prior to its cover date.

11. *The ASTRO\*CARTO\*GRAPHY Source Book of Mundane Maps for 1984*, copyright 1983 by Astro*Carto*Graphy, San Francisco, CA.

12. *Ibid.*

**Richard Nolle**

In the last 15 years Richard Nolle has published nearly 2,000 feature articles and columns in leading astrology magazines and journals, including *Dell Horoscope, American Astrology, Astrology Now, Astro-Psychological Problems, Astro\* Talk, KOSMOS, Mercury Hour, Today's Astrologer*, and the *NCGR Journal*. For the last three years he has published *STAR\*TECH*, a monthly magazine dedicated to empirical evidence of correlations between cosmic cycles and the entire spectrum of human experience.

Nolle has published several books, including *Chiron, Critical Astrology* and *Interpreting Astrology*. He also operates a cosmic calculation service, providing personal reports for the general public and advanced chart calculations for physicians, stock and commodity brokers, psychiatrists, and professional astrologers and students.

Nolle's educational background includes a B.A. (majors in philosophy and religion) from the University of Florida and graduate work in philosophy at Florida State University. After spending two years as an urban planner (in Orange County Florida, during the height of the Disney boom), he became a free-lance writer and researcher in 1973. Nolle now makes his home in Tempe, Arizona with his wife Maria and their son Dylan.

# THE SUPERMOON ALIGNMENT

What's a SuperMoon, and why should you care? It is not, I assure you, something you'll see sticking out the window of a car speeding down Fraternity Row during pledge week. Rather, it's a term I have coined to denote what is technically known as a *perigee-syzygy*: a syzygy (New or Full Moon) that occurs when the Moon is at its perigee (closest approach to Earth). There is ample evidence to suggest that the SuperMoon alignment is one of the most significant configurations ever discovered with respect to the field of Mundane Astrology in terms of its correlation with upheavals on the level of geophysics (including weather and seismic activity) and mass psychology (including social and economic disruptions). And it's something you'll have a chance to experience for yourself a number of times in the years ahead. What to expect? Read on. . . .

## A Bad Moon on the Rise

If you were anywhere along the Atlantic seaboard in 1979, you probably remember Hurricane David. The *New York Times* called it one of the worst storms to hit the Atlantic seaboard in the 20th century. Descriptions of the storm's fury made front-page news in the *Times* early in September that year:

> Hurricane David smashed into the Georgia-South Carolina coast this afternoon, then headed inland toward the capital city of Columbia, South Carolina, after lashing Savannah, Georgia and the barrier islands . . . in Charleston, huge waves broke over the High Battery Wall at 7:15 P.M. . . . five-foot seawalls, some recently built to stop already advancing erosion, were battered down and large areas of beach swept away.[1]

> At nightfall Tuesday, it had smashed ashore again with full hurricane force near Savannah, Georgia . . . where the hurricane settled directly over the city and pounded it relentlessly for more than three hours.[2]

> The storm whipped up already higher-than-normal tides, killing at least eight people and leaving more than 2.5 million residents of the New York metropolitan area without electricity . . . heavy surf pounded the Atlantic Shoreline, where abnormally high tides were running . . .[3]

The news media did a good job reporting the damage left in Hurricane David's wake, but one national magazine broke the story way ahead of the others. The September 1979 issue of *Dell Horoscope*, the world's leading popular astrology magazine, hit the newsstands in July—some six weeks before Hurricane David hit, mind you—with an article that began as follows:

> It is September 6, 1979; the wind blows hard from the sea onto the Atlantic coast of the United States. The Moon rises a little past full as the Sun sets, but the gale-driven clouds ensure that few people will be out to enjoy the sight for long. Earlier in the day, the morning high tide rolls and surges inland; but the worst comes after dark. A little before 10:00 P.M. (EDT), the dark waves boil over seawalls in Savannah, Georgia.[4]

That article was written in December 1978 (post-marked on the 29th, to be precise) and was typeset the following March. As predictions go, it was a rather good one. To be sure, I was a couple days off the mark in picking the exact date Savannah was deluged, but the fact remains that on September 6, 1979, the sea assaulted the Atlantic coast, just as I had written more than nine months in advance of the fact. In any case, SuperMoon effects are felt from *one to two days before and after the actual alignment* in the heavens.

That prediction was only the first of many I have published, which have been confirmed by subsequent events. The evidence is clear and mounting: SuperMoon alignments time significant events on the macro scale down here on Earth, from storms and flooding (even earthquakes) on the geophysical level to major turning points in the ebb and flow of the mass psyche.

Remember the August 9, 1987 SuperMoon? It was accompanied by some pretty notable seismic activity in the form of earthquakes felt in Peru and Chile. The Chile tremor registered 6.8 on the Richter scale, according to the Pacific Tsunami Warning Center in Honolulu, and was felt most strongly in Arica, Iquique, Tacna, Moquegua, and Arequipa. Arica was hit hardest: the town shook for two minutes shortly before noon on August 8, and when the tumbling stopped there were six people dead and 106 injured. Many buildings were severely damaged, power and phone service was cut off, and portions of the Pan-American Highway were blocked by landslides.

America's heartland felt SuperMoon storms on August 8, the day before the alignment. There were flash-flood watches in Iowa and Nebraska where heavy rains pushed the West Nishnabotna River to the 19-foot flood stage from Hancock to Randolph (Iowa). In Nevada and Colorado, a cold front triggered storms that lingered over the central Rockies. And on the actual day of the Super-Moon, a tropical depression formed in the Gulf of Mexico, threatening coastal interests in Texas and Louisiana.

The Leo '87 issue of STAR*TECH described the August 9 SuperMoon in advance as "a time of strong psychological polarization" and expressed the hope that it would bring "illumination, rather than confrontation."[5] While there surely were people who experienced a time of illumination coinciding with this particular alignment, they didn't make the news of the day. Instead, the news services carried accounts of riots and terrorism in Northern Ireland and a divisive strike in South Africa.

The Aquarius '87 issue of STAR*TECH predicted that the August 9 SuperMoon, owing to its sextile to Saturn and opposition to Venus and Mars, would bring "something in the way of an adjustment in the financial world (including the stock market)."[6] August 9 was indeed a watershed on the economic front, timing as it did a boom in the bull market on Wall Street and the advent of Alan Greenspan's tenure at the Fed. As we now know, it didn't take too long for the great October collapse to make the August market look like the good old days. Anyone who sold a Dow-Jones portfolio at the time of the August SuperMoon (when the market was near its last peak before the great crash) would have cashed in quite handily.

If you don't remember the August 1987 SuperMoon, perhaps you recall the one that came the following January. Describing that one in advance (in the Sagittarius '87 issue of STAR*TECH), I wrote:

> The SuperMoon that forms in the heavens on January 19, 1988 will be a new Moon at 28°21' Capricorn, conjunct the I. C. (4th House cusp) at Washington, D.C. According to the traditions of mundane astrology, property damages are likely in the U.S. un-

der an alignment of this sort, falling as it does on the
I.C. at the nation's capital. If such developments do
manifest, they are more likely to involve severe
weather rather than seismic activity . . .[7]

Once again, SuperMoon lived up to its advance bill-
ing. On January 17, a storm hit the California coast with
breakers up to 20 feet high, destroying a restaurant and
washing away a hotel in Redondo Beach, taking out the
city pier at Huntington Beach, and damaging numerous
beachfront homes in Malibu and elsewhere. The storm
drew its energy from a low-pressure system so strong that
it sent barometers in Los Angeles plunging to a reading of
29.25 inches, the lowest level measured in more than 100
years of record-keeping there. (As noted in my book *Interpreting Astrology*, SuperMoons tend to coincide with the
formation of massive low-pressure systems.)

Working its way eastward, the storm accounted for
many millions of dollars in property damage and a loss of
some two dozen lives before it was spent. Air travel was
brought to a standstill in many parts of the nation due to
bad weather. Chicago's O'Hare airport was closed, and
several plane crashes resulted in fatalities in Arkansas,
Colorado, Illinois, Missouri and Texas. Interstate high-
ways through much of America's heartland were closed as
well. All in all, it was yet another demonstration of the SuperMoon effect—one of the most powerful tools in the
predictive arsenal of the cosmic craft.

Once the flotsam and jetsam were cleared away, not
a few Golden State residents surveyed the damage around
them, remembered the *STAR*TECH* prediction, and sent
in their subscriptions. One in particular wrote:

> The SuperMoon article was especially timely.
> The January 19 SuperMoon tides wiped out a couple
> of my favorite restaurants in Redondo Beach and did
> incredible damage all along the southern California

coast. Gale force winds (blowing against the tide) are occurring as I write this, as the February SuperMoon takes place. What next?[8]

As it turned out, the SuperMoon storms rattling windows in California in February also left their mark a continent away in Brazil. During a five-day period that month, Rio de Janeiro was inundated with 12 inches of rain falling to the accompaniment of non-stop volleys of thunder and lightning. Rain-swollen rivers leaped their banks, and the surging flood that resulted swept through the streets, knocking down buildings and hurling automobiles about like so many tiny toys. Before it was done, there were 85 people dead, 200 injured and 4,800 homeless; 50,000 people had to be relocated for safety reasons as authorities feared a typhoid fever epidemic since the flooding had contaminated local water supplies with sewage.

I could go on and on, but by now I'm sure you get the picture: SuperMoon works. There can be no question that this is one of the most powerful cosmic alignments in what is technically termed Mundane Astrology, i. e., that branch of astrology dealing with large-scale (macro) events rather than personal (micro) events. Of course, the individual who happens to be caught in the crossfire of a macro cataclysm will no doubt feel it personally. When that happens to you, it doesn't feel micro at all. And with that in mind, it wouldn't hurt to get a handle on the SuperMoon phenomenon. That's the focus of this chapter, which not only explains what SuperMoon is, but when it happens. (See the table which lists all SuperMoon alignments for the 20th century at the end of this chapter. )

## Ebb and Flow, Above and Below
Tidal ebb and flow are powered by the gravitational attraction the Sun and Moon exert on Earth. Although the Sun is by far the more massive of the two, Luna's closer

proximity results in the lunar influence being a much more prominent factor in influencing the tides. In fact, the tide-raising force of the Moon is more than twice that of the Sun.

As anyone who frequents the seashore knows, a New or Full Moon is always accompanied by higher-than-normal tides. A quarter Moon, on the other hand, is always accompanied by lower-than-normal tides. The stronger New and Full Moon tides are called *spring* tides, while those accompanying the quarter Moon are termed *neap* tides. Astrology distinguishes the lunar phases as a particular class of aspects where an aspect is defined as an angular relationship involving two or more celestial bodies as seen from Earth. The New Moon is a *conjunction* aspect between the Sun and Moon, while the Full Moon is an *opposition* aspect between these two; a quarter Moon is a *square* aspect between the two luminaries.

The fact that New and Full Moons coincide with a pronounced increase in tidal action lends credence to the ancient astrological tradition, passed down through Ptolemy, which holds that the conjunction and opposition aspects are essentially equal in power and are far superior in strength to all other aspects. What we have here, in other words, is empirical confirmation based on physical evidence of an ancient astrological tradition.

Although not previously recognized for what it is, the SuperMoon seems to have been vaguely understood as a powerful alignment far back in the history of astrology. Astrological tradition is virtually unanimous in acclaiming the significance of New and Full Moon configurations. The SuperMoon is indeed one of these, albeit a very special case. And at least as far back as Claudius Ptolemy (2nd century C.E.)[9] astrologers have said that the Moon's influence is greatest when Luna is "swift of course," i.e., when the Moon's apparent motion is faster than normal. The SuperMoon qualifies as something special on this count, too, for the Moon's motion is greatest when the distance between Earth and the Moon is least, which it is when the Moon is at or near its perigee as it is in the case of a SuperMoon alignment.

Astrology and astronomy alike use the general term *syzygy* (pronounced SIZ-uh-jee) to denote both the New and Full Moon. Basically, a syzygy is an alignment between Earth and two or more celestial bodies. At New Moon, the Earth, Sun and Moon are lined up with the Moon in the middle. At Full Moon, the alignment occurs with Earth in the middle. As aspects go, any syzygy is powerful. But some are more powerful than others, resulting in dramatically different tidal effects from one syzygy to the next.

The Greek astrologer Hipparchus (ca. 125 B.C.E.) is widely credited with inventing the system of zodiacal signs (as opposed to the constellations of the same name) upon which modern astrology is based. Less well known in astrological circles is Hipparchus' discovery that the Moon does not maintain a constant distance from the Earth. Noticing that the Moon appears larger at certain times of the lunar month than others, Hipparchus reasoned that Luna's orbit at times carries her closer to Earth than usual. The closer approach he termed *perigee* (literally "closest to Earth"), while the maximum separation was called *apogee*.

Such astrological greats as Ptolemy and Kepler were also aware of the lunar perigee and apogee, but it was left to Isaac Newton to explain how and to what extent these factors affect the tides. Newton's theory of gravitation explained tidal phenomena as due to the gravitational attraction of the Moon and (to a lesser extent) the Sun. Aware of the apogee and perigee variations in the lunar orbit, and mindful that gravitational attraction between two bodies increases as the distance between them diminishes, Newton realized that the lunar perigee coincides with an amplified tide-raising influence.

In his monumental treatise *Principia* (1687), Newton backed up his theoretical deduction with observations he had made at the port of Bristol. He found that a normal spring tide, one coinciding with an ordinary syzygy, attained a tidal height of 10 feet. A spring tide which coincided with a perigee-syzygy, however, could raise the tide to 12 feet or more. (The effect is especially pronounced, Newton noted, "when the wind sets the same way as the tide."[10])

In 1978, an in-depth study of perigean spring tides was published by Fergus Wood, research associate with the U.S. National Ocean Survey (NOS), under the title *The Strategic Role of Perigean Spring Tides*. Wood's comprehensive treatise clearly shows that perigean tides are among the mightiest weapons in nature's arsenal of destruction. Searching through contemporary accounts reaching back over 300 years, Wood found that perigean tides have resulted in immense assaults on the coastal zones of North America, costing many thousands of lives and billions of dollars in property damage.

Such awesome displays of nature's wrath are not solely due to perigean tides. As Newton observed, they are caused by perigean spring tides augmented by strong offshore winds. But in this connection it is worth noting that astrometeorologists have long held that *any New or Full Moon tends to coincide with the formation of strong low-pressure centers in the Earth's atmosphere.* Low-pressure centers are the focal points of stormy weather. A hurricane, for example, is a massive low-pressure center. Thus, the same force which raises the tides also tends to produce the high winds needed to drive massive walls of water over the seashore, wreaking havoc on the lives and property of people who live in a fragile coastal environment.

Donald Bradley (writing under his astrological *nom de plume* Garth Allen) pointed out that "about twice as many tropical storms have whirled to hurricane intensity on the three days centered at New and Full Moon as on the three days following the quarter phases."[11] With this in mind, the special case of a perigee-syzygy would seem especially likely to generate the hurricane-force winds that augment the possibility of tidal destruction to coastal zones. Although this extrapolation from Bradley's deductions cannot be regarded as conclusive, anyone living on a hurricane-prone shoreline might wish to give the matter some thought the next time the Weather Bureau announces a hurricane alert.

There are a number of factors which must be taken into account in predicting dangerous perigean tides, and the weather is foremost among these. Without simultaneous offshore winds, a perigean tide poses no special danger to coastal interests. Also, as Fergus Wood writes, perigean spring tides "do not necessarily occur on the central day of perigee-syzygy. . . but can show up within several days before or after it."[12] With these factors in mind, it's a risky business to predict the exact date and location of a wind-driven perigean tidal assault on the coast. It's difficult to pin down or determine a date certain for the perigean tide as well as the possibility of storm winds accompanying the tide, and every coastal region on Earth is a potential target.

While the trick of predicting perigean spring tides is not easy, there is no question as to the devastation they can cause. The tide itself can wash away such coastal structures as piers, wharves and beach dwellings. Sewers can be backed up when the high tide flushes into sewage outfalls. Beaches are liable to be eroded away as the tides recede. Inland waterways are sometimes overloaded some distance from the sea as the tidal flow surges into river mouths. This can cause flooding far inland in the event of heavy rainfall as the runoff is unable to drain properly under these conditions.

Other effects of the perigean spring tide are less obvious, but no less perilous. Pollution is often stirred up by strong tidal currents, causing an upwelling of noxious wastes which can be harmful both to marine life and to people. Small craft and ships at anchor, floating on the higher-than-normal perigean spring tides, have been known to snap their anchor lines, which can result in loss or damage to the affected vessels, not to mention the danger to their crews. Tall-masted craft may be unable to pass safely under fixed bridges spanning bays, straits and rivers because they ride too high on the water. Obstacles to navigation may be concealed under the tidal surge, posing a significant threat to marine craft, which may run aground or even rip open upon striking submerged reefs, sandbars, rocks and other obstructions. Conversely, when perigean spring tides ebb, they recede much farther than is normally the case. This can be a boon for beachcombers in search of shells and the like, but it's a real hazard to marine vessels that could become stranded in channels rendered too shallow by the extreme ebb tide.

A perigee-syzygy can also pose a threat inland for two principal reasons. In the first place, the perigee-syzygy tends to coincide with atmospheric low-pressure systems, which can bring about dangerous storms inland as well as at sea. Further, there is evidence to suggest that the perigee-syzygy may also be a factor in earthquakes because of stress in the Earth's crust caused by the amplified gravitational forces at work in such a configuration. The 1987 earthquakes in Peru and Chile mentioned earlier are examples of this; others include the California earthquakes of November 22 and 26, 1976, which registered 3.8

and 6.3 on the Richter scale, respectively. Both California quakes came close on the heels of the perigee-syzygy of November 21.

At this point, it would be a Herculean task to predict which among the future SuperMoon alignments might coincide with disastrous coastal flooding, dangerous storms or earthquake activity since each alignment represents such a potential, which can be manifested anywhere in the world. While their particular consequences and geographic focal points cannot be foreseen in all their specifics at this point, at least we can know in advance when the SuperMoon alignment will take place. The included table lists all SuperMoons from 1900-1999, and if the past is any indication, this table is well worth a look. In particular, note that three of these alignments in the 1990s fall under the classification known as *proxigee-syzygy* (after Fergus Wood). This is a very special class of SuperMoon in which the Sun and Moon are opposed and in the same plane of declination and Earth is at or near aphelion (closest approach to the Sun). The combination of these factors makes for the most intense SuperMoon alignment of all. Mundane forecasters may, therefore, wish to take note of the indicated dates: **December 2, 1990; January 19, 1992;** and **March 8, 1993**.

### Let's Get Personal

Beyond the dramatic possibilities of tidal waves, earthquakes and great storms, the perigee-syzygy may also have a direct and personal significance for each of us as human beings. For millennia, astrologers have distinguished three principal branches of the cosmic craft: Mundane, which deals with events on a scale affecting masses of human beings; Genethliacal, which focuses on strictly personal experience; and Horary, the divinatory technique used to answer questions of virtually any kind. Up to this point, we have considered only what would be termed the most obvious mundane implications of the perigee-syzygy. But there is another mundane dimension to SuperMoon beyond its heavy-handed geophysical effects. What about possible correlations with human psychology and behavior, which en masse can alter the economic and political scheme of things as surely as a SuperMoon tide remakes a beachfront town?

Ironically, much of what the ancients considered as Mundane Astrology has passed into the realm of orthodox science, principally since Isaac Newton formulated the theory of gravitation which provided a logical and causal basis for relating solar, lunar and planetary alignments to such terrestrial phenomena as tides, climate, earthquakes and ionospheric disturbances. Throughout modern history, whenever an orthodox scientific explanation has been advanced to account for astrological teachings, the scientists have appropriated astrology and called it something else. Without so much as a thank you, they have pilfered astrology's true and rightful legacy. The sad truth is that astrology is considered superstition until science discovers how it works—whereupon it is considered science. Until a couple decades ago, plagiarisms of this sort stopped short of encroaching on the personal component of the cosmic craft, being confined to the mundane sphere. But the development in the field of biology of the so-called "biological clocks" theory has led many researchers to suspect that cosmic bodies do have a direct influence on terrestrial life forms.

Based on experimental evidence, some biologists now believe that earthly organisms time their behavior in some unknown way so as to coincide with certain celestial configurations. Why this should be so controversial is a puzzle to me. Terrestrial life has evolved over the course of billions of years in the context of an environment which includes cosmic effects. Where's the surprise in the notion that organisms would adapt to their environment? Controversy notwithstanding, one school of thought (pioneered by Dr. Frank Brown of Northwestern University) holds that the mysterious biological clocks are synchronized with the Sun and the Moon. If this is true, there may be some scientific basis for believing that SuperMoon has direct consequences for life forms on Earth—including each of us as individuals and all of us in the collective sense.

Human beings, no less than other life forms on Earth, are instinctively aware of the Moon's dominion. After all, our evolutionary heritage reaches back to the very oceans that rise and fall to a lunar rhythm. When homo sapiens first became consciously aware of the lunar cycle we cannot precisely know. But it appears that Paleolithic men and women were notching reindeer bones to represent lunar phases some 10 to 20 thousand years ago. The astrologers of ancient Babylon seemed to know something of the Moon's uncanny ties to biological life, for they maintained that the "Moon-God" makes "the sheep-fold and cattle pen to flourish."[13]

Myth and folklore hold similar opinions regarding the lunar influence. African Pygmies call the Moon *Pe*, which is said to be the principle of generation and fertility. In ancient times, the Hittites called the Moon *Arma*, which means "pregnant," and the Hindus regarded Luna as the regent of everything growing on Earth.

Traditional astrology is unanimous in granting the importance of the lunar influence on human beings. In the 2nd century, Ptolemy recognized that living creatures respond to the waxing and waning of the Moon as surely as the tides do. Ptolemy further described the Moon's influence as feminine in nature. Astrologers since Ptolemy have expounded on his original themes at great length.

From the Ptolemaic notion that instincts are keyed to the lunar rhythm, astrologers have gone on to attribute instincts and feelings to the lunar domain.

Systematic empirical observation of the lunar influence may have begun with Aristotle in the 4th century B.C.E. In his extensive work as a naturalist, Aristotle had noticed that the ovaries of sea urchins swell at the time of the Full Moon. Later, Cicero and Pliny asserted that oysters and other shellfish increase and decrease in number in rhythm with the lunar cycle, with lows coming at the New Moon and highs at the Full Moon.

In modern times, numerous correlations between biological activity and lunar cycles have been observed. Biologists have discovered a number of cycles that closely coincide with the Moon's movement through the heavens. Many of the so-called circadian cycles, for example, appear to be timed by Luna's passage over the horizon and meridian (roughly corresponding to the Ascendant and Midheaven of a horoscope). Although biologists are still divided in their opinions as to the cause of biological rhythms, one school of thought believes that the ultimate answer may involve cosmic bodies, principally the Sun and the Moon.

One possibility is that terrestrial organisms are able to sense changes in the Earth's magnetic field which are caused by Luna's motion relative to our home planet. At any point on Earth's surface, a plumb line will be displaced from the prime vertical by the Moon's passage through the sky. Perhaps biological clocks are synchronized by this signal. After all, diverse organisms are sensitive to changes in Earth's magnetic field, and it is well known that the geomagnetic field "alters hourly in direct accordance with the solar day, the lunar day, and the lunar month."[14]

Whatever it is that times terrestrial organisms to the

lunar rhythm, human beings are by no means exempt from the Moon's influence. The most obvious of all Moon-related cycles in human experience is menstruation. The average menstrual cycle approximates a lunar month. Late in the 19th century, the Swedish Nobel Prize winner Svante Arrhenius carefully recorded more than 11,000 menstrual periods and found that the onset of bleeding occurs more often during the waxing Moon than during the waning Moon—with a peak coming on the night before the New Moon. Since then, other researchers have conducted similar studies, some of which support Arrhenius' findings, while others do not.

While the connection between the Moon and the menstrual cycle remains unsettled, the fact remains that the average menstrual cycle is keyed to Luna's orbital cycle. Another lunar rhythm in the reproductive cycle is pregnancy, which lasts an average of ten lunar months. Admittedly, we're talking averages and cycles here because it's clear that all women do not ovulate on cue at the very same moment that the Moon makes some universal aspect in the heavens—and maybe we ought to count ourselves lucky for that—any more than all pregnancies last exactly ten lunar months. Perhaps the key to reconciling the observed deviations from these averages is to investigate whether each individual woman may be timed to her own unique lunar rhythm, which might be a function of her natal Sun-Moon aspect, but this is far beyond the scope of this chapter. In any event, the evidence is sufficient to suggest that the ancient astrological tradition which holds that women are somehow ruled by the Moon may not be so far-fetched after all.

In addition to menses and gestation, births are another human reproductive phenomenon which has been correlated with lunar rhythms. The Menaker study of more than a half-million births which had occurred in

New York City hospitals from 1948 to 1957 showed a maximum of births just after the Full Moon and a minimum immediately following the New Moon. Studies in other cities came up with different results, however, so the issue is far from settled. But in this connection it should be noted that different coastal locations exhibit differing tidal responses to the Moon. It is, therefore, at least possible that the various experimental observations of lunar birth cycles may have overlooked local factors which somehow modify the lunar influence. A biological case in point is the mayfly, an insect which in temperate regions times its swarming by the Sun, but uses the Moon as its cosmic clock in the tropics. This suggests that biological responses to the Moon may have local adaptations, and it may account for the differing results obtained by observers at different locations.

One of the more controversial aspects of Moon-coordinated human behavior is "Moon madness," or lunacy as it was known in times past. In the 16th century, Paracelsus claimed that mentally disordered people experience extremes of psychotic behavior at the New Moon. On the other hand, doctors in 18th century England believed just the opposite: the Full Moon coincides with psychotic outbreaks, they claimed. Prior to 1808, inmates at the Bethlehem hospital for the insane were beaten at regular lunar phase intervals in the belief that it would render the inmates less dangerous at the critical lunar cycles when mental aberrations were thought to be the strongest. If anything, the experience of the unfortunate Bethlehem inmates indicates that "lunatics" are not the only ones to be strangely affected by the Moon—their keepers are susceptible to lunacy, too. With this in mind, and recognizing that the lunar influence pervades all of Planet Earth, I sometimes wonder what difference it would make if the inmates or their keepers were in charge of the asylum. . . .

Police authorities often claim that crimes of various sorts reach a peak around the Full Moon. In a 1961 report to the American Institute of Medical Climatology, Inspector Wilfred Faust of the Philadelphia Police Department observed that the Full Moon brings on an increase in reported crimes of violence. Studies of homicides in Dade County, Florida and Cuyahoga County, Ohio, show a Full Moon murder peak. A similar study by the St. Louis Police Department failed to show a lunar murder cycle, but police officers there report that citizen complaints reach a peak at the Full Moon.

A possible explanation for lunar rhythms in human behavior may be that the Moon affects the nervous systems of individual human beings. At the Virginia Department of Health, Dr. Leonard Ravitz measured the difference in electric potential between the head and chest of mental patients. Over a period of years, certain patterns became obvious, and Ravitz concluded that changes in an individual's electric potential followed a solar as well as lunar rhythm. In particular, a 27-year-old schizophrenic in Ravitz's care showed a consistent tendency to exhibit exaggerated psychotic symptoms at the New and Full Moon, when instrument readings showed the greatest difference in electric potential. If a normal syzygy (New or Full Moon) is enough to send some people into a frenzy, the much stronger perigee-syzygy seems even more likely to coincide with extremes in human behavior, which explains my inclination to call this alignment a SuperMoon. It's enough to make a person wonder whether the course of wisdom in the event of a perigee-syzygy alignment of Sun and Moon would be as astrologer Elbert Wade suggests in connection with Full Moons in general: "Stay off the streets . . . use extra care in driving, and avoid going to the sort of places where trouble may strike."[15]

## Lunar Lore from Ptolemy to Today

Evidence and possible mechanisms regarding the lunar effect aside, the fact remains that astrology has for many centuries had a symbolic understanding of the Moon which is generally consistent with all of the empirical findings to date. For example, Llewellyn George considered the Moon to be "significant of things of a constantly changing or fluctuating character," such as "feelings and states of mind or health."[16] Likewise, Marc Edmund Jones characterized Luna as an "indication of feeling."[17] Frances Sakoian and Louis Acker described the Moon's personal impact as indicative of an individual's "type of immediate emotional response to life's situations."[18] According to Michael Meyer, the Moon is associated with "feelings, reactions and instincts . . . the bio-psychic functions and feeling-instinct responses."[19] Last but not least in our brief survey of the representative literature, Leonora Luxton wrote that the Moon "controls man's emotional response en masse as well as individually, "and adds that "mob response to any situation is the result of lunar influence."[20]

In light of the summary evidence and survey of the astrological literature discussed up to this point, the correlation between observed fact and astrological tradition is striking. The traditional association of the Moon with women parallels the demonstrated importance of lunar rhythms in menstruation, fertility, gestation, and the cyclic distribution of births. The astrological tradition relating the Moon to instinct and emotion finds empirical confirmation in crime statistics, psychotic behavior, and changes in the electrical potential of individual human beings. All these phenomena exhibit variations keyed to the lunar cycle, as we have seen. Of course, the evidence is still inconclusive on some points, but the general trend is plain to see: the Moon is linked to human behavior, even if the mechanism which underlies this link is still unknown. And since the SuperMoon alignment is a most extreme case of the lunar influence, it's no wonder that its significance has a certain logical priority over all other Moon manifestations down here on Earth. Accordingly, the question is not whether the perigee-syzygy has meaning at the personal (micro) and mundane (macro) levels; the real wonder is that astrology hasn't taken note of the SuperMoon effect until now. Or has it?

Astrological tradition is mute on the subject of the perigee-syzygy itself, but clues to its meaning may be inferred from the traditional indications associated with perigee and syzygy individually considered. Although some modern astrologers—those who consider "distance value" as a valid technique, at any rate—suggest that perigee indicates a heightened cosmic influence due to the decrease in distance between celestial bodies and Earth, ancient astrologers had little to say about perigee *per se*. However, as I mentioned previously, when a celestial body is at perigee, its motion relative to Earth is greatest, so perigee equates with rapid motion. This is worth noting in view of the ancient tradition which holds that a celestial body (such as the Moon) moving at greater than average speed ("swift in course") is more influential than when moving at average speed or slower ("slow in motion"). Thus, tradition implies that the lunar perigee, when the Moon is swift in course, coincides with a time of heightened lunar influence on Earth.

Where the syzygy itself (New or Full Moon) is concerned, tradition is not so reticent: "There are certain particular consequences which result from the New and Full Moon," Ptolemy wrote.[21] Among contemporary astrologers, Sakoian and Acker summarize the general trend of thinking on the subject of lunar syzygies as well as anyone. They write that the New Moon signifies a time when "emotional impulsiveness is combined with the tendency to concentrate all of one's forces in one area of expression . . . passive action can suddenly become aggressive and vice versa."[22] On the other hand, the Full Moon is said to indicate "a conflict between the conscious will and the unconscious mind and feelings," resulting in "relationship problems . . . restlessness, nervousness, or psychosomatic ailments."[23]

Syzygy and perigee are each separately acknowledged as important in the literature of astrology, that much is clear. What isn't clear is why it took so long for astrologers to put these two cosmic factors together. The fact is, SuperMoon is just the synthesis astrology has lacked for all these centuries where these factors are concerned—not the end-all and be-all by any means, but an important missing link that now has been found.

I am hopeful that the day will come when the psychology of lunar effects is empirically verified, just as the geophysical effects have been. If the scientific findings to date are any indication—and these include the Gauquelin work, primarily—whatever is ultimately upheld by the scientific method will include some elements of astrological tradition while discarding others. But until the experimental results are in, a reasonable guess is that the astrological symbolism of lunar effects may be as much a precursor of tomorrow's science as Ptolemy's link between the Moon and the tides proved to be the precursor of Newton's Law of Gravitation. With that in mind, consider the traditional symbolism. . . .

The dark perigee-syzygy alignment occurs when the Moon lies between the Earth and the Sun. Nights are darker in this case because the nocturnal luminary is absent from view. And if an eclipse occurs at this point, the Sun's rays are cut off in broad daylight. At the light perigee-syzygy, Earth is between the Sun and the Moon, nearer the diurnal luminary. Nights are brighter and bio-logical life is more active at this point. If an eclipse occurs under this alignment, the nocturnal luminary is temporar-ily extinguished.

Symbolically speaking, light is consciousness (day, Sun) and darkness is unconsciousness (night, Moon). Ap-plying these traditional concepts in a personal sense might lead us to expect that anyone born at the dark perigee-syzygy would tend to live life more on an instinctive level in close contact with feelings, the unconscious mind, and perhaps the collective unconscious as well. A light peri-gee-syzygy birth chart, on the other hand, would signify a heightened link to conscious and superconscious reality, an active rational intellect, and perhaps a relative lack of contact with instinctive levels of awareness, or at least a sense of conflict between the rational and the irrational. If one were born at a perigee New Moon, in other words, feelings and instinct would predominate, but if one were born at a perigee Full Moon, the intellect would tend to try to prevail over the instinctive nature. What I'm suggesting here, in short, is that the SuperMoon is essentially the same as a normal New or Full Moon—only more so. It repre-sents an extreme emphasis.

Judging from the letters I received from people who read my 1979 *Dell Horoscope* article on the SuperMoon alignment, it appears that the symbolism of this cosmic configuration really does ring true. One woman wrote about her father, who was born at the time of a perigee Full Moon, an eclipse yet. "No one can figure my father out," she wrote. "He is a very strange and solitary person who lives alone. No one in the family has anything to do with him, although we all live in the same town. He has never done any of us any physical harm, but we have been emo-tionally abused by him—he is very strange!"

Another correspondent, who was born coincident

with a perigee New Moon, described her life as "a crazy quilt—nothing much for sure and almost everything for maybe." After a difficult childhood (thanks to an alcoholic father), this woman ended up marrying an alcoholic, then living with yet another when the marriage broke up. Now alienated from her own children, who blame her for their lack of material advantages in life, this perigee-syzygy native sums up her life as follows: "I suppose I always wanted things out of my reach, and the things I could get just didn't seem that important to me."

One woman wrote to tell me about a friend of hers who was born on the SuperMoon of March 14, 1949—and who took his own life less than a week after the Super-Moon of May 3, 1977. "He was extremely psychic . . . his powers of ESP were amazing us all. Also, he was very hyper and ecstatic, spoke at great length about reincarnation . . ."

An anxious mother wrote about her daughter, who is a perigee Full Moon type. "She's like a walking time bomb inside," the mother wrote, "but very quiet outwardly. I've always felt very close to her, but other people have a hard time understanding her because they can feel her intensity. At times she tells me she feels like she's going to explode inside, and she becomes fearful of herself. Her worst enemy was her father—not a day went by that we didn't argue about her."

Not all the responses came from people whose experience of the natal perigee-syzygy was negative in character. Some people with this alignment report having a special gift, which they attribute at least in part to the Super-Moon configuration. One woman, a songwriter, wrote to say that she "can pick or create hit songs under a Full Moon, and by the time the New Moon comes around this is verified." Another declared that "a lifelong interest in mind study was born of the childhood realization that anything I wished for came to me." Yet another describes herself as "highly sensitive at any Full Moon, fanciful, and nervous . . . I can really cut a swath through the world, propelled by my Full Moon energy and charisma!"

I won't go into any more of the SuperMoon letters at this point because they tend to repeat the same issues over and over again. Aside from the obvious theme of pronounced emotional intensity, which is common to both types of syzygies, the letters offer an important further clue. A majority (although not all) refer to childhood *family difficulties*, discord with one's own family as an adult, and a feeling of being very special in some way—sometimes especially gifted, sometimes especially cursed. Tradition suggests that the Sun-Moon alignment is symbolic of one's father and mother, respectively, and, by extension, of the family in general. The SuperMoon often seems to indicate a powerfully charged and polarized family atmosphere that can result in separation or sorrow through one or both of the parents, and in many cases the broken or unhappy homelife pattern is repeated in the next generation. It may well be that domestic conflict, particularly in childhood, is part of the SuperMoon syndrome which accounts for the emotional intensity this alignment seems to signify.

I certainly don't mean to suggest that the perigee-syzygy is anything like a curse, even though many of the letters I received were from or about people who seem to have suffered more than their share of hard knocks in life. There were also those who wrote to say that they felt special by virtue of unique gifts or talents they possessed. The SuperMoon alignment is like anything else in that its potential can manifest both positively and negatively. What does seem to come through consistently is summed up by the key word of this configuration, as far as I am able to determine, and that is **intensity**. It's a factor worth looking for in your own chart as well as in the horoscopes of fam-

ily, friends, clients, etc. Whenever you run across a Super-
Moon chart, be alert to its special potential, both natally
and under the influence of subsequent transits, particularly lunations.

### SuperMoon on the Horizon . . .

I think it's fair to say that one doesn't have to be born
at a perigee-syzygy to feel its intensity, although I do suspect that the psyches of those who are born at such times
hint at the kind of atmosphere which prevails whenever a
SuperMoon occurs. Whenever this alignment takes place
(an average of several times a year), all life on Earth is subject to its influence in one way or another, either on the micro (personal level) or on the macro (mundane) level. Refer to the table at the end of this chapter, check out the SuperMoon alignments in your past, and see if they don't relate to significant emotional experiences in your life. Similarly, watch for the future SuperMoons, and take note of
the way they unfold for you. (If you use any system of progressions, be aware of progressed SuperMoon alignments
as well, whether direct or converse.) You too may find that
the perigee New Moon signifies a time that highlights the
instinct and the unconscious mind in a very special, even
powerful, way, while the perigee Full Moon generally
puts a similar degree of emphasis on the intellect and conscious mind (and relationships as well).

In addition to these essentially personal/psychologi-
cal indications, there is also the well-documented possibility that SuperMoon alignments can time the occurrence of
great natural upheavals, such as earthquakes, storms and
floods—any of which can have dire personal consequences for anyone who happens to be in harm's way at
the time. History shows that it has happened before, and I
have no doubt it will happen again, in which case it
wouldn't hurt to steer clear of flood-prone lowlands or

areas of seismic risk when this alignment takes place in the sky.

And let's not forget that mass psychology—a principal driving force in such areas of Mundane Astrology as politics and economics—is a collective which embraces individual psychology. If the individual is responsive to SuperMoon effects, then the collective must reflect them as well. Accordingly, look for collective unease (riots, stock market panics, etc.) when this alignment forms in the heavens. Again, these correlations have been observed in the past, which is reason enough to be aware of their potential in the future.

In closing, all I ask is that you look into the matter for yourself, and see if the SuperMoon doesn't earn a place in your astrological bag of tricks. Don't forget that mundane SuperMoon effects can show up anywhere from a couple days before to a couple days after the exact alignment itself, as Fergus Wood advised. And pay special attention to the extreme proxigee-syzygy type, as well as any Super-Moon where the luminaries are near the equinoctial points—in the Pisces/Aries and Virgo/Libra polarity, in other words. When these alignments loom on the horizon, take note of what follows in their wake . . .

## Notes

1. *New York Times*, September 5, 1989, pp. Al-A2.

2. *New York Times*, September 6, 1989, p. D20.

3. *New York Times*, September 7, 1989, p. Al.

4. Richard Nolle, "SuperMoon (Part 1)," *Dell Horoscope*, Vol. 45 No. 9 (September 1979), p. 26.

5. Richard Nolle, "Planet Watch," *STAR\*TECH*, Vol. 1 No. 7 (Leo 1987), p. 12.

6. Richard Nolle, "SuperMoon Strikes Again," *STAR\*TECH*, Vol. 1 No. 1 (Aquarius 1987), p. 6.

7. Richard Nolle, "SuperMoon Update," *STAR\*TECH*, Vol. 1 No. 11 (Sagittarius 1987), p. 20.

8. Barbara Stevenson, "My Word!" (letters to the editor), *STAR\*TECH*, Vol. 2 No. 2 (Pisces 1988), p. 15.

9. *Note*: C.E. (Common Era) is equivalent to A.D., and B.C.E. (Before the Common Era) is equivalent to B.C. These alternative calendar designations are used here in preference to their more common equivalents for ecumenical reasons.

10. *Sir Isaac Newton's Mathematical Principles*. Vol. 2. Trans. by Florian Cajori. Berkeley, CA: University of California Press, 1973, p. 481.

11. Garth Allen, "Crashing the Weather Barrier," *American Astrology*, Vol. 44 No. 6 (August 1976), p. 21.

12. Fergus Wood, *The Strategic Role of Perigean Spring Tides*, Washington, D.C.: U.S. Department of Commerce, 1978, p. 408.

13. C.J.S. Thompson, *The Mystery and Romance of Astrology*, Detroit, MI: Singing Tree Press, 1969, p. 53.

14. Lyall Watson, *Supernature*, New York: Bantam, 1974, p. 26.

15. Elbert Wade, "Coping With Full Moon Madness," *Dell Horoscope*, Vol. 43 No. 11 (November 1977), p. 41.

16. Llewellyn George, *A to Z Horoscope Maker & Delineator*. 28th edition. St. Paul, MN: Llewellyn, 1970, p. 259.

17. Marc Edmund Jones, *Astrology, How & Why It Works*, Baltimore, MD: Pelican, 1973, p. 239.

18. Frances Sakoian & Louis Acker, *The Astrologer's Handbook*, New York: Harper & Row, 1973, p. 278.

19. Michael Meyer, *A Handbook for the Humanistic Astrologer*, New York: Anchor, 1974, p. 70.

20. Leonora Luxton, *Astrology, Key to Self-Understanding*, St. Paul, MN: Llewellyn, 1978, p. 160.

21. *Ptolemy's Tetrabiblos*. Trans. by J.M. Ashmand. North Hollywood, CA: Symbols & Signs, 1976, p. 64.

22. Sakoian & Acker, *op. cit.*, p. 278.

23. *Ibid.*, p. 416.

# THE SUPERMOON ALIGNMENT

*User Notes:* The table on the following pages lists all SuperMoon alignments from 1900-1999. All dates and times are expressed in Universal Time (U.T.—also known as Greenwich Mean Time [G.M.T.]). All times are expressed in 24-hour clock terms: 1:00 P.M. is 13:00. To convert these times to your local standard time, add or subtract the appropriate number of hours, being careful to watch for date changes. Thus, anyone using Eastern Standard Time (EST) should subtract five hours from the times shown.

*Abbreviations:* Months are designated by the first three letters of their names as are zodiacal signs. The *Long.* column refers to zodiacal position, given in degree-sign-minute format. The *T* column refers to the type of SuperMoon lunation. The two basic types are New Moon (N) and Full Moon (F). Where these are also eclipses, the designation E is added. An asterisk (*) denotes an unusually strong SuperMoon alignment.

When SuperMoons by transit form major aspects to the natal chart, a highly emotional period is likely to follow.

An extreme case of SuperMoon (asterisked in the table) is the *proxigee-syzygy*, a Full Moon occurring within five hours of perigee with the Sun and Moon in the same plane of declination and Earth at or near perihelion (i.e., closest approach to the Sun). Proxigee-syzygies are rare indeed, happening once every 20 years or so. For an indepth discussion of the SuperMoon alignment, see the recently published book *Interpreting Astrology*.

| Date | Time | Long. | T |
|---|---|---|---|
| 1900 Jan 31 = 01:23 = 10 AQU 45 = N |
| 1900 Mar 01 = 11:25 = 10 PIS 27 = N |
| 1900 Mar 30 = 20:30 = 09 ARI 41 = N |
| 1900 Sep 09 = 05:06 = 16 PIS 03 = F |
| 1900 Oct 08 = 13:18 = 14 ARI 48 = F |
| |
| 1901 Mar 20 = 12:53 = 29 PIS 14 = N |
| 1901 Apr 18 = 21:37 = 28 ARI 09 = N |
| 1901 May 18 = 05:38 = 26 TAU 34 = NE |
| 1901 Oct 27 = 15:06 = 03 TAU 30 = FE |
| 1901 Nov 26 = 01:17 = 03 GEM 06 = F |
| |
| 1902 May 07 = 22:45 = 16 TAU 25 = NE |
| 1902 Jun 06 = 06:11 = 14 GEM 36 = N |
| 1902 Jul 05 = 12:59 = 12 CAN 33 = N |
| 1902 Dec 15 = 03:47 = 22 GEM 15 = F |
| |
| 1903 Jan 13 = 14:17 = 22 CAN 14 = F |
| 1903 Jun 25 = 06:11 = 02 CAN 30 = N |
| 1903 Jul 24 = 12:46 = 00 LEO 26 = N |
| 1903 Aug 22 = 19:51 = 28 LEO 31 = N |
| |
| 1904 Feb 01 = 16:33 = 11 LEO 25 = F |
| 1904 Mar 02 = 02:48 = 11 VIR 07 = FE |
| 1904 Aug 11 = 12:58 = 18 LEO 23 = N |
| 1904 Sep 09 = 20:43 = 16 VIR 42 = NE |
| 1904 Oct 09 = 05:25 = 15 LIB 29 = N |
| |
| 1905 Mar 21 = 04:55 = 29 VIR 55 = F |
| 1905 Apr 19 = 13:38 = 28 LIB 49 = F |
| 1905 Sep 28 = 21:59 = 05 LIB 05 = N |
| 1905 Oct 28 = 06:58 = 04 SCO 12 = N |
| |
| 1906 May 08 = 14:09 = 17 SCO 03 = F |
| 1906 Jun 06 = 21:11 = 15 SAG 13 = F |
| 1906 Nov 16 = 08:36 = 23 SCO 05 = N |
| 1906 Dec 15 = 18:54 = 22 SAG 55 = N |
| |
| 1907 Jun 25 = 21:27 = 03 CAP 08 = F |
| 1907 Jul 25 = 04:29 = 01 AQU 05 = FE |
| |
| 1908 Jan 03 = 21:43 = 12 CAP 08 = NE |
| 1908 Feb 02 = 08:36 = 12 AQU 07 = N |
| 1908 Aug 12 = 04:59 = 19 AQU 03 = F |
| 1908 Sep 10 = 12:23 = 17 PIS 22 = F |

| Date | Time | Long. | T |
|---|---|---|---|
| 1909 Feb 20 = 10:52 = 01 PIS 11 = N |
| 1909 Mar 21 = 20:11 = 00 ARI 35 = N |
| 1909 Sep 29 = 13:05 = 05 ARI 44 = F |
| 1909 Oct 28 = 22:07 = 04 TAU 51 = F |
| |
| 1910 Apr 09 = 21:25 = 19 ARI 08 = N |
| 1910 May 09 = 05:33 = 17 TAU 43 = NE |
| 1910 Nov 17 = 00:25 = 23TAU 47 = FE |
| 1910 Dec 16 = 11:05 = 23 GEM 38 = F |
| |
| 1911 May 28 = 06:24 = 05 GEM 48 = N |
| 1911 Jun 26 = 13:19 = 03 CAN 48 = N |
| 1911 Dec 06 = 02:52 = 12 GEM 52 = F |
| |
| 1912 Jan 04 = 13:29 = 12 CAN 51 = F* |
| 1912 Feb 02 = 23:58 = 12 LEO 48 = F |
| 1912 Jul 14 = 13:13 = 21 CAN 41 = N |
| 1912 Aug 12 = 19:57 = 19 LEO 42 = N |
| |
| 1913 Jan 22 = 15:40 = 02 LEO 03 = F |
| 1913 Feb 21 = 02:03 = 01 VIR 52 = F |
| 1913 Aug 31 = 20:38 = 07 VIR 48 = NE |
| 1913 Sep 30 = 04:56 = 06 LIB 25 = NE |
| |
| 1914 Mar 12 = 04:18 = 20 VIR 46 = FE |
| 1914 Apr 10 = 13:28 = 19 LIB 50 = F |
| 1914 Oct 19 = 06:33 = 25 LIB 02 = N |
| 1914 Nov 17 = 16:02 = 24 VIR 28 = N |
| |
| 1915 Apr 29 = 14:19 = 08 SCO 11 = F |
| 1915 May 28 = 21:33 = 06 SAG 27 = F |
| 1915 Dec 06 = 18:03 = 13 SAG 33 = N |
| |
| 1916 Jan 05 = 04:45 = 13 CAP 32 = N |
| 1916 Jun 15 = 21:41 = 24 SAG 24 = F |
| 1916 Jul 15 = 04:40 = 22 CAP 20 = FE |
| |
| 1917 Jan 23 = 07:40 = 02 AQU 45 = NE |
| 1917 Feb 21 = 18:09 = 02 PIS 34 = N |
| 1917 Aug 03 = 05:10 = 10 AQU 17 = F |
| 1917 Sep 01 = 12:28 = 08 PIS 29 = F |
| |
| 1918 Mar 12 = 19:52 = 21 PIS 26 = N |
| 1918 Apr 11 = 04:34 = 20 ARI 29 = N |
| 1918 Sep 20 = 13:01 = 26 PIS 45 = F |

| Date | Time | Long. | T |
|------|------|-------|---|
| 1918 Oct 19 | 21:34 | 25 ARI 41 | F |
| 1919 Mar 31 | 21:04 | 10 ARI 06 | N |
| 1919 Apr 30 | 05:30 | 08 TAU 49 | N |
| 1919 May 29 | 13:12 | 07 GEM 06 | NE |
| 1919 Nov 07 | 23:35 | 14 TAU 31 | FE |
| 1919 Dec 07 | 10:03 | 14 GEM 15 | F |
| 1920 May 18 | 06:25 | 27 TAU 00 | NE |
| 1920 Jun 16 | 13:41 | 25 GEM 04 | N |
| 1920 Jul 15 | 20:25 | 23 CAN 00 | N |
| 1920 Dec 25 | 12:38 | 03 CAN 27 | F |
| 1921 Jan 23 | 23:07 | 03 LEO 26 | F |
| 1921 Jul 05 | 13:36 | 12 CAN 57 | N |
| 1921 Aug 03 | 20:17 | 10 LEO 55 | N |
| 1921 Sep 02 | 03:33 | 09 VIR 07 | N |
| 1922 Feb 12 | 01:17 | 22 LEO 33 | F |
| 1922 Mar 13 | 11:14 | 22 VIR 06 | FE |
| 1922 Aug 22 | 20:34 | 28 LEO 56 | N |
| 1922 Sep 21 | 04:38 | 27 VIR 24 | NE |
| 1922 Oct 20 | 13:40 | 26 LIB 23 | N |
| 1923 Apr 01 | 13:10 | 10 LIB 47 | F |
| 1923 Apr 30 | 21:30 | 09 SCO 30 | F |
| 1923 Oct 10 | 06:05 | 15 LIB 54 | N |
| 1923 Nov 08 | 15:27 | 15 SCO 12 | N |
| 1923 Dec 08 | 01:30 | 14 SAG 56 | N |
| 1924 May 18 | 21:52 | 27 SCO 39 | F |
| 1924 Jun 17 | 04:41 | 25 SAG 42 | F |
| 1924 Nov 26 | 17:15 | 04 SAG 12 | N |
| 1924 Dec 26 | 03:46 | 04 CAP 07 | N |
| 1925 Jul 06 | 04:54 | 13 CAP 35 | F |
| 1925 Aug 04 | 11:59 | 11 AQU 34 | FE |
| 1926 Jan 14 | 06:34 | 23 CAP 21 | NE |
| 1926 Feb 12 | 17:20 | 23 AQU 15 | N |
| 1926 Aug 23 | 12:38 | 29 AQU 37 | F |
| 1926 Sep 21 | 20:19 | 28 PIS 05 | F |
| 1927 Mar 03 | 19:24 | 12 PIS 14 | N |
| 1927 Apr 02 | 04:24 | 11 ARI 26 | N |

| Date | Time | Long. | T |
|------|------|-------|---|
| 1927 Oct 10 | 21:14 | 16 ARI 34 | F |
| 1927 Nov 09 | 06:36 | 15 TAU 52 | F |
| 1928 Apr 20 | 05:25 | 29 ARI 53 | N |
| 1928 May 19 | 13:14 | 28 TAU 17 | NE |
| 1928 Nov 27 | 09:05 | 04 GEM 54 | FE |
| 1928 Dec 26 | 19:55 | 04 CAN 50 | F |
| 1929 Jun 07 | 13:56 | 16 GEM 18 | N |
| 1929 Jul 06 | 20:47 | 14 CAN 15 | N |
| 1930 Jan 14 | 22:21 | 24 CAN 03 | F* |
| 1930 Feb 13 | 08:39 | 23 LEO 56 | F |
| 1930 Jul 25 | 20:42 | 02 LEO 09 | N |
| 1930 Aug 24 | 03:37 | 00 VIR 15 | N |
| 1931 Feb 03 | 00:26 | 13 Leo 13 | F |
| 1931 Mar 04 | 10:36 | 12 VIR 54 | F |
| 1931 Apr 02 | 20:05 | 12 LIB 07 | FE |
| 1931 Sep 12 | 04:26 | 18 VIR 27 | NE |
| 1931 Oct 11 | 13:06 | 17 LIB 15 | NE |
| 1932 Mar 22 | 12:37 | 01 LIB 41 | FE |
| 1932 Apr 20 | 21:27 | 00 SCO 34 | F |
| 1932 May 20 | 05:09 | 28 SCO 58 | F |
| 1932 Oct 29 | 14:56 | 05 SCO 59 | N |
| 1932 Nov 28 | 00:43 | 05 SAG 35 | N |
| 1933 May 09 | 22:04 | 18 SCO 48 | F |
| 1933 Jun 08 | 05:05 | 16 SAG 57 | F |
| 1933 Jul 07 | 11:51 | 14 CAP 53 | F |
| 1933 Dec 17 | 02:53 | 24 SAG 44 | N |
| 1934 Jan 15 | 13:37 | 24 CAP 44 | N |
| 1934 Jun 27 | 05:08 | 04 CAP 52 | F |
| 1934 Jul 26 | 12:08 | 02 AQU 48 | FE |
| 1934 Aug 24 | 19:37 | 00 PIS 56 | F |
| 1935 Feb 03 | 16:27 | 13 AQU 56 | NE |
| 1935 Mar 05 | 02:40 | 13 PIS 36 | N |
| 1935 Aug 14 | 12:43 | 20 AQU 48 | F |
| 1935 Sep 12 | 20:18 | 19 PIS 08 | F |
| 1935 Oct 12 | 04:39 | 17 ARI 56 | F |
| 1936 Mar 23 | 04:13 | 02 ARI 22 | N |

| Date | Time | Long. | T |
|------|------|-------|---|
| 1936 Apr 21 | = 12:33 | = 01 TAU 13 | = N |
| 1936 Sep 30 | = 21:01 | = 07 ARI 30 | = F |
| 1936 Oct 30 | = 05:58 | = 06 TAU 38 | = F |
| | | | |
| 1937 May 10 | = 13:17 | = 19 TAU 27 | = N |
| 1937 Jun 08 | = 20:43 | = 17 GEM 36 | = NE |
| 1937 Nov 18 | = 08:09 | = 25 TAU 35 | = FE |
| 1937 Dec 17 | = 18:52 | = 25 GEM 26 | = F |
| | | | |
| 1938 Jun 27 | = 21:10 | = 05 CAN 32 | = N |
| 1938 Jul 27 | = 03:53 | = 03 LEO 28 | = N |
| | | | |
| 1939 Jan 05 | = 21:30 | = 14 CAN 40 | = F |
| 1939 Feb 04 | = 07:55 | = 14 LEO 37 | = F |
| 1939 Aug 15 | = 03:53 | = 21 LEO 26 | = N |
| 1939 Sep 13 | = 11:22 | = 19 VIR 46 | = N |
| | | | |
| 1940 Feb 23 | = 09:55 | = 03 VIR 39 | = F |
| 1940 Mar 23 | = 19:33 | = 03 LIB 01 | = FE |
| 1940 Oct 01 | = 12:41 | = 08 LIB 11 | = NE |
| 1940 Oct 30 | = 22:03 | = 07 SCO 20 | = N |
| | | | |
| 1941 Apr 11 | = 21:15 | = 21 LIB 35 | = F |
| 1941 May 11 | = 05:15 | = 20 SCO 07 | = F |
| 1941 Oct 20 | = 14:20 | = 26 LIB 48 | = N |
| 1941 Nov 19 | = 00:04 | = 26 SCO 16 | = N |
| 1941 Dec 18 | = 10:18 | = 26 SAG 07 | = N |
| | | | |
| 1942 May 30 | = 05:29 | = 08 SAG 10 | = F |
| 1942 Jun 28 | = 12:09 | = 06 CAP 09 | = F |
| 1942 Dec 08 | = 01:59 | = 15 SAG 21 | = N |
| | | | |
| 1943 Jan 06 | = 12:38 | = 15 CAP 20 | = N |
| 1943 Feb 04 | = 23:29 | = 15 AQU 17 | = NE |
| 1943 Jul 17 | = 12:21 | = 24 CAP 03 | = F |
| 1943 Aug 15 | = 19:34 | = 22 AQU 05 | = FE |
| | | | |
| 1944 Jan 25 | = 15:24 | = 04 AQU 33 | = NE |
| 1944 Feb 24 | = 01:59 | = 04 PIS 21 | = N |
| 1944 Sep 02 | = 20:21 | = 10 PIS 13 | = F |
| 1944 Oct 02 | = 04:22 | = 08 ARI 51 | = F |
| | | | |
| 1945 Mar 14 | = 03:51 | = 23 PIS 13 | = N |
| 1945 Apr 12 | = 12:30 | = 22 ARI 14 | = N |
| 1945 Oct 21 | = 05:32 | = 27 ARI 28 | = F |

| Date | Time | Long. | T |
|------|------|-------|---|
| 1945 Nov 19 | = 15:13 | = 26 TAU 56 | = F |
| | | | |
| 1946 May 01 | = 13:16 | = 10 TAU 33 | = N |
| 1946 May 30 | = 20:49 | = 08 GEM 49 | = NE |
| 1946 Dec 08 | = 17:52 | = 16 GEM 03 | = FE |
| | | | |
| 1947 Jan 07 | = 04:47 | = 16 CAN 03 | = F |
| 1947 Jun 18 | = 21:26 | = 26 GEM 47 | = N |
| 1947 Jul 18 | = 04:15 | = 24 CAN 43 | = N |
| | | | |
| 1948 Jan 26 | = 07:11 | = 05 LEO 15 | = F* |
| 1948 Feb 24 | = 17:16 | = 05 VIR 01 | = F |
| 1948 Aug 05 | = 04:13 | = 12 LEO 38 | = N |
| 1948 Sep 03 | = 11:21 | = 10 VIR 51 | = N |
| | | | |
| 1949 Mar 14 | = 94:03 | = 23 VIR 53 | = F |
| 1949 Apr 13 | = 04:08 | = 22 LIB 54 | = FE |
| 1949 Sep 22 | = 12:21 | = 29 VIR 09 | = N |
| 1949 Oct 21 | = 21:23 | = 28 LIB 09 | = NE |
| | | | |
| 1950 Apr 02 | = 20:49 | = 12 LIB 32 | = FE |
| 1950 May 02 | = 05:19 | = 11 SCO 15 | = F |
| 1950 May 31 | = 12:43 | = 09 SAG 29 | = F |
| 1950 Nov 09 | = 23:25 | = 17 SCO 00 | = N |
| 1950 Dec 09 | = 09:28 | = 16 SAG 44 | = N |
| | | | |
| 1951 May 21 | = 05:45 | = 29 SCO 23 | = F |
| 1951 Jun 19 | = 12:36 | = 27 SAG 25 | = F |
| 1951 Jul 18 | = 19:17 | = 25 CAP 21 | = F |
| 1951 Dec 28 | = 11:43 | = 05 CAP 56 | = N |
| | | | |
| 1952 Jan 26 | = 22:26 | = 05 AQU 56 | = N |
| 1952 Jul 07 | = 12:33 | = 15 CAP 19 | = F |
| 1952 Aug 05 | = 19:40 | = 13 AQU 17 | = FE |
| 1952 Sep 04 | = 03:19 | = 11 PIS 32 | = F |
| | | | |
| 1953 Feb 14 | = 01:10 | = 25 AQU 03 | = NE |
| 1953 Mar 15 | = 11:05 | = 24 PIS 34 | = N |
| 1953 Aug 24 | = 20:21 | = 01 PIS 21 | = F |
| 1953 Sep 23 | = 04:16 | = 29 PIS 51 | = F |
| 1953 Oct 22 | = 12:56 | = 28 ARI 50 | = F |
| | | | |
| 1954 Apr 03 | = 12:25 | = 13 ARI 13 | = N |
| 1954 May 02 | = 20:22 | = 11 TAU 53 | = N |
| 1954 Oct 12 | = 05:10 | = 18 ARI 21 | = F |

| Date | Time | Long. | T |
|------|------|-------|---|
| 1954 Nov 10 | = 14:29 | = 17 TAU 40 | = F* |
| 1954 Dec 10 | = 00:57 | = 17 GEM 26 | = F |
| | | | |
| 1955 May 21 | = 20:59 | = 00 GEM 01 | = N |
| 1955 Jun 20 | = 04:12 | = 28 GEM 05 | = NE |
| 1955 Nov 29 | = 16:50 | = 06 GEM 42 | = FE |
| 1955 Dec 29 | = 03:44 | = 06 CAN 39 | = F |
| | | | |
| 1956 Jul 08 | = 04:38 | = 15 CAN 59 | = N |
| 1956 Aug 06 | = 11:25 | = 13 LEO 57 | = N |
| | | | |
| 1957 Jan 16 | = 06:21 | = 25 CAN 52 | = F |
| 1957 Feb 14 | = 16:38 | = 25 LEO 44 | = F |
| 1957 Aug 25 | = 11:32 | = 01 VIR 59 | = N |
| 1957 Sep 23 | = 19:18 | = 00 LIB 29 | = N |
| | | | |
| 1958 Mar 05 | = 18:28 | = 14 VIR 41 | = F |
| 1958 Apr 04 | = 03:45 | = 13 LIB 52 | = FE |
| 1958 Oct 12 | = 20:52 | = 19 LIB 01 | = NE |
| 1958 Nov 11 | = 06:34 | = 18 SCO 22 | = N |
| | | | |
| 1959 Apr 23 | = 05:13 | = 02 SCO 19 | = F |
| 1959 May 22 | = 12:56 | = 00 SAG 41 | = F |
| 1959 Nov 30 | = 08:46 | = 07 SAG 24 | = N |
| 1959 Dec 29 | = 19:09 | = 07 CAP 20 | = N |
| | | | |
| 1960 Jun 09 | = 13:02 | = 18 SAG 40 | = F |
| 1960 Jul 08 | = 19:37 | = 16 CAP 36 | = F |
| 1960 Dec 18 | = 10:47 | = 26 SAG 32 | = N |
| | | | |
| 1961 Jan 16 | = 21:30 | = 26 CAP 32 | = N |
| 1961 Feb 15 | = 08:10 | = 26 AQU 25 | = NE |
| 1961 Jul 27 | = 19:50 | = 04 AQU 31 | = F |
| 1961 Aug 26 | = 03:13 | = 02 PIS 39 | = FE |
| | | | |
| 1962 Feb 05 | = 00:10 | = 15 AQU 43 | = NE |
| 1962 Mar 06 | = 10:31 | = 15 PIS 23 | = N |
| 1962 Apr 04 | = 19:45 | = 14 ARI 33 | = N |
| 1962 Sep 14 | = 04:11 | = 20 PIS 52 | = F |
| 1962 Oct 13 | = 12:33 | = 19 ARI 42 | = F |
| | | | |
| 1963 Mar 25 | = 12:10 | = 04 ARI 08 | = N |
| 1963 Apr 23 | = 20:29 | = 02 TAU 58 | = N |
| 1963 May 23 | = 04:00 | = 01 GEM 19 | = N |
| 1963 Nov 1 | = 13:55 | = 08 TAU 25 | = F |

| Date | Time | Long. | T |
|------|------|-------|---|
| 1963 Nov 30 | = 23:54 | = 08 GEM 03 | = F |
| | | | |
| 1964 May 11 | = 21:02 | = 21 TAU 10 | = N |
| 1964 Jun 10 | = 04:22 | = 19 GEM 19 | = NE |
| 1964 Dec 19 | = 02:41 | = 27 GEM 14 | = FE |
| | | | |
| 1965 Jan 17 | = 13:37 | = 27 CAN 15 | = F |
| 1965 Jun 29 | = 04:52 | = 07 CAN 14 | = N |
| 1965 Jul 28 | = 11:45 | = 05 LEO 10 | = N |
| 1965 Aug 26 | = 18:50 | = 03 VIR 18 | = N |
| | | | |
| 1966 Feb 05 | = 15:58 | = 16 LEO 24 | = F |
| 1966 Mar 07 | = 01:45 | = 16 VIR 02 | = F |
| 1966 Aug 16 | = 11:48 | = 23 LEO 10 | = N |
| 1966 Sep 14 | = 19:13 | = 21 VIR 31 | = N |
| | | | |
| 1967 Mar 26 | = 03:21 | = 04 LIB 47 | = F |
| 1967 Apr 24 | = 12:03 | = 03 SCO 37 | = FE |
| 1967 Oct 03 | = 20:24 | = 09 LIB 56 | = N |
| 1967 Nov 02 | = 05:48 | = 09 SCO 07 | = NE |
| | | | |
| 1968 May 12 | = 13:05 | = 21 SCO 51 | = F |
| 1968 Jun 10 | = 20:13 | = 19 SAG 59 | = F |
| 1968 Nov 20 | = 08:01 | = 28 SCO 04 | = N |
| 1968 Dec 19 | = 18:19 | = 27 SAG 56 | = N |
| | | | |
| 1969 Jun 29 | = 20:04 | = 07 CAP 52 | = F |
| 1969 Jul 29 | = 02:45 | = 05 AQU 49 | = F |
| | | | |
| 1970 Jan 07 | = 20:35 | = 17 CAP 09 | = N |
| 1970 Feb 06 | = 07:13 | = 17 AQU 05 | = N |
| 1970 Aug 17 | = 03:15 | = 23 AQU 49 | = FE |
| 1970 Sep 15 | = 11:09 | = 22 PIS 12 | = FE |
| | | | |
| 1971 Feb 25 | = 09:48 | = 06 PIS 09 | = NE |
| 1971 Mar 26 | = 19:23 | = 05 ARI 29 | = N |
| 1971 Oct 04 | = 12:19 | = 10 ARI 37 | = F |
| 1971 Nov 02 | = 21:19 | = 09 TAU 48 | = F |
| | | | |
| 1972 Apr 13 | = 20:31 | = 24 ARI 00 | = N |
| 1972 May 13 | = 04:08 | = 22 TAU 30 | = N |
| 1972 Oct 22 | = 13:35 | = 29 ARI 15 | = F |
| 1972 Nov 20 | = 23:06 | = 28 TAU  44 | = F* |
| 1972 Dec 20 | = 09:45 | = 28 GEM 37 | = F |

| Date | Time | Long. | T |
|------|------|-------|---|
| 1973 Jun 01 = 04:34 = 10 GEM 33 = N |
| 1973 Jun 30 = 11:39 = 08 CAN 32 = NE |
| 1973 Dec 10 = 01:35 = 17 GEM 51 = FE |
| | | | |
| 1974 Jan 08 = 12:36 = 17 CAN 51 = F* |
| 1974 Feb 06 = 23:24 = 17 LEO 48 = F |
| 1974 Jul 19 = 12:06 = 26 CAN 27 = N |
| 1974 Aug 17 = 19:02 = 24 LEO 29 = N |
| | | | |
| 1975 Jan 27 = 15:09 = 07 LEO 03 = F |
| 1975 Feb 26 = 01:15 = 06 VIR 49 = F* |
| 1975 Sep 05 = 19:19 = 12 VIR 36 = N |
| 1975 Oct 05 = 03:23 = 11 LIB 16 = N |
| | | | |
| 1976 Mar 16 = 02:53 = 25 VIR 39 = F |
| 1976 Apr 14 = 11:49 = 24 LIB 39 = F |
| 1976 Oct 23 = 05:10 = 29 LIB 55 = NE |
| 1976 Nov 21 = 15:11 = 29 SCO 27 = N |
| | | | |
| 1977 May 03 = 13:03 = 12 SCO 58 = F |
| 1977 Jun 01 = 20:31 = 11 SAG 13 = F |
| 1977 Dec 10 = 17:33 = 18 SAG 33 = N |
| | | | |
| 1978 Jan 09 = 04:00 = 18 CAP 32 = N |
| 1978 Jun 20 = 20:30 = 29 SAG 08 = F |
| 1978 Jul 20 = 03:05 = 27 CAP 04 = F |
| | | | |
| 1979 Jan 28 = 06:20 = 07 AQU 44 = N |
| 1979 Feb 26 = 16:45 = 07 PIS 29 = NE |
| 1979 Aug 08 = 03:21 = 15 AQU 00 = F |
| 1979 Sep 6 = 10:59 = 13 PIS 16 = FE |
| | | | |
| 1980 Feb 16 = 08:51 = 26 AQU 50 = NE |
| 1980 Mar 16 = 18:56 = 26 PIS 21 = N |
| 1980 Apr 15 = 03:46 = 25 ARI 20 = N |
| 1980 Sep 24 = 12:08 = 01 ARI 35 = F |
| 1980 Oct 23 = 20:52 = 00 TAU 36 = F |
| | | | |
| 1981 Apr 04 = 20:19 = 14 ARI 58 = N |
| 1981 May 04 = 04:19 = 13 TAU 37 = N |
| 1981 Jun 02 = 11:32 = 11 GEM 50 = N |
| 1981 Nov 11 = 22:26 = 19 TAU 27 = F |
| 1981 Dec 11 = 08:41 = 19 GEM 13 = F |
| | | | |
| 1982 May 23 = 04:40 = 01 GEM 44 = N |

| Date | Time | Long. | T |
|------|------|-------|---|
| 1982 Jun 21 = 11:52 = 29 GEM 47 = NE |
| 1982 Jul 20 = 18:57 = 27 CAN 43 = NE |
| 1982 Dec 30 = 11:33 = 08 CAN 27 = FE |
| | | | |
| 1983 Jan 28 = 22:26 = 08 LEO 26 = F |
| 1983 Jul 10 = 12:18 = 17 CAN 41 = N |
| 1983 Aug 08 = 19:18 = 15 LEO 40 = N |
| 1983 Sep 07 = 02:35 = 13 VIR 55 = N |
| | | | |
| 1984 Feb 17 = 00:41 = 27 LEO 32 = F |
| 1984 Mar 17 = 10:10 = 27 VIR 01 = F |
| 1984 Aug 26 = 19:25 = 03 VIR 43 = N |
| 1984 Sep 25 = 03:11 = 02 LIB 14 = N |
| 1984 Oct 24 = 12:08 = 01 SCO 16 = N |
| | | | |
| 1985 Apr 05 = 11:32 = 15 LIB 38 = F |
| 1985 May 04 = 19:53 = 14 SCO 17 = FE |
| 1985 Oct 14 = 04:33 = 20 LIB 47 = N |
| 1985 Nov 12 = 14:20 = 20 SCO 09 = NE |
| 1985 Dec 12 = 00:54 = 19 SAG 56 = N |
| | | | |
| 1986 May 23 = 20:45 = 02 SAG 25 = F |
| 1986 Jun 22 = 03:42 = 00 CAP 27 = F |
| 1986 Dec 01 = 16:42 = 09 SAG 12 = N |
| 1986 Dec 31 = 03:10 = 09 CAP 08 = N |
| | | | |
| 1987 Jul 11 = 03:33 = 18 CAP 20 = F |
| 1987 Aug 09 = 10:17 = 16 AQU 19 = F |
| | | | |
| 1988 Jan 19 = 05:26 = 28 CAP 21 = N |
| 1988 Feb 17 = 15:54 = 28 AQU 12 = N |
| 1988 Aug 27 = 10:56 = 04 PIS 23 = FE |
| 1988 Sep 25 = 19:07 = 02 ARI 55 = F |
| | | | |
| 1989 Mar 07 = 18:19 = 17 PIS 10 = NE |
| 1989 Apr 06 = 03:33 = 16 ARI 19 = N |
| 1989 Oct 14 = 20:32 = 21 ARI 28 = F |
| 1989 Nov 13 = 05:51 = 20 TAU 50 = F |
| | | | |
| 1990 Apr 25 = 04:27 = 04 TAU 43 = N |
| 1990 May 24 = 11:47 = 03 GEM 03 = N |
| 1990 Dec 02 = 07:50 = 09 GEM 52 = F* |
| 1990 Dec 31 = 18:35 = 09 CAN 50 = F |
| | | | |
| 1991 Jun 12 = 12:06 = 21 GEM 02 = N |

| Date | Time | Long. | T |
|------|------|-------|---|
| 1991 Jul 11 | = 19:06 | = 18 CAN 59 | = NE |
| 1991 Dec 21 | = 10:23 | = 29 GEM 03 | = FE |
| | | | |
| 1992 Jan 19 | = 21:28 | = 29 CAN 04 | = F* |
| 1992 Feb 18 | = 08:04 | = 28 LEO 55 | = F |
| 1992 Jul 29 | = 19:35 | = 06 LEO 54 | = N |
| 1992 Aug 28 | = 02:42 | = 05 VIR 03 | = N |
| | | | |
| 1993 Feb 06 | = 23:55 | = 18 LEO 13 | = F |
| 1993 Mar 08 | = 09:46 | = 17 VIR 50 | = F* |
| 1993 Apr 06 | = 18:43 | = 16 LIB 58 | = F |
| 1993 Sep 16 | = 03:10 | = 23 VIR 16 | = N |
| 1993 Oct 15 | = 11:36 | = 22 LIB 08 | = N |
| | | | |
| 1994 Mar 27 | = 11:10 | = 06 LIB 33 | = F |
| 1994 Apr 25 | = 19:45 | = 05 SCO 22 | = F |
| 1994 Nov 03 | = 13:35 | = 10 SCO 54 | = NE |
| 1994 Dec 02 | = 23:54 | = 10 SAG 35 | = N |
| | | | |
| 1995 May 14 | = 20:48 | = 23 SCO 35 | = F |
| 1995 Jun 13 | = 04:04 | = 21 SAG 42 | = F |

| Date | Time | Long. | T |
|------|------|-------|---|
| 1995 Dec 22 | = 02:22 | = 29 SAG 45 | = N |
| | | | |
| 1996 Jan 20 | = 12:51 | = 29 CAP 45 | = N |
| 1996 Jul 01 | = 03:58 | = 09 CAP 36 | = F |
| 1996 Jul 30 | = 10:35 | = 07 AQU 32 | = F |
| | | | |
| 1997 Feb 07 | = 15:06 | = 18 AQU 53 | = N |
| 1997 Mar 09 | = 01:15 | = 18 PIS 31 | = NE |
| 1997 Aug 18 | = 10:55 | = 25 AQU 32 | = F |
| 1997 Sep 16 | = 18:51 | = 23 PIS 56 | = FE |
| | | | |
| 1998 Mar 28 | = 03:14 | = 07 ARI 15 | = N |
| 1998 Apr 26 | = 11:41 | = 06 TAU 03 | = N |
| 1998 Oct 05 | = 20:12 | = 12 ARI 23 | = F |
| 1998 Nov 04 | = 05:18 | = 11 TAU 35 | = F |
| | | | |
| 1999 May 15 | = 12:05 | = 24 TAU 14 | = N |
| 1999 Jun 13 | = 19:03 | = 22 GEM 20 | = N |
| 1999 Nov 23 | = 07:04 | = 00 GEM 32 | = F |
| 1999 Dec 22 | = 17:31 | = 00 CAN 25 | = F |

**Chris McRae, PMAFA**

Chris McRae, an Aquarian with Aries Rising and Moon in Taurus, began studying astrology in 1965. In 1971 she started teaching and counseling, and she received her professional accreditation with the American Federation of Astrologers in 1974. From 1973-1982, she taught a six-semester course at Grant MacEwan College in Edmonton, Alta., Canada. In 1977 she founded and became the President of the Edmonton Astrological Society, and she also has been on the Board of Directors for the American Federation of Astrologers.

Mrs. McRae has lectured all over the United States, Canada, Australia, and New Zealand and has frequently appeared on convention faculties. In 1982 she received the FCA Astrological Hall of Fame Uranus award for "Innovative Ideas and Outreach Nationally and Internationally."

Mrs. McRae's first book, *The Geodetic World Map,* was published in 1987 by the AFA. It is one of the most innovative concepts introduced into astrology, assigning zodiacal symbology systematically to any location on Earth in order to ascertain how a person functions there. Political, economic and geophysical activity can be observed as transits affect various locations.

# THE GEODETIC EQUIVALENT
# METHOD OF PREDICTION

The Geodetic Equivalent is essentially a set of house cusps which can be drawn up, by a very simple process, for any geographic location using longitude and latitude coordinates. Action occurs when transits, including lunations and eclipses, activate these cusps.

It is fascinating and rewarding to watch world events unfold as they respond to these contacts. It is even more rewarding to be able to predict the unfolding events. We see the drama of the planetary interplay in the sky, but our challenge is to know *where* the drama will unfold. The Geodetic system is a powerful tool in this determination because we do not need to wonder if we are using the correct birth chart of a city or a nation. The Geodetic cusps are predetermined and constant.

Geodetics can also be used to predict how an individual would respond to any location by applying natal, or even progressed, planets to the Geodetic wheel of that location and watching transits time events. Think about that for a moment as a predictive tool! Who will win the race? Who will win the contest? Who will win the election? Nothing significant can happen in a locality without contact with the Geodetic cusps for that place.

I have not been able to determine who developed the concept of Geodetics. To my knowledge, the first book written on the subject was called *The Geodetic Equivalents* by Sepharial, first published around 1920 and reproduced by the American Federation of Astrologers. In that wee booklet, the author comments that it was passed to him, but does not mention by whom. Several earlier mundane astrologers, such as L. Edward Johndro, Frederic Van Norstrand, and even Manly P. Hall, used Geodetics.

Since discovering the concept, I have done considerable research and have been lecturing on its principles and uses at major conventions and astrological societies since 1979. Some of this research was presented in my book *The Geodetic World Map*, published by the American Federation of Astrologers in 1988. I believe that the most valuable contribution this book makes, other than showing some of the uses of the Geodetic, is the visual map presentation of the angles to facilitate observation.

## How to Set Up a Geodetic Wheel & Map

The basic premise is that every geographic longitude has a zodiacal reference. In other words, the zodiac, beginning at 0 degrees Aries, is laid out eastward from Greenwich, degree for degree. This becomes the Midheaven of any chosen location.

| East Longitude | | 0 to 30 | Degrees = | 0 to 30 Aries |
|---|---|---|---|---|
| " | " | 30 to 60 | " = | 0 to 30 Taurus |
| " | " | 60 to 90 | " = | 0 to 30 Gemini |
| " | " | 90 to 120 | " = | 0 to 30 Cancer |
| " | " | 120 to 150 | " = | 0 to 30 Leo |
| " | " | 150 to 180 | " = | 0 to 30 Virgo |
| **INTERNATIONAL DATE LINE** | | | | |
| West | " | 180 to 150 | " = | 0 to 30 Libra |
| " | " | 150 to 120 | " = | 0 to 30 Scorpio |
| " | " | 120 to 90 | " = | 0 to 30 Sagittarius |
| " | " | 90 to 60 | " = | 0 to 30 Capricorn |
| " | " | 60 to 30 | " = | 0 to 30 Aquarius |
| " | " | 30 to 00 | " = | 0 to 30 Pisces |

GUIDE FOR CONSTRUCTION OF GEODETIC MAP—Placidus

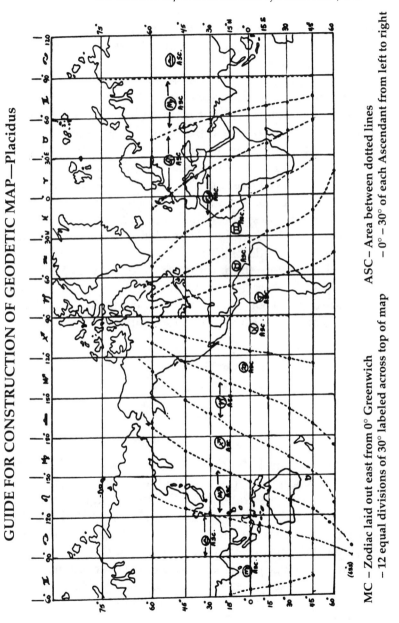

MC – Zodiac laid out east from 0° Greenwich

– 12 equal divisions of 30° labeled across top of map

ASC – Area between dotted lines

– 0° – 30° of each Ascendant from left to right

Refer to Figure 1, where this is visually presented across its top margin, encompassing the area running north and south.

The following are some examples of how to determine the specific Midheaven for any location. The longitude of Munich is 11E33. Its Midheaven is therefore 11:33 Aries. In a Table of Houses, at Munich's latitude of 48N09, you will find the other cusps.

The longitude of Singapore is 103E51. Rather than refer to the above table, simply divide this by 30 to find the number of complete signs. The balance becomes the degrees and minutes of the next sign. Therefore the MC of Singapore is 103:51 ÷ 30 = 3 complete signs, and 13:51 into the 4th sign would be 13:51 Cancer.

To facilitate finding the MC's for locations in West Longitude, subtract the longitude from 360 degrees, then divide by 30 to obtain the number of complete signs. New York City will be used as an example. Its longitude is 73W57.

$$
\begin{array}{l}
359{:}60 \\
\underline{-\ 73{:}57} \\
286{:}03 \\
\underline{-270.00}\ \div\ 30 = 9 \\
16{:}03\ \text{Capricorn}
\end{array}
$$

It is your individual choice as to which Table of Houses you prefer to use. I use the Placidus system, but some astrologers prefer Koch. Of course, the angles will be the same for both systems, but the 11th, 12th, 2nd and 3rd cusps vary from mere minutes to several degrees. That is a very valid consideration because *ALL* the cusps are important in Geodetic predicting. In checking over 200 charts using both house systems and very small orbs, I find both tell the story, but sometimes through slightly different contacts.

You may wish to create for yourself a set of Geodetic wheels for all of the capital cities from which major news is emanating. Many of these are already computed in *The Geodetic World Map*. However, in order to observe planets activating angles, I created a large wall map showing all the Midheavens and Ascendants globally. The effort proved to be more than worthwhile.

Displaying the Midheavens only requires drawing the vertical lines every 30 degrees of longitude as seen in Figure 1. To find the Ascendants, work with one sign at a time. For example, using the Ascendant of 0 degrees Sagittarius, start at latitude 60 degrees north and check the Table of Houses until you find the 0 degree Sagittarius Ascendant at that latitude. Look to the top of the column to find the corresponding Midheaven. Mark this spot on your map with a small *x*. This can be done with about half a degree of accuracy on a large wall map. Continue doing this for every 15 degrees of latitude, then connect your *x*'s to see where the 0 degree Sagittarius Ascendant would be at any latitude. This needs to be done for each zodiacal sign on the Ascendant. Use Figure 1 as your guide. However, to save time, all the positions are listed at the back of *The Geodetic World Map* as well as placed on a map.

The visual impact of the map began to open up new vistas of perception that were not anticipated. Patterns of events began to emerge, as well as events between countries showing correlation not easily seen except on a grid system. When a particular activity occurs on, say, a particular Cardinal degree, it is possible to visually check the map for any area with that Cardinal degree on its Midheaven or Ascendant to determine potential areas of similar activity, which indeed there often is. But not on every degree all of the time. The key word is *potential*. Certain areas are more vulnerable to certain types of activities at certain times, whereas some activities never occur at this location. It would be ridiculous predicting a tsunami in the middle of Montana. Be judicious!

## Country and City Rulerships

As we cast our eyes across the Geodetic map, even the small one reproduced here, we can see how locations respond to their Geodetic Midheavens and Ascendants. The Midheaven is symbolic of how that country wishes the world to see it and what the people collectively consider most important. The Ascendant represents the attitude of the people in general. We will look at only a few, and you can study this more comprehensively yourself.

It does not make a great deal of sense to attribute only one sign as ruler of a country as vast as Russia or even the United States or Canada. Geodetically, Russia has seven Midheavens and four Ascendants. The United States has four Midheavens and six Ascendants. Canada has four Midheavens and seven Ascendants. Of course, the Geodetics of the capital city reflect the Government of the country, but the regional diversity of these three large nations is reflected through the Geodetics. It makes governing a great deal more complex than that of a nation encompassing only one or two signs. For example, the eastern area of both the United States and Canada, which falls under a Capricorn Midheaven, contains the seats of Government and the main financial sections, and each reflects a more conservative attitude than the West Coast. As we move westward, we go through the Sagittarius Midheaven , and we are all familiar with the adage "Go West, young man, and make your fortune." All of California, where freedom of expression, casualness and "do your own thing" is prevalent, falls under an Aquarian Ascendant. However, San Francisco has a Geodetic Scorpio Midheaven, and Los Angeles, a Sagittarius Midheaven. Anyone familiar with these two cities can relate immediately to the differences of temperament and attitude.

The area of the globe that falls under the Pisces Midheaven and Cancer Ascendant, both Water signs, sent forth the great sea captains of old to claim the New World for the Motherland. This area also contains the greatest number of seaports in the world.

Please note that Imperial Japan, the Land of the Rising Sun, has a Leo Midheaven and Scorpio Ascendant. This country, according to legend, was founded by a direct descendant of the Sun goddess. The flag is the Sun in the middle of a plain white background. The Scorpio Ascendant is a reflection of the people's business and financial ability. The Tokyo Stock Exchange is currently the most powerful in the world. Playing the stock market is a national pastime.

It is interesting to note that some of the older mundane concepts of country rulerships assigned Cancer to China while others assigned Libra. Note that Geodetically the Midheaven is Cancer and the Ascendant is Libra. No wonder this controversy existed! The Cancer Midheaven is reflected by the long dynasties that ruled the country, and it is here that family tradition is both honored and worshipped. The Great Wall of China was built to keep out invaders.

The same exercise reveals how cities reflect their Geodetic angles. It is applicable and amusing to note that Las Vegas, which falls under the influence of a Sagittarius MC and Aquarius Ascendant, has been labeled the gambling and divorce capital of the world. Detroit, which is the largest automobile-manufacturing center in the world as well as a major industrial hub in the United States, has a Capricorn MC and Aries Ascendant. Mars rules mechanics. According to *Funk and Wagnalls Encyclopedia*, the ratio of privately owned automobiles in Detroit is among the highest in America, not because it is where they are manufactured, but because the public transportation systems are inadequate to meet the demands. Thus, the people solve the problem in their own Arien way.

In my opinion, it is time we left the old country rulerships where they belong—in the pages of antiquity as historical items. They were originally designed by Ptolemy, who divided the world into four quadrants running through the Mediterranean Sea from west to east, and the Aegean Sea from north to south. At that time, this was considered the center of the world. Ptolemy had a fairly logical system of sign designation, but as the world expanded the new assignments were added somewhat randomly because the original system could not be applied. Changes have been made over the years, but updating is certainly needed. Astrologers who have been working with Geodetic Equivalents agree that these make more sense and give a larger scope of interpretation than the old rulerships.

### Relocational Predictions

Relocation has proved to be one of the most exciting areas of Geodetic observations. We can use Geodetics in our personal lives to determine a permanent relocation. We can watch our natal and/or progressed planets cross over the Geodetic angles, and even the intermediate cusps, as we travel. This system can also be used with unprecedented success in placing the charts of political and military leaders, sports figures, trendsetters, etc., into the Geodetic wheels where their destiny unfolds. One simply cannot win or achieve in an area unless his/her chart connects with the Geodetic cusps of that location. We will look briefly at the personal application, then work with some examples of famous people.

A complete relocational concept consists of placing your planets, including your Midheaven, Ascendant, Arabian Points, or anything else you use, inside the Geodetic cusps of the chosen location. This will show your *potential* in that area. Place your progressions and transits on the outside of the wheel to observe transpiring events. If you are looking for a location to highlight a particular natal planet on a Geodetic Midheaven, convert that planet to the pertinent geographic longitude. For example, if the planet was at 16 Gemini 22, this would be 76:22 East Longitude. (Aries is 30 degrees + 30 degrees for Taurus + 16:22.) Refer to the map for cities located on this longitudinal line. However, it is often easier to intuitively pick a location, placing your planets in its Geodetic house cusps to see how they respond.

As mentioned above, also watch your planets cross the angles or other cusps of a location while traveling. I was once traveling by automobile from the United States back into my own country, Canada. For some reason, the customs official singled me out for a complete customs inspection. He began dismantling my car and strewing my belongings all over the sidewalk, and the louder I protested, the worse my predicament became until he also had the contents of my suitcases strewn upon the sidewalk. As he walked away, I could not resist one more barrage of protest, whereupon he whirled back around and removed two tires from my car. When he finally finished, it took me all afternoon to sort out, repack and put my car back together. It was not until years later, when I began studying Geodetics, that I realized that my *Mars* was on the Geodetic 9th House cusp of that location. Incidentally, he did not find anything illegal.

*Neptune* can correlate with lost items, confused reservations, food poisoning or perhaps a profound religious experience. *Jupiter* relates to fun, overindulgence and overspending. *Venus* relates to love and good companionship. These are a few examples, and you can gather more from your astrological knowledge.

While I was writing this, I took a reprieve from the computer and sauntered away to read today's newspaper, *The Edmonton Journal*, July 25, 1989. The following news item caught my attention:

> LONDON, British Prime Minister Margaret Thatcher appointed new foreign and defence secretaries yesterday, fired two other cabinet ministers and switched around several more. It was one of the biggest government shakeups since she won power . . . battling to halt her government's slide in popularity . . .

Naturally, I checked the current transits to the chart I have with her natal planets in the Geodetic cusps of London.

But before looking at the transits for the above event, observe Thatcher's natal chart in the London Geodetic and recall her tough economic policies that swept her into power. (All charts are calculated using Placidus houses.)

Her MC conjuncts the G.E. 3rd cusp, Ascendant squares the 2nd cusp, Uranus squares the 6th/12th, N. Node trines the MC, Moon quincunxes the MC, Mars quincunxes the 11th, Mercury trines the 12th, Ascendant/Saturn squares the 2nd/8th, Venus squares the 3rd/9th, and Jupiter quincunxes the 2nd.

She became Prime Minister on May 3, 1979. The previous New Moon conjuncted the 11th House of Commons. The previous Lunar Eclipse of 23° Virgo squared the 6th of labor unions. She wrested power from P.M. Callaghan by promising to face up to the unions (6th) and reverse British capitalism by putting down much of the country's socialist programs. Transiting Jupiter was conjunct her N. Node and trine the G.E. MC. Note her natal Jupiter is in the 6th, and ruling it. The transiting Sun was trine her Jupiter.

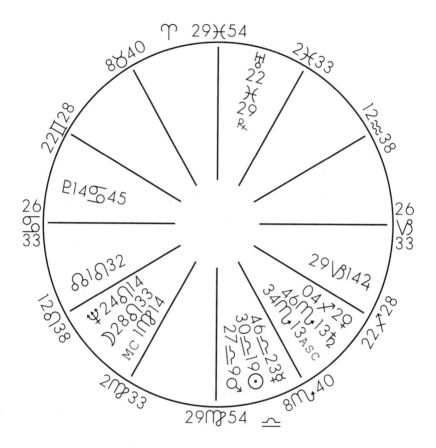

**Geodetic Cusps—London, England**

**Prime Minister Margaret Thatcher**
**October 13, 1925      8:50 A.M. GMT**
**00W38      52N55**
**Grantham, England**
**Source: AFA**

**Transits July 24, 1989**

The Sun trine the G.E. MC, semi-sextile the 3rd cusp and her MC, conjunct her N. Node.

The N. Node quincunx the G.E. Ascendant.

Mercury square the 11th/5th, sextile her Mars.

Venus quincunx the G.E. MC, conjunct her MC.

Mars trine the 6th cusp, sextile the 12th cusp, conjunct her Neptune.

Jupiter square the G.E. MC/IC, quincunx the 7th cusp, sextile her Moon.

Saturn/Neptune trine the 11th cusp, square her Mars.

Uranus trine the 3rd cusp, quincunx her N. Node, trine her MC.

Pluto stationary square the 2nd/8th (16′ orb) conjunct her Ascendant and Saturn.

(London's Geodetic 9th cusp quincunxes the Falkland Islands' 4th cusp, orb of 29′. Falkland Islands' 3rd/9th falls across London's 12th/6th. Their MC's are sextile and their Ascendants are square.)

### Sideline—U.S. Politics

The following is an "after the fact" exercise, but interesting just the same in explaining why George Bush, rather than Michael Dukakis, went to Washington. The birth data was given in *Mercury Hour*, January 1989 edition, under Marc Penfield's "Chart Mart."

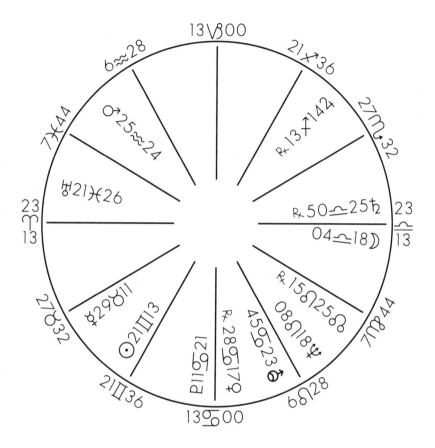

**Geodetic Cusps—Washington, D.C.**

**George Bush**
**June 12, 1924      Between 11 A.M. & Noon**
**71W05      42N15**
**Milton, Mass.**
**Source: Mother to Lois Rodden**

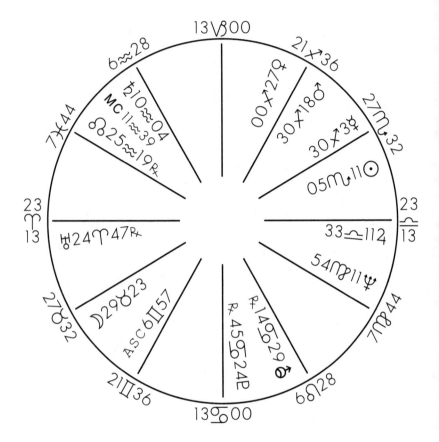

**Geodetic Cusps—Washington, D.C.**

**Michael Dukakis**
Nov. 3, 1933      5:50 P.M. EST
71W07      42N20
Brookline, Mass.
Source: Hospital, Frances McEvoy

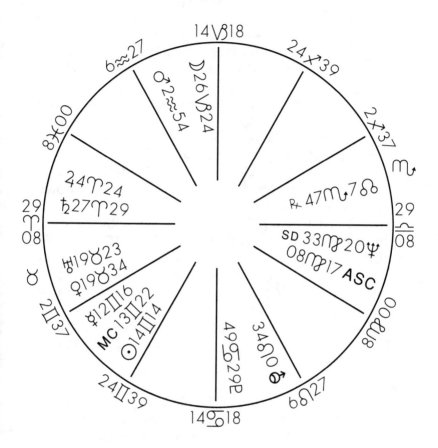

**Geodetic Cusps—Ottawa, Canada**

**Joe Clark**
**June 5, 1939      12:30 P.M. MST**
**113W50      50N35**
**High River, Alta.**
**Source: Doug Brown**

## Joe Who????

Joe Clarke was the only Western Canadian ever to hold the lofty position of Prime Minister of Canada, but only for 6¹/₂ months. The West hoped he would be able to heal some of the wounds they have always considered Ottawa to have inflicted upon "its territory." He was elected May 22, 1979, was handed the Seal on June 4, and his government was ousted by a "no confidence" vote on December 13, 1979 when it presented its budget to Parliament. His nickname was "Joe Who?"

Under the present Government he holds the portfolio of Minister of Foreign Affairs and has finally lived down his previous name.

His natal Sun, MC and Mercury are in the Geodetic 2nd House of budget quincunx the G.E. MC. His natal Nodes square the 11th cusp (Parliament), Saturn conjuncts the G.E. Ascendant, Mars trines the 2nd cusp and Pluto squares the G.E. Ascendant. When his government was defeated, transiting Uranus quincunxed the 3rd cusp, Saturn quincunxed the G.E. Ascendant, Mars conjuncted the 6th cusp, Mercury quincunxed the G.E. Ascendant, and the Nodes squared the 2nd cusp within a 10' orb.

## Canada and U.S. Relations

As we observe the Geodetic cusps for Washington, D.C., and Ottawa, Canada side by side, it becomes evident that the destinies of the two countries are entwined, at least as long as the capitals remain where they are! There may even be more significance than meets the eye in the fact that the U.S. MC is one degree earlier than the MC of Canada. Every Canadian knows that "it happens in the U.S. first" and then filters up to Canada.

But Canada has 29° Aries on the Ascendant and always seems to be in a state of crisis in terms of its personal identity as it struggles to shed the influence of American-

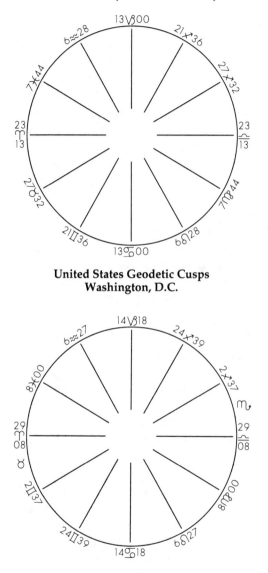

**United States Geodetic Cusps**
**Washington, D.C.**

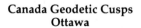

**Canada Geodetic Cusps**
**Ottawa**

ism. One of the greatest areas of influence comes via the communications media. The Canadian Radio and Television Commission has given the Canadian Broadcasting Corporation until 1991 to provide 90% Canadian content. Everyone in Canada knows that this is virtually impossible, particularly with the present budget restraints. It would do little good anyway because the barrage of *Miami Vice*-type programming would always find its way across the border since it is what the people prefer to watch. It is probably not an exaggeration to state that most Canadians watch more American television by cable than their own channels.

At this writing, both countries are experiencing the Saturn/Neptune conjunction on their Geodetic Midheavens and have yet to experience the Uranus transit in 1991 and 1992. In 1991 the U.S. will deal with Uranus stationary retrograde on its MC; the following year it will be Canada's turn.

For Canada, 1989 was the year when the reality of the Free Trade Deal with the U.S. began unfolding. It became a major election issue in 1988 when people voted not for their Party as much as for or against free trade. No one seemed to fully understand the issues or the implications as contradictory opinions were strongly expressed. The potential long-term advantage seems to be to create a larger market for Canadian manufactured goods, but the interim period will take years. In the meantime, thousands of job losses are being blamed on the FTD as industry gears for the changes. Also, many social programs, such as Unemployment Insurance Benefits and Old Age Security, are being drastically cut in Canada because of pressure from the United States that their manufacturers cannot compete with the social programs of Canada, which would create unfair pricing standards.

When negotiations began in 1986, Uranus was exactly conjunct Washington's Geodetic 9th House cusp. The U.S. and Canada agreed on the pact on October 3, 1987. At that time, Uranus was conjunct Ottawa's Geodetic 9th House and trine Washington's Ascendant. Jupiter conjuncted the midpoint of the Ascendants of the two countries. Mars trined the U.S. 2nd cusp and squared Canada's 3rd/9th. Venus, ruler of the 7th in both charts, sextiled the U.S. 9th cusp. Mercury squared Canada's 11th/5th, creating hot and heavy debates in Parliament. The Prime Minister was trying to rush the vote through the House because his term of office was running out and he wanted historical credit for the deal. It passed Parliament all right, but the Senate blocked it until after the upcoming election.

On January 2, 1988, when the two countries actually signed the Agreement, Saturn was conjunct Ottawa's 9th cusp and quincunx Washington's 2nd cusp.

September 19, 1988—FTD passed by U.S. Congress.

November 8, 1988—George Bush became U.S. President.

November 21, 1988—Brian Mulroney won the Canadian election and just managed to get the FTD through the Senate on December 30. The U.S. had imposed a deadline of December 31. All during November, Uranus at 29 degrees Sagittarius was trine Ottawa's Ascendant. The issue was so controversial that some commentators thought that it could separate the country, but then, separatist issues never seem to be far from the surface in Canada. On December 31, Pluto was at 14 Scorpio 35 sextile Ottawa's MC by an orb of 17′. Pluto had already passed the sextile to Washington's MC by 1° 35′. Jupiter was conjunct Washington's 2nd cusp and quincunx Ottawa's 9th. Mercury was trine Washington's 2nd cusp and square Canada's Ascendant. The Sun was at 10° Capricorn.

One additional comment: Prime Minister Mulroney's Mars is in Ottawa's Geodetic 9th House trine the Ascendant with an orb of only 24'. He was like the proverbial "cat on a hot tin roof "to get the Deal passed before the election so he would be credited for this accomplishment.

## World Events

For the past 10 years, I have kept a Geodetic file of events transpiring, or I should say "erupting," in Teheran. Only the highlights will be mentioned; otherwise this article would far exceed the parameters given. Also, not all of the aspects will be listed. They are too numerous and boring for the casual reader. If you wish more detail, you need only apply the transits from your ephemeris for any date given.

Before actually discussing the Teheran issue, it is important to make a slight digression. In following very potent activity, be it geophysical disruptions or revolutionary political upheavals, it is important to realize that events do not operate like a blind snapping up or down. There is a build-up of energy or influence as matters develop. This occurs in the form of eclipses, lunations, and/ or slow transits moving into place, and when all is ready they are often triggered by a faster transit touching off the most vulnerable point in the setup. In this regard, it is important to observe eclipse patterns, particularly Solar Eclipses in pairs, and their accompanying transits. A new pair is, of course, usually formed every six months at the opposite sides of the zodiac, one being a North Nodal Eclipse and the other being a South Nodal Eclipse. When these are less than 10 degrees apart, their potency seems to be increased.

In 1975 we had a pair of Solar Eclipses in Fixed signs at 20° Taurus and 10° Scorpio. Then the 10° Scorpio eclipse paired up with the next eclipse in 1976 at 9° Taurus, which paired up with the following one at 0° Scorpio. In 1977 and

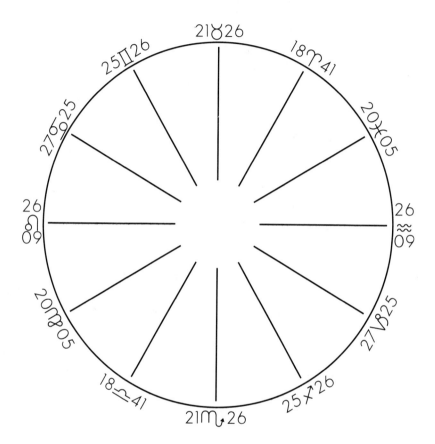

**Geodetic Cusps—Teheran, Iran**
**Placidus**
**Koch Cusps:**

11th 28♊20
12th 28♋07
2nd 24♍41
3rd 23♎16

1978 the eclipse pairs moved into Aries/Libra. Then there was only one in Pisces, which meant that the patterns were back into Fixed signs for 1979, 1980, 1981 and 1982. This is the longest and most concentrated period during this entire century of eclipses in Fixed signs. The Persian Gulf has always been a hotbed of political upheaval and intrigue, and it is easy to see why when we realize that their Geodetic Midheaven is Taurus and their Geodetic Ascendant is Leo, coupled with the fact that they are located in a densely populated and ancient global area.

With such a concentration of Fixed eclipse pairs, one could perceive in advance, by using Geodetics, that much upheaval would result in this global area. Uranus activated Teheran's MC/IC and ASC/DSC from 1979-1982, to be followed by Pluto from 1991-1994.

During 1975-76, with the eclipses closer to Baghdad's MC and Ascendant, Iraq was more in the news than Iran. Leaders tried to negotiate a peace to quell a 14-year rebellion among the Kurds, which was partially financed by Iran, but as fast as an agreement was signed, fighting resumed and nothing was settled. Then, a very rich oil strike in Iraq ranked them second to Saudi Arabia in oil reserves. These two events alone planted the seeds from which much trouble grew.

Meanwhile in Iran, hostilities were building against the Shah and his one-party dictatorial system. Demonstrators against the Government were either shot or imprisoned as an estimated 100,000 political prisoners packed the jails. Spending was out of control as the deficit rose to approximately one billion dollars. The Shah signed a 10-billion-dollar arms contract with the U.S. in exchange for oil, but strikes began crippling the industry. By 1977, fast-paced developments had caused runaway inflation, massive unemployment and a horrendous balance of payment deficit.

In 1978, events reached a stage of crisis. Islamic traditionalists were protesting against the rapid modernization. These flames of protest were fanned until demonstrators nationwide were demanding the Shah's removal. The country became virtually paralyzed by strikes. Police fired on demonstrators. In 1978 alone, according to *Funk & Wagnalls Standard Reference Encyclopedia Yearbook* (1978), more than 4,000 were slain. Anger had mounted against the thousands of U.S. people holding prestigious jobs in the oil industry. All of this was being orchestrated by the Ayatollah Khomeini from his exile in Paris.

Finally, on January 16, 1979 the Shah left the country. Looking only at the action on the Geodetic cusps, transiting Uranus was conjunct the 4th cusp and sextile the 2nd. Neptune was square the 2nd/8th. The Sun and Mars were conjunct the 6th, quincunx the Ascendant and quincunx the 11th, forming a Yod.

The Ayatollah Khomeini returned to his homeland on February 1 as Venus in Sagittarius conjuncted Teheran's Geodetic 5th cusp and trined the Ascendant. On April 1 he proclaimed an Islamic Republic of Iran to be ruled by a religious council. Pluto was within minutes of conjuncting the 3rd/9th axis. Neptune was within minutes of squaring the 2nd/8th. Uranus was still on the 4th. Retrograde Jupiter at 29° Cancer was conjunct the 12th cusp. Mars was within 14 minutes of squaring the 5th/11th. Mercury was slowing to its station prior to going direct and had formed a quincunx to the Ascendant.

On May 1, 1979, when the Ayatollah Motahari was assassinated, Mars was within 11 minutes of conjuncting the 9th cusp and Neptune squared the 8th.

On November 4, 1979, Muslim students seized control of the U.S. Embassy in Teheran, taking hostages. Pluto was forming a Yod with the MC and the 8th cusp. Uranus was conjunct the 4th cusp and Mars squared the MC/IC.

On the U.S. Geodetic cusps for Washington, Uranus was inconjunct the 3rd cusp, Saturn was quincunx the Ascendant and Jupiter was quincunx the 11th cusp.

Khomeini became ruler for life under the new constitution on December 3, 1979. There was a Full Moon that day in Teheran's Geodetic 10th House.

The Shah died on July 27, 1980. Uranus was stationary direct within four minutes of Teheran's 4th cusp, and Neptune squared with Pluto quincunxing the 8th. He died in Cairo where his natal Pluto, ruler of his Ascendant, was exactly conjunct Cairo's 12th cusp. His natal Sun was exactly conjunct Cairo's 4th.

On September 22, 1980, war began between Iraq and Iran with the bombing of the Abadan oilfields. Pluto formed a Yod to the MC and 8th cusp of Teheran's Geodetic wheel, Neptune was quincunx the MC and square the 2nd/8th, Mars quincunxed the 9th cusp, and Mercury conjuncted the 3rd cusp.

On January 20, 1981, the U.S. hostages were released from Teheran. Pluto trined the 11th cusp, Neptune conjuncted the 5th cusp and Mars sextiled the 9th cusp of Teheran. Transits to the Washington Geodetic cusps included Pluto conjunct the 7th cusp, Neptune trine the Ascendant and Uranus conjunct the 8th cusp.

On August 20, 1988, a cease-fire was called between Iran and Iraq, putting an end to the eight-year war. At that time the Sun was conjunct and Uranus was forming a trine to the Ascendant of Teheran.

On June 3, 1989, Ayatollah Khomeini died. Mars trined the 4th cusp, Mercury sextiled the 12th, Venus (MC ruler) quincunxed the 6th cusp, the North Node quincunxed the 12th cusp, and Transpluto squared the MC/IC and trined the 8th cusp.

Please note that orbs for the aspects used are all very small. In many instances they measure mere minutes, and at the maximum they run two to three degrees.

The problems are far from over in this hotbed of political and religious intrigue. I am sure that from now on when you observe eclipses, lunations, or major transits crossing over or forming a stationary position at 21 or 26 degrees of any Fixed sign you will be alerted to new developments in that area.

While the Teheran Geodetic chart is still fresh in the mind of the reader, it would be appropriate to place Salman Rushdie's natal planets into it (see chart on the following page). He is the author of *The Satanic Verses*. After its publication in London, the Ayatollah Khomeini sent out an order on February 7, 1989 for Rushdie's assassination because he felt the book was blasphemous. According to a report in *The Edmonton Journal*, February 25, 1989, "Iranian clerics put a bounty equal to $6.2 million Canadian on his head." Rushdie defended his right to free speech in a free world, which Khomeini would not honor, and Rushdie had to go into hiding. Even though he was not born in Teheran, was not living there, and his book was not published there, part of his fate was attached to that location and his planets would naturally tie into the Teheran Geodetic chart. Since London, England's Geodetic cusps are also in this text, you may wish to apply Rushdie's planets to that chart also.

Without adding any more charts to this article, it would be appropriate to mention briefly the trigger points in a couple more items which are currently in the news at the time of this writing. This helps to show that it is not necessary to search diligently to find action appropriate to Geodetic cusps in order to "make" a system work. They appear constantly in current news items.

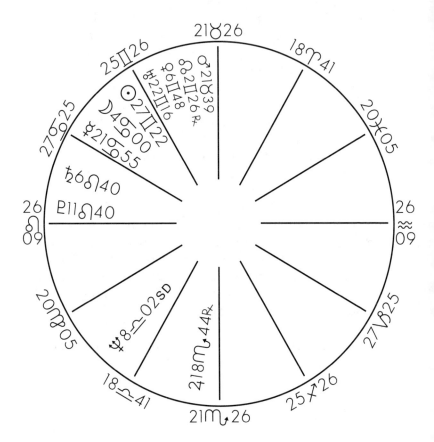

**Geodetic Cusps—Teheran, Iran**

**Salman Rushdie**
**June 19, 1947**
**Time Unknown**
**72E51      18N56**
**Bombay, India**
**Source: Marc Penfield, *Mercury Hour*, July 1989**

## Armenian Earthquake – 6.7

Date:       December 7, 1988
Time:       10:41 A.M.
Place:      Tbilisi, Armenia, USSR
            Longitude: 44E55   Latitude: 41N45
Source:     *The Edmonton Journal*, December 8, 1988
Headline:   "Thousands feared dead as quake rocks Caucasus."

This was reported to be the worst earthquake in 80 years to hit the Caucasus region. The world rushed emergency supplies and manpower to aid thousands who were buried, injured or homeless. The death toll was estimated to be between 80,000 to 100,000 as buildings and apartment blocks tumbled like matchsticks.

The eclipse axis of 27 Pisces 42 and 18 Virgo 40 stretched across the Geodetic 2nd/8th Houses for this area. The Saturn/Uranus conjunction at 27° Sagittarius in October squared the first eclipse point, setting up a potentially dangerous situation looking for a location. The New Moon on November 9 conjuncted the 4th cusp and trined the 8th. The Full Moon on November 23 was in the 10th but made no aspects. But Pluto conjuncted the 4th House cusp. Transpluto was conjuncting the Ascendant. The trigger appeared to be the Sun, which made an exact square to the 8th House cusp and a quincunx to the Midheaven with an orb of a few minutes.

## Tiananmen Square, Beijing, China

Date:       June 4, 1989
Time:       10:23 A.M.
Place:      Beijing, China
            Longitude: 116E25   Latitude: 39N55
Source:     *The Edmonton Journal*, June 4, 1989
Headline:   "Beijing bloodbath ends student sit-in."

This was a fight for democracy. Chinese troops opened fire on student demonstrators with machine guns, cutting a swath of dead bodies through the throngs. A human cry resounded around the world in a protest of the violence perpetrated by a government against its citizens.

The Geodetic Midheaven of Beijing is 26 Cancer 24 and its Ascendant is 22 Libra 44. All of this began as Mars at 22 Cancer 29 was approaching the MC and squaring the Ascendant within 15'. Mercury retrograde, approaching its stationary position to go direct, was within minutes of forming a trine with the 12th cusp and a sextile with the 6th. Transpluto in the 10th closely squared the 2nd/8th axis.

### New Madrid, Missouri

In 1987-88 there was a potent eclipse axis T-square buildup that is worthy of mention. It began on September 22, 1987 with the Solar Eclipse at 29 Virgo 34. Six months later on March 17, 1988, the Solar Eclipse occurred at 27 Pisces 42. As previously mentioned, when an eclipse pair forms an opposition of less than 10 degrees, it appears to be powerful and worthy of observation. In February 1988, Mars, Saturn and Uranus all reached 0 degrees of Capricorn, with Neptune already in early Capricorn.

This apex of a T-square with the eclipse pair would earmark all Cardinal Midheavens and Ascendants on the map. One such location runs right through New Madrid, Missouri where a great earthquake occurred in 1811 that was so strong it caused the great Mississippi River to flip out of its banks while the ground heaved like ocean waves. The other location runs through the interior of China. An Ascendant line of 0 degrees Capricorn runs through an earthquake zone in the Northwest Territories, Canada.

I watched the New Madrid area and was relieved

**Geodetic Cusps**
**New Madrid, Missouri**

that another great quake had not occurred. When discussing this with Joyce Wehrman, she informed me that she had data on an unusually large number of small ones on that fault line. There were also record-breaking tropical storms along that line in the Gulf of Mexico.

However, Alaska experienced a quake, as did the 0 degree Capricorn Northwest Territories. A 7.6 shaker occurred in the interior of China on November 6, 1988, through the 0 degree Cancer Midheaven and 0 degree Libra Ascendant.

The question arises as to when the next big one will hit the U.S. Midwest. The Geodetic wheel is hereby given so others can watch the future action. We need to watch the three Solar Eclipses of 1992 which are as follows: January 4 at 13° Capricorn, June 30 at 9° Cancer, and December 23 at 3° Capricorn. Saturn will also near the 12th cusp, Mars will pass over both the Ascendant and the 4th cusp, and Transpluto will quincunx the 11th cusp. Then in May 1993 a Solar Eclipse at 0° Gemini will quincunx the Geodetic Midheaven. Also in 1993, Neptune/Uranus will quincunx the 6th cusp.

It would truly be a great service to mankind to be able to forecast all of the great disasters in the world, but we must recognize that there are a great number of variables, and it requires study to sharpen both our tools and our wit. The Geodetic Equivalent has come closer to this reality than anything that I have found in astrology to date. The process is simple, the aspects are tight, eliminating some of the potential error factors, and its message comes through.

There may be other resources and other research foundations that could prove to be of value to us and us to them, but until we can tap into these we as astrologers are basically on our own. It may turn out that they need us more than we need them.

It is this author's desire that more astrologers become involved with this system so that together we can grow a great deal faster.

### Nicholas Campion

Nicholas Campion was born in 1953 and began his studies of astrology in 1971. Educated at Queens' College, Cambridge, he read history and took graduate studies at London University, reading history and politics at the School of Oriental and African Studies and international relations at the London School of Economics.

His books include *An Introduction to the History of Astrology, Mundane Astrology* (with Michael Baigent and Charles Harvey), *The Book of World Horoscopes* and *The Practical Astrologer*.

He is a former President of the Astrological Lodge of London.

# THE AGE OF AQUARIUS:
# A MODERN MYTH

"It is probable that there is no branch of Astrology upon which more nonsense has been poured forth than the doctrine of the precession of the equinoxes."

—Charles Carter
*Astrology Quarterly*, Vol. 21, p. 111

The Age of Aquarius is one of the great clichés of modern astrology. It is widely believed, both by modern astrologers and a great many people who have come into contact with astrology, that because of the astronomical phenomena known as the "precession of the equinoxes," the world is currently entering, or is about to enter, a new phase of history known as the Age of Aquarius. While only a small proportion of astrological literature is devoted to this subject, astrological texts in general are peppered with generalizations about the coming Aquarian Age. This esoteric notion has been nurtured by an independent but associated belief that the world is about to enter a New Age. These two ages, the New Age and the Age of Aquarius, are held by most people to be one and the same thing, a belief which I hope to show is both mistaken and responsible for a great many half-truths, errors and illusions.

In this chapter I will argue that the broad structure of

New Age belief is but one modern embodiment of a mille-narian tradition independent of any astrological association with or derived from the precession of the equinoxes, let alone the supposed astrological qualities of the Age of Aquarius.

In addition, because New Age thought encourages the simplest possible perspective on historical development, it has resulted in an excessively crude attitude toward the use of astrology in the technical analysis of history. As precession is regarded as the major cause of historical change, so the complex theories of planetary cycles are ignored. Similarly, as all historical evidence is seen as relating primarily to a single astronomical factor, the quality of historical research is frequently no more than that which would be required of a ten-year-old child. I will, therefore, argue both that New Age beliefs are irrelevant to any supposed effect arising from precession, and that the devout belief in the Age of Aquarius to which most astrologers adhere is positively destructive of good astrological practice.[1]

Criticism of the New Age movement must be based on historical and sociological arguments, in which respect the material presented here represents but a précis of a much larger work. I hope it will be understood that it has been possible to do no more than outline the case here and that the details must await future publication.

It is vital for the proper study of Mundane Astrology that astrologers develop and maintain a sound astrological approach combined with strict adherence to solid historical research. It is, unfortunately, necessary to criticize work which so often falls below even the minimum standards which would be required in any profession or branch of human study other than astrology. Only astrologers so readily put up with substandard work, and chief among this work is that on the Age of Aquarius.

## Millenarianism

As a means of historical and political understanding, astrology offers a system of technical analysis based on the measurement and interpretation of planetary cycles. This is, and always has been, its major strength. However, it also has long been associated with a number of religious and philosophical attitudes to history, which to the believer have offered meaning and hope, but for the seeker after knowledge have damaged and obscured historical and astrological understanding.

The principal historical theory associated with astrology is **millenarianism**. The word *millenarianism* is derived from the Latin *millenium*, "a thousand," and refers to the Persian, Jewish and Christian belief that world history is divided into neat periods of one or two thousand years. There are two, or in later accounts, three of these phases, each of which embodies a particular spiritual Zeitgeist. For example, in the Christian version the first phase is that of the Old Testament, ruled by God; the second is that of the New Testament, the era of Christ; and the third, heralded by the second coming of Christ, is that of the Holy Spirit.

The history of millenarianism is a vast subject in itself, too complex for this present essay.[2] However, I do wish to make a number of salient points about classic millenarian theory, which are directly relevant to our understanding of modern New Age beliefs.

1. It is believed that prior to the beginning of the next phase of history human society will have reached a state of terminal decline. This will culminate in a global trauma, either man-made, natural, divinely inspired, or a combination of the three.

2. Appropriate evidence is sought and found to justify such theories. Witness the ease with which Chris-

tian fundamentalists exploit the Bible to justify their proposition that Armageddon is approaching.

3. It is predicted that the coming age will be a distinct improvement on the present one, although in some theories it is forecast that decline will eventually return.

4. In the Judaeo-Christian version and in some pagan accounts, the coming phase will be inaugurated by the appearance of a world savior, messiah or son of God.

5. The entire historical process moves forward according to a plan that is in outline preordained, and in some cases, divinely inspired.

6. It is the duty of every citizen of the world to actively prepare for the next phase of history. Thus, Christians must prepare for the second coming of Christ through a combination of devout lifestyle and the conversion of unbelievers. Marxists must create the conditions for socialist revolution.

7. Finally, and perhaps most importantly, it is believed that the transformation from one age to the next is imminent. That is to say, the approaching historical trauma and the consequent return to the golden age must take place during the lifetime of the believer.

It will be noted that there is a paradox arising from the contradiction between the concept that history is broadly predetermined, but each individual must make a free choice to work towards the fulfillment of the historical plan. This paradoxical theory was defined by the philosopher Karl Popper as *historicism*. The voluntary participation of the individual in the necessities of history he termed *activism*.[3]

Although the major psychological impulse behind millenarianism is clearly religious, astrology has played a vital role in the formulation of millenarian theory. Jewish and Christian millenarianism drew on ancient cosmology, while Marxism, the most potent form of modern millenarianism, is, in its broad structure, directly derived from Christian millenarianism, the coming of Christ replaced by the proletarian revolution and the Kingdom of God by communism.

Millenarianism has exerted a profound impact on European thought and has inspired many a social upheaval. It was, and is, a force to be reckoned with and, as I shall argue, it lies at the very heart of the modern New Age movement.

### Astrological Millenarianism—The Platonic Year

The earliest extant written account of a comprehensive theory of astrological history is recorded by Plato in the *Timaeus* and elaborated in other works such as the *Republic* and the *Laws*.[4] Plato assumed that historical epochs began and ended when all the planets formed a mean conjunction at the exact location they occupied at their creation, which takes place once every 36,000 years. The period of history defined by Plato is known as the Great Year, or in honor of the great philosopher himself, the **Platonic Year**. Subsequent commentators assumed that Plato regarded the point of creation as 0° Aries, although in his later account of around 280 B.C., the Babylonian astrologer Berossus argued that the relevant degrees were 0° Cancer and 0° Capricorn. When all the planets formed a mean conjunction at 0° Cancer, Berossus claimed, the world was consumed by fire. When the conjunction occurred at 0° Capricorn, the destruction was by water. Berossus' theory was accepted by most classical authors and retained wide currency in Medieval and Renaissance Europe. Louis Le Roy, Regius Professor of Greek at the College de France in Paris, still regarded it as the linchpin of astrological history in 1576.[5] In Le Roy's scheme, as in so many theories over the previous 1500 years, the great Platonic planetary cycle subsumed series of lesser cycles, moving from the long-term cycle of Jupiter/Saturn conjunctions down to the monthly lunation cycle.

Plato's concern was not solely with the measurement and analysis of history but with the active integration of the individual with the historical process. His attitude to this process was thoroughly millenarian and historicist. He believed that the current phase of history represented a tragic collapse of civilized values, that a major cataclysm was approaching, that the golden age would then return, and that it was the duty of every citizen to encourage this preordained plan to fulfill itself. Whereas in Jewish or Christian millenarianism it was a devout lifestyle and obedience to God which were the prerequisites for an improvement in the direction of historical change, Plato specified a disciplined lifestyle combined with a rigorous program of *education*. The philosophical man in the Platonic universe was he who lived an austere life and dedicated himself to the pursuit of truth via the study of the abstract arts, chiefly music, mathematics and geometry. The insistence in Platonic millenarianism that an educational program was central to individual participation in the historical process is one that has come to be an essential component of contemporary New Age theories.

## The Precessional Year

The Precessional Year, the period of time that it takes the equinoxes to precess through the zodiac, is often misnamed the Platonic Year. It is, of course, nothing of the kind. The Platonic Year was rooted in the concept of planetary cycles. The modern great year, by contrast, is based in the measurement of stellar motion against the background of the zodiac as a consequence of the phenomenon of precession.

Precession is a physical consequence of the Moon's, and to a lesser extent, the Sun's gravitational attraction for the equatorial bulge of the Earth. The result is an oscillation of the Earth's axis, which in turn causes the pole of the equator to move in a circular motion around the pole of the ecliptic, a phenomenon known as *nutation*.

The intersection of the planes of the ecliptic and the equator are, therefore, subject to a continual westward motion, the effect on observational astronomy being a gradual shift of the position of the Sun at the equinoxes against the background of the fixed stars. The rate of precession is 50.25" per annum, or 1° 23' 5" per century.[6]

In precessional astrology the time taken by the Vernal Equinox to precess through 30 degrees is known variously as a Platonic Year, a Platonic Month or a Great Age. The longer period denoted by one complete revolution is also known as a Great Year. However, I shall refer to the shorter period as a Precessional Month and the longer as a Precessional Year.

By the tradition, which is now a century old, each Precessional Month takes its character from the sidereal sign, or *morphomaton*, in which the Sun is situated at the Vernal Equinox.[7] It is generally agreed that this event currently takes place with the Sun in the sidereal sign or constellation of Pisces, giving rise to the belief that the current historical phase is the Precessional Month or Age of Pisces. Because the vernal point precesses, the signs take precedence in reverse order. The previous age was therefore that of Aries, while the approaching epoch is the Age of Aquarius.

It is perhaps because the length of one great month

approximates to one 2000-year millenium in the Christian scheme of history that the precessional great ages have been so readily adapted to existing millenarian beliefs.

## Precession in Classical Astronomy

Belief in the precessional ages is now so deeply entrenched that most astrologers accept their role in history without question, and it is generally assumed that the ages were recognized in the ancient world. Advocates of occult and fantasy schools of thought, largely influenced by Mme. Blavatsky's writings, believe that they were discovered tens or even hundreds of thousands of years ago on the mythical continents of Atlantis or Lemuria. Many serious astrologers, with greater justification, assume that the ages were acknowledged by classical scholars such as Plato or by the Jews and Christians of 2000 years ago.

The belief that Plato was aware of precession is based on the coincidence that, like his Platonic Year of 36,000 years, the Precessional Year of 25,872 years seems to involve a sexagesimal system of counting. It is argued that Plato's figure of 36,000 was, therefore, a misunderstanding of the real rate of precession. This proposition was confused by the medieval belief that the duration of one complete precessional cycle was 36,000 years and by the general ignorance of most commentators since then, especially astrological writers. If Plato was aware of precession, it is astonishing that neither he nor his pupil Aristotle betrayed any hint of their knowledge in their extensive astronomical writings.[8] The fact is that Plato was concerned almost exclusively with the motions of the planets which he thought could be explained according to the principles of the numbers 3 and 6.

The truth, as far as we know it, is that Hipparchus was the first classical author to mention precession around 130 B.C. This does not, however, mean that he discovered it; all we can say with certainty is that he was aware of it. Thomas Kuhn wisely recorded that precession "seems to have been noticed first by Hipparchus during the second century B.C."[9] Kuhn also remarks that although a number of Hipparchus' successors mentioned precession, others denied the existence of the effect or described it quite differently.

The first astrologer known to have mentioned precession was Claudius Ptolemy, the Alexandrine scholar, who made observations between about 121 and 151 A.D. but ignored it as a factor in astrology.[10] It is generally thought that in Ptolemy's time the existing sidereally based zodiac coincided with the modern tropical zodiac. In other words, 0° Aries in the sidereal zodiac coincided with the Sun's position at the Vernal Equinox. It, no doubt, seemed a simple matter to Ptolemy to rationalize the situation by defining 0° Aries as the vernal point rather than as the beginning of the constellation of Aries, but the legacy he bequeathed to his successors has not been an easy one. With the shift of the constellations in relation to the tropical Ptolemaic zodiac in the following centuries, they gradually became redundant, while the zodiac itself eventually ceased to have any connection to the awesome symbolism of the fixed stars.

## The Precessional Year in the Modern Period

During the Middle Ages, when it was believed that the Precessional Year and the Platonic Year of 36,000 years were one and the same thing, it was by inference believed that precession did have a role in history and was, therefore connected to the periodical cataclysms which punctuated Platonic Years. I have come across no reference to any other astrological significance which may have been conferred upon precession. Indeed, I have found no evidence for the proposition that astrologers prior to the late

19th century regarded precession as much more than an irritating embarrassment, let alone a guide to the passage of the great historical ages, whose character is derived from the signs of the zodiac.

It was in the hands of the 16th-century French historian and astrologer Jean Bodin that for the first time precession exerted a creative influence on astrological thought, offering both the basis of a critique of medieval astrology and a steppingstone towards a reformed modern approach. Disturbed by the shift of the constellations in relation to the zodiac, Bodin proposed the foundation of a reformed Mundane Astrology in which he argued that the, in his view, discredited tropical zodiac should be ignored, while greater attention should be paid to the relationship between planetary cycles and historical chronology.[11]

After Bodin's death, the concern with chronology which he had aroused was taken up by others, although not always in the form he envisaged. Ironically, scholars such as James Ussher and Isaac Newton related their chronological research to precession rather than planetary cycles, though it must be said that, unlike Bodin, their interest in the movement of the fixed stars was concerned purely with measurement of celestial motions rather than the interpretation of astrological meaning. During the 18th century it became clear that precession was a valuable aid to the study of Indian history, although this interest was, like Ussher's and Newton's, not in the least astrological in terms of celestial influence. Rather it was seen that precession offered a valuable chronological tool. The consequence was that by the end of the 18th century educated people were aware of the astronomical phenomenon of precession, the Western tradition of Platonic Years and, as a direct result of Orientalist studies, the Hindu belief in great astrological ages, the Yugas.

Such ideas rapidly infiltrated the burgeoning esoteric fringe. In 1813 the French occultist Fabre D'Olivet mentioned precession in connection with the Yugas in his edition of *Golden Verses of Pythagoras*. In 1822 the English antiquarian Samson Arnold Mackey published his *Mythological Astronomy of the Ancients Demonstrated* in which he, for the first time, hinted at an astrological effect from precession through the constellations. However, astrologers were slow to catch on, and I have found no first reference to the Precessional Months as we know them prior to 1879, and no reference to the Age of Aquarius itself prior to 1883.[12]

By the end of the 19th century, such astrological speculations had fused with a Neo-Platonic, Qabbalist, Rosicrucian mystical tradition whose mystical lineage may be traced quite clearly to the Renaissance and which had quite separately given birth to the idea of a New Age of spiritual enlightenment.[13]

Such genteel millenarianism as emanated from men of the caliber of Swedenborg and William Blake was welded into a powerful social force when it encountered the visionary Theosophical philosophy of H. B. Blavatsky. Blavatsky herself had little to say about precession, but subsequent Theosophical writers, all heavily influenced by her, were in no doubt that the world was on the brink of a New Age which was to be heralded by a cataclysm and the coming of a World Teacher. Indeed, modern New Age millenarianism owes its spirit and doctrines almost entirely to Theosophy.

From the 1900s to the 1980s, influential Theosophical astrologers such as Alan Leo and Dane Rudhyar have devoted a great deal of thought to the New Age for whom it was, of course, equivalent to the Age of Aquarius. Indeed, the majority of astrologers who have written on the Age of Aquarius have been Theosophists, and it is doubtful if the idea would have achieved such general currency without Theosophy's potent contribution.

## The Beginning of the Age of Aquarius

Since Ptolemy's time, precession has posed a problem for astrology, undermining the conventional reliance on the tropical zodiac. The invention of the notion of the Age of Aquarius has done nothing to ease such uncertainty. Indeed, attempts to define the temporal limits of the Age are themselves riddled with doubt, and the plain fact is that opinions on the beginning of the Age are purely subjective. In other words, they clearly have no basis in any agreed astronomical or historical consensus. Even Cyril Fagan's scholarly work on precession, outlined in *Zodiacs, Old and New*, loses its validity if we call into question the entire process of trying to establish a precise beginning for the Aquarian Age.

So far, I have collected from astrological literature about 80 published dates for the beginning of the Age, ranging from 1761 to 3500.[14] These dates fall into four categories as follows:

1. Dates which are purely symbolic, having no astronomical basis. The most obvious of these is the millenarian proposition that the Age of Aquarius will begin in 2,000 A.D.

2. Dates based on astrological factors independent of Aquarian symbolism.

3. Dates based on Aquarian symbolism. One such is 1962, the year of the great conjunction of planets in Aquarius.

4. Dates based on attempts to define the cusp between the constellations of the sidereal signs Pisces and Aquarius. These vary according to individual

preference and, as I shall argue, the whole attempt to define this cusp is largely futile.

The sheer variety of dates proposed for the beginning of the Age of Aquarius is surely of great significance for our understanding of the entire question. The unavoidable conclusion is that the belief that the Age of Aquarius is beginning at the present time is, therefore, justifiable on neither astrological nor astronomical grounds but is clearly a manifestation of traditional millenarianism.

## The Nature of the Age of Aquarius

From around 1880, belief in the coming Age of Aquarius spread fast, assisted by Thesophical excitement at the prospect of an imminent New Age. The general view of the New Age's nature and characteristics was formed in the 1880s and has changed little since then. It is immediately clear from the following authoritative statement, given in 1962 by Cyril Fagan, that the qualities of the modern New Age differ little from those of any other New Age suggested since the recorded history of millenarianism began over 2,500 years ago.

> During this Age the whole world will be just one big happy family, speaking the same language and freely mingling and intermarrying one another. Nations, monarchies, sovereign governments, republics, communistic states, separate communities, clans and tribes will be things of the past. National, political and religious labels, which now factionalize the world into many contending camps, such as British, American, Germany (sic), Russian, Capitalist, Communist, Christian, Hindu, Moslem and so forth, will disappear. Frontiers, customs barriers and color bars will vanish, and

with them the hierarchical, caste and clan systems. In such a society there will obviously be no need for armies or armaments of any description. This desirable state of affairs will not be brought about by conquest; but by a complete psychological revolution taking place in the consciousness of all individuals.[15]

The arrival of the Age of Aquarius will, then, necessitate a political revolution more complete than any in the history of human civilization, but unlike other revolutions the external revolution will flow naturally and easily from the internal revolution which must take place in the psyches of each and every human being.

It must be said, though, that the characteristics of the New Age relate to common conceptions of the returning golden age and were current in the 19th century prior to any discussion of the Age of Aquarius.[16]

## THE EVIDENCE

There are two classes of evidence customarily brought forward to demonstrate the proposition that the world is entering the Age of Aquarius. Both are based on the arbitrary selection of half-digested facts manipulated to present a preconceived conclusion. The first relies on the interpretation of historical evidence, the second on the analysis of contemporary developments.

### Historical Evidence

The effect of precession on civilization is supposed to be felt primarily through spiritual evolution. It, therefore, makes sense to attempt to identify the principal features of the religions of previous ages. Unfortunately, with the sole exception of Jung's essay on the Age of the Fishes and Robert Hand's essay which will soon be discussed, every other attempt I have seen displays a cavalier disregard for even elementary standards of historical research, a contempt for the truth, and a breathtaking abandonment of any concept that astrologers should strive for the highest possible standards in their work. The nature of historical events is misrepresented, there is little attempt to make any serious correlation with precession itself, and the arguments are heavily Eurocentric, being drawn almost exclusively from Western history.[17]

At its worst, this material enters the realms of the fantastic, proclaiming literal nonsense about Atlantis or human evolution from thought-forms. One is reminded of children who believe in fairies rather than supposedly educated adults engaged in a search for the truth, and it is astonishing that such work is published, let alone read.

At its most acceptable, parallels are drawn between the animal ruler of the Age in question and the animals featured in the corresponding religious imagery. For example, the Age of Taurus of the 3rd and 4th millenia B.C. is said to be demonstrated in the widespread worship of the bull. The Age of Aries saw the worship of the ram, and the Age of Pisces brought the fish symbolism of Christianity.

In the case of the Piscean Age, one is struck by just how un-Piscean it has been.[18] Yet in a magnificent piece of double-speak, the brutality of the Piscean Age is explained as a consequence of the suppression of Piscean values, an explanation justified by reference to various Jungian doctrines. Surely then, if the Piscean Age expressed qualities directly opposed to the sign's supposed astrological nature, will the Age of Aquarius be one of Leonine authority rather than Aquarian brotherhood?

## Contemporary Evidence

Of course, historical examination may reveal the effects of precession in the past, but without necessarily demonstrating that the Age of Aquarius is almost upon us.

This task is left to the interpretation of current developments in order to demonstrate Aquarian characteristics,
much as a Christian fundamentalist might interpret international affairs in light of the *Book of Revelation* or a Marxist
is perpetually on the lookout for signs of the crisis of capitalism which, it is forecast, will herald the socialist revolution.

Believers in the imminence of the New Age generally
find the evidence for their assumptions in whatever contemporary or historical developments appear to be, or
have been, progressive. The American, French and Russian revolutions together with radicalism of the 1960s variety are all seen as Aquarian, as are broader movements
such as feminism. Technological achievements such as
space travel and computerization are all categorized as
Aquarian. However, individual items of evidence are collected without regard to their nature or relative importance. Features which would be far better assigned to
other signs are given to Aquarius for *a priori* reasons under
a neat circular argument which runs as follows: The Age of
Aquarius is beginning; therefore, anything that transpires
now must be a symptom of the Age of Aquarius; the fact
that such events are happening is proof that the Age of
Aquarius is beginning. Such is the logical and intellectual
bankruptcy of the New Age movement.

A certain amount of self-censorship is also required,
for Saturn, Aquarius' traditional planetary ruler, is deeply
antipathetic to change of any sort. Only radical Uranus,
the sign's modern secondary ruler, evokes New Age sym-
pathies, so only the Uranian face of Aquarius is mentioned. Thus is the astrological tradition deemed incon-
venient.

Indeed, the general approach is colored by a deep ignorance of the complicated traditions of astrological historiography. For example, on its most simple level the revo-

lution in both transport and radio communications during the 20th century, which is usually ascribed to the approach of the Aquarian Age, may be more appropriately related to the opposition of Neptune and Pluto in Gemini to Jupiter and Uranus in Sagittarius, which took place between 1890 and 1900. Similarly, the computer revolution of the last few decades may be related to the mutation of the Jupiter/Saturn conjunction into Air signs. The space race, one would have thought, was Sagittarian. I am not concerned with the truth or otherwise of such statements, merely with the existence of an astrological tradition relying on the analysis of planetary cycles, which is far richer and more diverse than anything offered by the belief in great ages.

### New Age Millenarianism

It is clear that New Age philosophy corresponds to all the characteristics of millenarianism laid down previously.

1. It believes that the present age is one of decline, but that the Age of Aquarius, a golden age, is imminent.

2. It is also widely believed that a global crisis will precede the Age of Aquarius.[19]

3. The crisis will be alleviated both by the reappearance of the World Teacher and by individual activist effort.

4. Every contemporary event is interpreted as evidence of the coming of the Age. Every past event reveals the effects of precession on history.

We must also draw attention to a number of other features of New Age thought which connect it to the millenarian tradition. Chief amongst these is its *literalism* in which mystical concepts are translated into crude reality.

Hence, we find a literal belief in the existence of a fabulous golden age to which the world is about to return or in the imminent arrival on Earth of a new World Teacher. Then there is New Age historicism, the combination of belief in a predetermined future with the obligation of every individual to assist in the creation of that future. It is this historicism which lies at the root of New Age education—the belief in the importance of personal transformation if history is to follow its allotted course. Activism in the New Age movement, which takes the form of personal transformation and growth via a range of therapeutic, spiritual and educational disciplines, including astrology, will be the subject of a future paper. Needless to say, all these activities must be pursued in the service of the great historical plan, the preordained arrival of the Age of Aquarius.

### The Impact of Precession

Once the layers of New Age mythology have been stripped away, the true contribution of precession to the history of astronomy and astrology becomes clear. As we have seen, precession presented a problem for both physical astronomy and interpretative astrology from Ptolemy until the 17th century. Eventually, in the 16th and 17th centuries, the irritation it caused to the intellectual models of the medieval era triggered revolution in three areas.

Firstly, Nicolaus Copernicus was prompted to begin the work which was to revolutionize cosmology by establishing the heliocentric solar system.[20]

Secondly, the French historian and political scientist Jean Bodin abandoned the tropical zodiac, arguing instead for an astrology based on planetary cycles which could be observed and measured without ambiguity. Bodin was one of the first figures in the astrological reform program, which found its highest expression in the work of Kepler.

Thirdly, historical studies were transformed by Bodin's insistence that planetary cycles must be correlated with strict historical chronology based on rigorous research.

In practice, Bodin contributed little towards his goal of building a verifiable cyclically based Mundane Astrology, and within a century of his death historical and astrological studies had diverged, leaving academic historians with little more than contempt for astrology and astrologers by and large completely ignorant of history.

## THE USES OF PRECESSION IN ASTROLOGY

The question remains, then, as to what application the painfully slow precession of the equinoxes does have in astrology, aside from the creation of a mythology for the modern era, an ideology for the New Age movement.

The problem, of course, is that the rate of precession is so slow that within historical time it has been so slight as to offer us few clues. Recorded history began in the Near East in the third millenium B.C., and after that date records are slight for many eras and many regions of the world. For earlier periods we must rely on archaeological evidence, which is both scarce and notoriously difficult to date, and ultimately the geological record.

### Precession and Geological Time

If precession is a long-term phenomenon, correlations should be sought with equally long-term terrestrial phenomena. So far, little work has been done in this field.

The best evidence for a long-term effect from precession is offered by the study of climate. In his book *Future Weather and the Greenhouse Effect*, the science journalist John Gribbin gives an account of a number of climatic cycles of aproximately 25,000 years in length. We are still, however, in unknown territory and much work remains to be done.

Dr. Christine Janis, a palaeontologist, has attempted to correlate vertebrate evolution with a Great Great Great Great Precessional Year (a G4 year) of 43,200,000 years. First at a lecture at the Astrological Lodge in London and subsequently in the *Astrology Quarterly*, Janis drew connections between this cycle and terrestrial evolution.[21] This is all very provocative, and Janis did show connections between her scheme and three of the four major extinction periods, including that of the dinosaurs. However, her system is fatally flawed by an essentially arbitrary attribution of G4 years to signs of the zodiac. For example, she allots the present age to Aries on the grounds that this sign is traditionally associated with modern man, arguing that it began with the appearance of the first recognizably human ancestors about two million years ago. Using this as a base, she measures evolution against precession back to the G4 Age of Pisces which, in her system, commenced around 477,200,000 years ago. While Janis's work indicates the broad nature of the connections that may be made between geological time and precession, by choosing to link her chronology to a fixed zodiac of 12 signs and, like so many others, selecting an arbitrary starting point, Janis imposes an interpretative model on her work which may obscure more significant findings.

### Stellar Precession

As we have seen, the fundamental problem with all attempts to build an astrological theory around the astronomical fact of precession is the lack of any adequate astronomical framework. Of the 80 starting points for the Age of Aquarius that I have collated, some claim no relationship to precession while among the others some 70 different starting points are assumed for the sidereal zodiac. The stumbling block is the need for a fixed sidereal zodiac of 12 equal signs with precisely measured cusps, a need which perhaps satisfies some human desire to forecast that the Age of Aquarius will begin on such and such a date. The reason for this need to determine the precise beginning of the Age of Aquarius is surely that once such a forecast has been issued the faithful can look forward with hope in their hearts to the blessed golden age.

The obvious alternative (but one which is less satisfying from the millenarian point of view, for it means that successive precessional months will overlap) is to use the *morphomata*, or actual stellar constellations. As far as I know, this model was first used by Jung in his 1951 essay "The Sign of the Fishes," yet in view of the fact that his theoretical comments on precession were lifted directly and without attribution from various Theosophical and other recent writers, I would expect that he was drawing on existing published work. The great advantage of such a system is that it allows the precise dating of observed physical astronomical phenomena and may, therefore, form the basis of a realistic comparison between astronomical events arising from precession on the one hand and historical chronology on the other.

Jung gave a date of 146 B.C. for the conjunction of the first star of the constellation Pisces with the vernal point. He then confined himself to theoretical speculation on the nature of the Age of Pisces rather than historical analysis, allowing himself only the observations that the precession of the constellation's midpoint over the vernal point coincided with the European Renaissance and that the vernal point itself will precess into Aquarius sometime between 2,000 and 2,200 A.D. This will not mark the neat beginning of the New Age, however, for the existence of an overlap between the constellations means that the Spring Equinox will continue to occur in Pisces until almost the end of the third millenium.

However, while Jung's musings on Piscean symbolism, which merely amplifed those of the early Theosophists, have been accepted as gospel by the New Age movement, his shift of the emphasis from fixed equal sidereal signs to morphomata has been largely ignored, evidence surely of the New Age movement's love of simple answers and detestation of the intellectual quest. To the best of my knowledge, only one astrologer, Robert Hand, has continued Jung's work in print, and of the many lectures given every year on the New Age I know of only two in the U.K. which have addressed the question of stellar precession .[22]

Robert Hand's arguments, contained in his work "The Age and Constellation of Pisces," are published in his collected *Essays on Astrology*. His work makes use of Pisces' astrological symbolism in an intelligent, thought-provoking manner, manipulating astrological tradition with a knowledge and understanding of historical developments, and should be studied and absorbed by all aspiring New Age astrologers.

Hand erects a theoretical construct in which arguments concerning the correlations between precession and the development of consciousness are based on the successive conjunctions of the vernal point with the fixed stars of the constellation of Pisces. His principal thesis connects the beginning of the Piscean Age with *a shift in Western philosophy away from cyclical theories of infinite time towards the conception of a* **finite linear progression** *from a once-and-for-all creation to a future global destruction.*

Within this scheme he identifies four phases:

1. 111 B.C.–371 A.D. Precession through the West Fish correlated with the development of Christianity from mystical origins to state religion.

2. 371–1351. Precession to the midpoint of the cord

connecting the two fish correlated with the supremacy of Christianity in Europe.

3. 1351–1817. Precession from the midpoint of the cord to the East Fish correlated with the disintegration of Catholicism, the Renaissance, the Reformation, the rise of Humanism.

4. 1817–2813. Precession through the East Fish: so far correlates with the Age of Reason, the Scientific revolution and the rise of scientism.

In view of the gradual nature of precession, these dates must be seen as correlating with trends rather than precise events, and may be seen as the central points of cuspal periods of at least 70 and perhaps 140 years, these being the periods required for one or two degrees, respectively, to precess over the vernal point.

Running through Hand's work is a skepticism and ability to distance himself from historical comment which is borne of his historical education. His work is useful to my current thesis in that it opens the way to an astrological sociology of astrology itself. By attempting to discern a dialectical process within the development of Piscean Age belief, Hand allows us to locate astrological beliefs within that process. In addition, his discussion of the changes in consciousness associated with precession takes millenarianism, and therefore by implication what I have defined as New Age millenarianism, into account. For example, we may see New Age millenarianism as a symptom of the general alienation which followed the ideological revolution which is itself connected to the precession of the vernal point into the West Fish in 1817. New Age beliefs, therefore, become not an accurate and truthful account of the transition into the Age of Aquarius, but an unthinking consequence of deeper changes which are only half-recognized and not at all understood, a symptom of precession rather than an accurate account of its effects.

Indeed, if we can see any truth in Hand's proposition that the Age of Pisces has correlated with a linear, finite approach to terrestrial history, it becomes clear that apocalyptic millenarianism, which has flourished under this approach, is itself an essential part of Piscean Age philosophy.

Generally speaking, Hand considers precession only in terms of the conjunctions of celestial phenomena with the vernal point. However, it would be legitimate to use other aspects, especially the so-called event-manifesting hard aspects based on the division of the circle by two or four. Might not the precession of a star over one of the other Cardinal points reveal something of significance? It is intriguing, for example, that Antares and Aldebaran reached 0° Capricorn and 0° Cancer in the years 391 and 392, respectively, from where they squared the vernal point. This was only some 20 years after Christianity became the state religion of the Roman Empire, reinforcing Hand's argument that this event may be related to stellar precession. However, we are still faced with the problem that precession is so slow in relation to historical development that any insights it may offer are few and far between in relation to those offered by the analysis of planetary cycles.

### Mathematical Precession

From Ptolemy's time onwards, it was widely believed that the true rate of precession was one degree every 100 years, or one complete cycle every 36,000 years. This, of course, was the ideal number which in Platonic philosophy determined the duration of one complete Platonic Year. In Plato's historical scheme, one complete cycle of the universe consisted of two Great Years, one embodying growth, the other decay, making a total of 72,000 years.

This is 1000 times the true figure for the period of precession through one degree. Even Christine Janis's G4 Year is exactly equivalent to 100 Hindu Kali Yugas or 10 Maha Yugas. Such connections as these, some based on mistaken assumptions, others which are perfectly reasonable, point to two conclusions:

> 1. The cycle of precession may be mathematically related to Platonic and Pythagorean numerology.
>
> 2. The cycle of precession itself may not be a determining cycle in the sense that it is responsible for any correlations which may be made between it and terrestrial cycles, but it may when together with those events normally classed as effects of precession, a product of the mathematical laws identified by Plato and which in Platonic philosophy regulate the universe, or at least our section of it. [23]

We may search for other short-term cycles which may have no obvious immediate astronomical correlation but do conform to Platonic mathematics and may, therefore, be related to precession as a higher harmonic phase of the low harmonic which manifests in precession. In other words, theoretically a $3^1/_2$-year cycle in human or animal behavior might, in a sense, represent the same order of phenomenon as does precession.

For the best available information on cycles, we must turn to the work of the Foundation for the Study of Cycles, founded by Edward R. Dewey. The Foundation publishes a regular journal describing its research and the identification of apparently regular cycles, some in human activities, others in plant or animal behavior or climatic phenomenon.

A summary of the Foundation's work up to 1971 is given in *Cycles: The Mysterious Forces That Trigger Events* by Edward R. Dewey and Og Mandino. This work lists some 90 cycles which may be related to the common mathematics which connect Platonic numerology with precession, few of which offer exact connections, but many of which are intriguing. For example, a series of 5.91-year cycles covering business failure, railroad stock prices and grouse abundance deviate only slightly from the ideal 6-year period one would expect in a Platonic scheme. Yet Dewey's equation of these cycles with a 5.91-year Sunspot Cycle draws our understanding of precession into the realm of short-term astronomical cycles. So, the 5.91-year cycles may be imperfect from the Platonic point of view, yet one Precessional Month consists of approximately 365 such cycles, a figure which is approximately the number of days in the solar year, that is, the number of complete revolutions made by the Earth during its orbit of the Sun. The twelve 18.2-year cycles listed by Dewey are roughly equivalent to a division of the 72-year period of precession by four.

Such free association between the numbers measuring one cycle and another is a characteristic of Neo-Platonist and Qabbalist numerology, and while the patterns revealed may be pleasing, they may offer little in the way of useful information. Yet, it may be that such investigations offer the best clue to an understanding of the cyclic nature of precession free from millenarian New Age superstition. The work in this field remains to be done, and all we can do at the moment is suggest avenues for research.

## Conclusion

We may speculate that the notion of the Age of Aquarius entered astrological mythology because it is simple and appealed to astrologers who were, because of the 17th-century collapse of intellectual astrology, largely ignorant of their own tradition. The astrologers of the 19th century were obliged, so to speak, to reinvent the wheel, and in the process many old traditions were dropped and some new practices invented. As far as Mundane Astrology is concerned, the problem has been exacerbated by the naive willingness of so many modern astrologers to regard themselves as apolitical and apart or aloof from the world of conventional politics. Indeed, among many New Age devotees, even a knowledge of politics is considered liable to sully the soul. Most are, therefore, reluctant to investigate the complexities of Mundane Astrology. The problem is compounded by the fact that much of the literature on the Age of Aquarius is produced by members of esoteric fringe cults who are generally inspired by an often superficial acquaintance with Oriental religions and ancient mythology and who combine an ignorance of all but astrological clichés with a devout belief in the imminent dawning of the New Age.[24]

The abandonment of the serious study of history through astrology has left a gap which has been filled by the theory of great ages, which requires almost no technical knowledge of astrology and but a child's grasp of history. It may, therefore, be used to make a point without any need for time-consuming studies or corrupting investigation of politics.

We may, perhaps, look kindly on New Age beliefs if we regard wishful thinking as being in some way helpful. After all, if people believe that they should behave well in the service of history, the world will be a better place.[25] New Age beliefs offer a useful ideology, providing a social glue and reinforcing the aspirations of particular groups of people. The New Age movement offers a safety net to those who may be unsure of their individuality and who require a collective purpose to give some meaning to their lives.[26]

This is all very well, but millenarianism has also been responsible for appalling suffering. In living memory, the brutality of Stalinism and the savagery of the Pol Pot regime in Cambodia, excesses which were fueled by Marxist millenarianism, were both dedicated to the creation of the New Age. The puerile simplicities of astrological New Age millenarianism fed directly into Fascist ideology from the 1890s to 1930s, a fact which should stand as a terrible reminder of the perils of the sort of sloppy, nonsensical and infantile thinking which characterises the New Age religion and plagues modern astrology. Those who imagine that the New Age movement is all sweetness and light should remember the horror of Jonestown.[27]

## Notes

1. Charles Carter was not above criticism in this respect. Yet, at least that wise astrologer was aware of the pitfalls and voiced his opinion in typically stringent terms in *An Introduction to Political Astrology* (p. 73):

"In the West we have heard about the so-called Aquarian Age, which is to follow that of Pisces, and for some unexplained reason, is to be so much pleasanter to inhabit, until the very mention of this term fills the careful astrologer with apprehension. For it is questionable whether many who talk about it, and even some of those who write about it, understand what is meant."

Rupert Gleadow echoed Carter's words in *Your Character in the Zodiac* (p. 137) [now titled *The Zodiac Revealed*]: "In general, however, the expression the 'Aquarian Age' means only 'the next phase of the future,' and is used by people who do not know or care about its origin."

2. I am planning a history of astrology and millenarianism to be published by Routledge in 1991 under the title *The Great Year*.

3. See Karl Popper, *The Poverty of Historicism*, London, 1986.

4. The most important texts for Plato's political cosmology

are the *Timaeus*, trans. R. Bury, and the *Republic*, trans. Paul Shorey, both published by Heinemann Educational Books, Inc.

5. For Berossus, see Stanley Mayer Burstein, *The Babyloniaca of Berossus*, Undena Publications, 1978. For Louis Le Roy, see his *Of the Interchangeable Course* or *Variety of Things in the Whole World*, London, 1594.

6. The precise figure given in *The MacMillan Dictionary of Astronomy* is 50.2564 + 0.0222T arc seconds per annum where *T* is the time in Julian centuries from 1900. The Vernal Equinox precesses through 30 degrees in approximately 2156 years, a figure often simplifed by astrological writers to 2,000 years or 2,100 years, and through 360 degrees in approximately 25,872 years.

7. The sidereal zodiac is defined according to the background of the fixed stars whereas the tropical zodiac is defined by the equinoxes and solstices. The tropical zodiac is conventionally used in the West, the sidereal in India. The *morphomata* are the irregular physical constellations.

8. See John L. Dreyer's *History of the Planetary Systems from Thales to Kepler*, pp. 278-9.

9. Thomas S. Kuhn, *The Copernican Revolution: Planetary Astronomy in the Development of Western Thought*, Harvard University Press, Cambridge, Mass. and London, 1957, p. 269.

10. An excellent summary of the historical background to precession and its measurement is given by Walter Koch in "Vernal Point and Era of Aquarius," *In Search*, Vol. 2, nos. 1 & 2, Spring 1959.

11. For an account of Bodin's contribution to astrology, see "Astrological Historiography in the Renaissance: The Work of Jean Bodin and Louis Le Roy" in *Clio and Urania Confer: History and Astrology*, edited by Annabella Kitson.

12. Alfred Pearce, *The Text Book of Astrology*, p. 10; Gerald Massey, *The Natural Genesis*, Vol. 2, pp. 378-503.

13. According to Robert Ellwood, the modern concept of the New Age may be traced to the 18th-century mystic Emanuel Swedenborg (1688-1772), whom he calls "the major bridge between the old medieval alchemist or Rosicrucian in his dark laboratory, and the spiritualist seance on the American frontier of the modern Theosophical lecture." Swedenborg believed that

in a spiritual sense the second coming of Christ took place in 1757. Ellwood comments that Swedenborg's emphasis upon this invisible consummation must be a precursor to modern "'New Age' or 'Aquarian Age' ideas." *Religious and Spiritual Groups in Modern America*, Prentice-Hall, Inc., New Jersey, 1973, pp. 64-6.

Another figure of interest is Alphonse-Louis Constant (1810-1875), who as Eliphas Levi became one of the most renowned occultists of the modern age. I have not found any mention in Levi's works of the Age of Aquarius, although he and the other French occultists were deeply influenced by the concept of a New Age initiated by the return of the Holy Spirit. See Christopher McIntosh's *Eliphas Levi and the French Occult Revival*, Weiser, New York, 1972.

14. Nicholas Campion, *The Book of World Horoscopes*, pp. 397-403.

15. Cyril Fagan, "Interpretation of the Zodiac of Constellations" *Spica*, Vol. 1, No. 1, October 1961, pp. 5-14.

16. See for example the description of the New Age anticipated by the French Naundorffists in Christopher McIntosh's *Eliphas Levi and the French Occult Revival*.

17. Whereas most historical accounts of precession are Eurocentric on account of their authors' ignorance, Robert Hand, whose work is of an entirely superior caliber, argues coherently that Eurocentrism is inevitable for philosophical reasons. See "The Age and Constellation of Pisces," *Essays on Astrology*, Para Research, Inc., Glouster, Mass., 1982, p. 152.

18. The proposition that the Christian era has been most un-Piscean was first put by Mme. Blavatsky in *The Secret Doctrine*, Vol. 3, p. 348.

19. In the 1930s Alice Bailey believed that the crisis had already taken place in the form of the Great War. See *The Externalisation of the Hierarchy*, Lucis Publishing Co., New York, 1968, p. 4.

20. See Thomas Kuhn, *op cit.*, p. 221.

21. Christine Janis, "Vertebrate Evolution and the Great, Great, Great Great Year," *Astrology Quarterly*, Vol. 53, No. 4 and Vol. 54, No. 1, first published in the *Astrological Review*, Winter 1972.

22. To be precise, Geoffrey Cornelius at the Astrological Lodge on June 18, 1984, and Maggie Hyde in her Carter Memorial Lecture at the Astrological Asociation and Astrological Lodge in September 1984.

23. The conventional sequence of causal or acausal connections in astrology commences with God, then moves to the stars, the planets, and ultimately to the Earth. Neo-Platonism inserts numbers between God and the stars, an addition which is generally ignored. However, this is neither the time nor the place for a debate on the philosophy of astrology.

24. I would like to leave the last word on this particular subject to the great Dr. Walter Koch:

> Since astrology today has become a kind of substitute religion, many writers are seeking a field herein for the projection of their wishful world concepts and religious hopes. It seems likely that Rudolf Steiner first presented his all-inclusive ideas in a lecture on doctrines of eras. Then came Hans Kunkel, whose fascinating style bewitched all readers, and finally the decadents whose calculations enshrined Hitler as the exponent of the aquarian age, and who today fill the columns of the weekly periodicals with their phantasies (sic). One should regard these things, if one believed, as opinions, convictions, or as articles of faith, but they are not part of the substance of which the structure of astrological teachings is composed.
>
> If any significance regarding the "streaming" of time is to be sought in astrological principles, it cannot be a question of the aquarian age, which still lies in the dim distance. The cross-sections that are marked by the discovery of new planets offer themselves much more prominently. Thus the Uranian age of revolution and the present era began about 1789 with the discovery of Uranus in 1781. The machine age, democracy, socialism and communism began around 1846 with Neptune, and around 1930, the

Plutonic era of dictatorships and atom bombs. We live under the heartless threat of means of mass annihilation and not in the golden era of a new, transformed Saturn. Mankind has been enslaved both before and after them. No longer through the church or feudal lord, but through propaganda, capital and the totalitarian state. And therefore, all pronouncements about supposed aquarian tendencies of the present are only wishful beliefs and expectations for the future, but not reality for today.

Walter Koch, "Vernal Point and the Age of Aquarius," *In Search*, Vol. 2, No. 2, Spring 1959, p. 81.

Koch's assessment of the New Age movement as primarily religious is supported from a Christian point of view by Martin Israel who regards it as "a paganism brought up to date with gnostic accretions culled from psychic sources and heavily flavored by theosophical speculations derived from unorthodox offshoots of the world's major religions." *The Quest for Wholeness*, cited in *The Christian Parapsychologist*, Vol. 8, No. 2, June 1989, p. 69.

25. Rupert Gleadow, who was profoundly skeptical of the Age of Aquarius, wrote that "its only virtue is that it encourages us to look on the future, despite rebuffs, as something for which we must continue to do our best." *Your Character in the Zodiac* [*The Zodiac Revealed*], p. 137.

26. For the only existing attempt to offer a genuine sociological analysis of the New Age movement, see Mircea Eliade, *Occultism, Witchcraft & Cultural Fashions: Essays in Comparative Religions*, University of Chicago Press, 1978.

27. Among the many abuses perpetrated by New Age gurus, the most grotesque must be that of Jim Jones, whose followers committed mass suicide at their colony of Jamestown in Guyana in 1979.

# Bibliography

Aivanhov, Omraam Mikhail. *Aquarius, Herald of the Golden Age.* 2 Vols. Fréjus, France: Editions Prosveta, 1981.

Baigent, Michael, et al. *Mundane Astrology.* Wellingborough, Northamptonshire, England: The Aquarian Press, 1984.

Bailey, Alice A. *The Destiny of the Nations.* London: Lucis Press, 1949.

———. *Discipleship in the New Age.* 2 Vols. New York: Lucis Publishing Co., 1968, 1971.

———. *Education in the New Age.* New York: Lucis Publishing Co., 1971.

Begg, Ean. *Myth and Today's Consciousness.* London: Coventure, 1984.

Bennet, Julius. *The Riddle of the Aquarian Age.* London: London Astrological Research Society, 1925.

Blavatsky, H. P. *Isis Unveiled.* 2 Vols., Pasadena, Calif.: Theosophical University Press, 1976.

———. *The Secret Doctrine: The Synthesis of Science, Religion & Philosophy.* Los Angeles, Calif.: The Theosophy Company, 1982.

Burstein, Stanley Mayer. *The Babyloniaca of Berossus.* Sources and Monographs from the Ancient Near East. Vol. 1. fascicle 5. Malibu, Calif.: Undena Publications, 1978.

Campion, Nicholas. *The Book of World Horoscopes.* Wellingborough, Northamptonshire, England: The Aquarian Press, 1988.

———. "Astrological Historiography in the Renaissance: The Work of Jean Bodin and Louis Le Roy." *Clio and Urania Confer: History and Astrology.* ed. Annabella Kitson, London, 1989.

Carter, Charles. *An Introduction to Political Astrology.* London, 1951.

Costard, George. *The Use of Astronomy and Chronology Exemplified*. London, 1764.

Curtiss, H. A. and Curtiss, F. H. C. *The Message of Aquaria*. Reprint. (1921) Albuquerque, NM: Sun Publishing Co., 1981.

De Santillana, Giorgio. *The Origins of Scientific Thought*. London, 1961.

De Santillana, Giorgio and Von Dechend, Hertha. *Hamlet's Mill*. London, 1969.

Dewey, Edward R, and Mandino, Og. *Cycles: The Mysterious Forces that Trigger Events*. London, 1971.

D'Olivet, Fabre. *Golden Verses of Pythagoras*. Wellingborough, England: Thorsons, 1975.

Dreyer, John L. *History of the Planetary Systems from Thales to Kepler*. London, nd.

Eliade, Mircea. *The Myth of the Eternal Return*. Bollingen Series XLVI. Trans. by Willard R. Trask. Princeton: Princeton University Press, 1974.

————. *Occultism, Witchcraft and Cultural Fashions: Essays in Comparative Religions*. London and Chicago: University of Chicago Press, 1978.

Ellwood, Robert. *Religious and Spiritual Groups in Modern America*. New Jersey: Prentice-Hall, Inc., 1973.

Fagan, Cyril. "Interpretation of the Zodiac of Constellations," *Spica*, Vol. 1, No. 1, October 1961, pp. 5-14.

————. *Zodiacs, Old and New*. London, 1951.

Ferguson, Marilyn. *The Aquarian Conspiracy*. London: Paladin Books, 1986.

Gleadow, Rupert. *The Origin of the Zodiac*. London, 1968.

Gordon, Henry. *Channelling in the New Age*. Buffalo, New York: Prometheus Books, 1988.

Gribbin, John. *Future Weather and the Greenhouse Effect*. London, 1983.

Hand, Robert. "The Age and Constellation of Pisces," *Essays on Astrology*. Glouster, Mass.: Para Research, Inc., 1982.

Heindel, Max. *The Message of the Stars*. London, 1918.

———. *The Rosicrucian Cosmo-Conception*. London: Fowler, 1929.

Howard, Michael. *The Occult Conspiracy*. London: Rider & Co., 1989.

Israel, Martin. *The Quest for Wholeness*. London, 1989.

Janis, Christine, "Vertebrate Evolution and the Great, Great, Great, Great Year" *Astrology Quarterly*, Vol. 53, No. 4 and Vol. 54, No. 1, Winter 1978/79 and Spring 1979. Originally published in the *Astrological Review*, Winter 1972.

Jung, C. G. *Aion: Researches into the Phenomenology of the Self*. (The Collected Works of C. G. Jung: No. 9, Part 2) Trans. by R. F. C. Hull. London: Routledge and Kegan Paul, 1959.

Koch, Walter. "Vernal Point and Era of Aquarius," *In Search*, Vol. 2, Nos. 1 & 2, Winter 1958/59 & Spring 1959.

Leo. *Passing into Aquarius*. London: Andrew Dakers, nd.

Levi. *The Aquarian Gospel of Jesus the Christ*. London: L. N. Fowler, 1980.

Lewis, G. C. *An Historical Survey of the Astronomy of the Ancients*. London, 1862.

Mackey, Samson Arnold. *Mythological Astronomy of the Ancients Demonstrated*. Minneapolis, Minn.: Wizzards Bookshelf, 1973.

McIntosh, Christopher. *Eliphas Levi and the French Occult Revival*. New York: Samuel Weiser, Inc., 1972.

Manuel, F. *Shapes of Philosophical History*. London, 1965.

Massey, G. *The Natural Genesis*. London, 1883.

Mercier, Raymond. "Studies in the Medieval Conception of Precession," *Archives Internationales d'Histoire des Sciences*.

Muller, Max. *Ancient Hindu Astronomy and Chronology*. Oxford, 1862.

Neugebauer, O. *The Exact Sciences in Antiquity*. Oxford, 1957.

Norelli-Bachelet, P. *The Gnostic Circle*. New York: Samuel Weiser, Inc., 1978.

Plato. *Laws*. Trans. by R. G. Bury. London, 1926.

————. *Timaeus*. Trans. by R. G. Bury. London, 1929.

————. *Republic*. Trans. by Paul Shorey. London, 1930.

Plutarch. "Life of Sulla" in *Libes*. Ed. R. M. Hutchins. London, 1957.

Popper, Karl. *The Open Society and Its Enemies*. 2 Vols. London, 1945.

————. *The Poverty of Historicism*. London, 1986.

Preston, E. W. *The Earth and its Cycles*. London, 1931.

Reid, Vera W. *Towards Aquarius*. New York: Arco Publishing, Inc., 1944.

Rudhyar, Dane. *Astrological Timing*. London, 1969.

————. *Occult Preparations for a New Age*. London: Theosophical Publishing House, 1975.

Sedgwick, John. *Harmonics of History*. New York: Philosophical Library, Inc., 1975.

Sibbald, Luella. *The One With the Water Jar: Astrology, The Aquarian Age and Jesus of Nazareth*. San Francisco, Calif.: Guild for Psychological Studies, 1978.

Simms, Maria Kay. *Twelve Wings of the Eagle: Our Spiritual Evolution through the Ages of the Zodiac*. San Diego, Calif.: ACS Publications, 1988.

Steiner, Rudolf. *Cosmic Memory: Atlantis and Lemuria*. London and San Francisco: Harper and Row, 1981.

———. *Occult Science: An Outline*. Trans. by George Adams and Mary Adams. London: Rudolf Steiner Press, 1969.

———. *World History in the Light of Anthroposophy*. Trans. by George Adams and Mary Adams. 2nd ed. London: Rudolf Steiner Press, 1977.

Sturgess, Jon. *The Piscean Age and the Aquarian Age*. 1969.

Sucher, W. O. *Man and the Stars*. Reprint. (1952) Llangadog: Elidyr Press, 1981.

Tippett, Michael. *Moving into Aquarius*. St. Albans: Paladin Books, 1974.

Trevelyan, Sir George. *Operation Redemption: A Vision of Hope in an Age of Turmoil*. 2nd ed. Walpole, New Hampshire: Stillpoint Publishing, 1985.

———. *A Vision of the Aquarian Age*. London: Coventure, 1984.

Warcup, Adam. *Cyclic Evolution: A Thesophical View*. London: Theosophical Publishing House, 1986.

Webb, James. *The Occult Establishment*. Glasgow, 1981.

Winchell, A. *Sketches of Creation*. London, 1870.

Yeats, W. B. *A Vision*. London: Macmillan Publishing Co., 1937.

**Nancy Soller**

An art major, education minor and former teacher, Nancy Soller has been studying astrology for 16 years and making weather predictions for Llewellyn's *Moon Sign Book* since 1981.

Besides writing articles on weather prediction by astrometeorology, she conducts ongoing research of weather in the United States and is currently engaged in the study of the timing of major earthquakes which occurred between 1982 and 1984.

# WEATHER WATCHING
# WITH AN EPHEMERIS

*Astrometeorology* is the science of weather prediction by means of planetary positions. Its origins are lost in pre-history, but Aristotle wrote on the subject, and the great 2nd century Greek astronomer Claudius Ptolemy dealt with the nature of the planets concerning weather prediction in his *Tetrabiblos*. Astrometeorology did not advance during the Dark Ages or the Middle Ages, but by the 17th Century Johannes Kepler, building on the work of Tycho Brahe, earned fame by making long-range weather predictions based on planetary positions. Kepler then went on to discover the laws of planetary motion.

Noted advances in astrometeorology next occurred in London where a certain D. Goad published his *Astro-meteorogia*, which became the textbook for astrologers working in this field. Also in London, Sir Isaac Newton, by means of planetary positions, predicted weather anomalies that occurred 23 years after his death.

Astrometeorology suffered when science disclaimed astrology, but 20th-century advances in this field are due in part to George J. McCormack, an American who tried unsuccessfully to interest the United States Weather Bureau in this discipline. Unlike most of his predecessors, McCormack had the advantage of being able to study the effects of Uranus, Neptune and Pluto, making much greater accuracy possible. McCormack's work is treated in

Joseph F. Goodavage's book *Our Threatened Planet*, an excellent aid for anyone interested in this field of study.

Weather watching with an ephemeris is fun and easy. While Ingress charts are needed for making accurate seasonal predictions, an intelligent amateur, armed with the right ephemeris, can pick out high-risk rain and wind dates months in advance.

The right ephemeris is a necessity, however. For making daily predictions for 1990, *The American Ephemeris 1981-1990* should be used; *The American Ephemeris 1991-2000* should be used for the rest of the century. Both of these ephemerides have daily aspectarians which give the correct times (in Greenwich Mean Time) when aspects and Ingresses occur. *The American Ephemeris for the 20th Century* does *not* have a daily aspectarian and *cannot* be used for daily weather prediction without a lot of complicated math. Yet it does have times for the Ingresses and can be used to make seasonal predictions.

*The American Ephemeris 1981-1990* and *The American Ephemeris 1991-2000* can be ordered from ACS Publications, P.0. Box 34487, San Diego, California, 92103-0802; 1-800-637-2312.

## Daily Predictions

Picking out high-risk dates for precipitation and wind is very rewarding to those who live in areas where the weather changes often. This is done by selecting *weather-changing aspects* of the planets in the daily aspectarian of an ephemeris. The weather-changing aspects are the **major** aspects, which are the conjunction ( $\sigma$ ), parallel ( $\parallel$ ), sextile ( $\ast$ ), square ( $\square$ ), trine ( $\triangle$ ), and opposition ( $\sigma^{o}$ ).

The planets associated with *precipitation* are Venus ( $\mathcal{Q}$ ), Saturn ( $\hbar$ ), and Neptune ( $\Psi$ ). Whenever these planets form a major aspect to each other, the Sun ( $\odot$ ) or another planet, precipitation is likely.

Mercury ( ☿ ), Mars ( ♂ ), Uranus ( ♅ ), and Pluto ( ♇ ) are associated with *wind*. Whenever these planets form an aspect to each other, the Sun or another planet, wind may be expected. In addition, major aspects of Mercury and Uranus tend to lower temperatures; major aspects of Mars and Pluto tend to raise temperatures.

When a wind planet forms a major aspect to a rain planet, both wind and rain may be expected.

Most of the aspects in the daily aspectarian involve the Moon. These may be ignored except for *Sun square Moon* and *Sun opposing Moon*. Sun square the Moon indicates that the Moon is at its quarter and that rain is likely even though it is not indicated in any other way for that day. Sun opposing the Moon indicates that the Moon is full. This usually results in clear weather the day the aspect is perfect, but the following day may result in a dumping of precipitation that is not indicated in any other way.

Minor aspects of the planets to each other and the Sun may be ignored except for the *contraparallel*, which sometimes triggers a weather change.

Naturally, unusually wet seasons may see precipitation even on days not indicated by planetary positions, and unusually dry seasons may skip precipitation even on days indicated as wet. In addition, precipitation involving **Saturn** may last for several days.

Two further notes on daily predictions by the amateur: where wind predictions are concerned, the *trine* and *sextile* aspects of the wind planets result in breezes that flap clothes *gently* on a line; the *square* and *opposition* result in winds that may be defined as *brisk*, strong or whistling, up to destructive. Also, major aspects of **Neptune** to the Sun or other planets will sometimes result in fog rather than precipitation.

In making daily weather predictions it is important to remember that a weather change may take place east of your point of observation, missing you entirely. It is also possible for a weather change to begin so far to the west that it fizzles out before reaching your point of observation.

Weather observers who can set charts can greatly increase the accuracy of their daily predictions. A chart set for your location for the minute the aspect is perfect will indicate whether the weather change will occur in your location. *If either aspecting planet or the planet and the Sun is prominent, the change will affect your location.* Prominent means that the planet is forming a conjunction, opposition, square or trine to the **Midheaven** of the chart or is in an **angular house** (1st, 4th, 7th or 10th). The orb of influence is 8°.

Charts set for the minute the Moon is new ( ☉ ☌ ☽ ) or the Moon is full ( ☉ ☍ ☽ ) will tend to show two-week periods of time when unusually wet or unusually dry weather is likely. In the case of an unusually wet two-week period, Venus, Saturn or Neptune will be prominent in the chart. If a two-week period will be unusually dry, Mars or Pluto will be prominent. Again, the orb of influence is 8°.

In order to set charts to refine daily predictions, it is necessary to determine local sidereal time when the aspect or lunation is perfect. Instructions are given at the end of this chapter.

### Seasonal Predictions

Seasonal predictions are made from Ingress charts. Ingress charts are local charts set for the equinoxes and solstices, or the moment the Sun enters Aries (spring), Cancer (summer), Libra (fall), and Capricorn (winter). In order to set an Ingress chart it is necessary to determine local sidereal time at the time of the Ingress. (See the end of this chapter.)

**Mercury** prominent on an Ingress chart signifies strong winds and atypical cooler or colder weather. **Venus** prominent on an Ingress chart indicates a season with more than the average precipitation. **Mars** prominent indicates weather that will be hotter and drier than normal. **Jupiter** brings good weather. Jupiter prominent in a Capricorn Ingress chart indicates a mild winter. A prominent **Saturn** indicates cold, wet weather. A prominent **Uranus** signifies a dry, windy drought, unless Uranus happens to be in a Water sign. **Neptune** prominent signifies precipitation and mild temperatures, and **Pluto** operates in much the same way as Mars, bringing higher temperatures and little precipitation.

Once an Ingress chart is set up, it is studied to determine which influences will be the strongest. Any planet conjuncting the Midheaven will have the strongest influence on the weather, followed by any planet on the IC, and then by any planet squaring the Midheaven. Planets in angular houses are next. These are the planets in the 1st, 4th, 7th and 10th Houses. The orb of influence for planets aspecting the Midheaven is 8°; the closer the aspect is to exact, the more strongly it will influence the weather.

The *sign* that a planet is in at any given time is also important in making seasonal predictions. Any planet transiting through a Water sign tends to bring more moisture than it normally would. Planets in Fire signs tend to raise temperatures and create dry conditions. This influence by sign can be seen both on Ingress charts and by transit.

The *declination* of planets also plays a part in weather prediction. Many planets in northern declination tend to raise temperatures in the Northern Hemisphere; many planets in southern declination tend to warm the Southern Hemisphere.

## Planetary Conjunctions

Planetary conjunctions provide additional information about coming weather conditions. The conjunctions of the faster-moving inner planets—Mercury, Venus and Mars—are important only if they are prominent in an Ingress chart, and they bring brief weather changes by transit. Conjunctions of the slow-moving *outer planets*, however, have long-lasting effects on the weather and do not have to be prominent in an Ingress chart to do so.

By far, the most dramatic effects of the slow-moving outer planets involve **Saturn**. Conjunctions of Saturn usually accentuate the weather characteristics of the other planet.

In June of 1980 the Summer Ingress found a conjunction of Saturn and Mars squaring the Midheaven in locations west of St. Louis. It was an extremely hot, dry summer on the Plains, and as the hot weather moved east, emergency shelters were set up in St. Louis for the aged who could not afford air conditioning.

Immediately following the summer of 1980, Jupiter overtook Saturn, forming a new conjunction which brought extremely cold weather in the winter of 1980-1981 and cooler-than-normal temperatures in both the spring and fall of 1981.

During much of 1982 and almost all of 1983, Saturn was in conjunction with Pluto. At this time the trade winds and currents of the Pacific reversed, carrying a thick, warm layer of water to offshore Peru. This was the famous El Niño which created severe problems for seabirds and the fishing industry by preventing the rising of nutrient-rich, cool sub-surface water.

In addition to problems off South America, the Saturn/Pluto conjunction coincided with drought in India, Sri Lanka, the southern Philippines, Hawaii, southeast Africa, Indonesia and Australia.

The flooding and storms off our West Coast the winter of 1982-83 were not due to this conjunction but to the presence of Venus on the Midheaven of Ingress charts set for California, Oregon and Washington.

A Jupiter/Uranus conjunction, extending from December 1982 to November 1983, further complicated the weather picture during this period of time.

Starting in September of 1987, Saturn moved into conjunction with Uranus, bringing dry conditions which culminated in the drought of 1988. In the July 4, 1988 *U.S. News and World Report*, Betsy Carpenter stated that the jet stream had split in two and shifted, some of it traveling over northern Canada, some of it traveling south over Mexico, bringing these areas the moisture which usually fell on the Plains and the Midwest.

Other weather anomalies occurred in 1988. The heaviest monsoon rains in 70 years flooded Bangladesh, and a plunge in ocean temperatures off equatorial South America was called La Niña to distinguish it from the warm ocean temperatures of El Niño.

By January of 1989, Saturn was moving past Uranus and forming a new conjunction with Neptune. This should result in extremely wet conditions in the summer and fall of 1989 on into the year 1990. The year 1989 was an extremely interesting period in which to study conjunctions of Saturn because Saturn was within 8° of both Uranus and Neptune for most of the year.

Conjunctions of **Jupiter** last about a year. The Jupiter/Saturn conjunction has already been discussed; Jupiter/Uranus conjunctions are likely to result in chill winds. Conjunctions of Jupiter with Neptune generally result in low pressure, high humidity, fog and abnormally high precipitation. The influence of Jupiter's conjunctions do not seem to be as dramatic as the influence of Saturn's conjunctions, unless the Jupiter conjunction falls in a prominent place in an Ingress chart.

It should also be noted that local conditions during conjunctions of the outer planets can be modified by planets prominent in Ingress charts at the time of the conjunction.

The conjunctions of the planets beyond Saturn present some special problems in weather prediction. The three outer planets move so slowly that their conjunctions are truly rare, and they apparently bring long-lasting changes to the weather which act a little more subtly than the conjunctions of Saturn. The conjunctions of these planets are Uranus/Neptune, Uranus/Pluto and Neptune/Pluto.

Neptune was last conjunct Pluto before the turn of the century in the 1880s and '90s. Since Pluto had not been discovered at that time, the influence of this conjunction was not noted. We know nothing about its effect, although studies of what weather records exist from that time may give some clues to its behavior in the future.

The **Uranus/Pluto conjunction** occurred during the 1960s, becoming perfect in 1965 and 1966. This conjunction coincided with drought in the Northeast and brought weather anomalies to other parts of the world. The *U.S. News and World Report* of April 18, 1966 discussed the drought in the Northeast, which was in its fifth year then, and also reported recent droughts in India, Australia and South Africa; unusually bad winter storms on the Plains; a drenching of Florida; and extremely heavy rains in Brazil. Jerome Namias, chief of the Weather Bureau's Extended Forecast Division at that time, speculated that the Northeast's drought was probably due to an unusual movement of cold Arctic currents meeting the Gulf Stream off the coast of Newfoundland. Namias believed that temperature contrasts caused by the meeting of these two currents formed a storm center which sucked in dry, cool air from the drought area.

Weather records from 1961 to 1969 for Portland, Maine, Boston, New York City and Philadelphia show that the Uranus/Pluto drought was more severe when the conjunction was *applying* rather than separating and that 1965, the year the conjunction was perfect, saw the lowest annual precipitation at each locality. Annual rainfall in 1965 was 28.15 inches at Portland, 23.71 inches at Boston, 26.09 inches at New York City and 29.34 inches at Philadelphia. The 1944-1983 mean annual rainfalls at these cities are 42.54, 41.50, 43.72 and 41.38, respectively. Records from other cities in these areas echo such statistics.

The Uranus/Pluto conjunction was probably responsible for the extremely common phenomena of *hyperactivity* noted in children born in the late 1960s and early 1970s. When the Moon forms a hard angle to Uranus in a nativity, emotional tension results; when the Moon forms a hard angle to Pluto, there is a tendency towards impulsiveness. In the Sixties when the two were conjunct, the Moon formed hard angles to the conjunction four times each month. Children born on these critical days often had a tendency towards impulsive, out-of-bounds behavior. Since this conjunction is now history, we will be dealing less and less with hyperactivity.

The last and most recent conjunction of planets that orbit beyond Saturn is the **Uranus/Neptune conjunction**. It began forming in January of 1989 and these planets will remain linked until December of 1997. The conjunction will be perfect in 1993. Although this conjunction is already in effect, its influence has been masked by the Saturn/Neptune conjunction which was in effect until February of 1990. Now the effects of the Uranus/Neptune conjunction will be seen and its influence felt.

How will this conjunction affect the weather? Uranus and Neptune were last in conjunction during the

1810s and 1820s. This was before Neptune was discovered and also before modern weather records were kept. All weather information from that time in the United States comes from the journals of a few amateur weather-watchers who tended to make observations of fleeting and dramatic weather phenomena along with records of current events. There are virtually no weather records existing from those days which would be useful in the way modern weather records are in studying this conjunction.

Weather records do exist, however, from the time of the last Uranus/Neptune *opposition*, which occurred between l903-1914. Because a planetary opposition tends to act in the same way as a planetary conjunction—but not as dramatically—we can get a few clues to the type of weather to expect in the 1990s.

Uranus is associated with cold and drought, unless it is in a Water sign, in which case moisture is indicated. Neptune is associated with moisture and mild temperatures. In the 1990s, however, as in the period between l903-1914 and the last conjunction, Uranus will not be in a Water sign.

What happened between 1903 and 1914? Weather records for those years indicate slightly below-average precipitation at sample locations in the *interior* between the Rockies and the Appalachians except for Bismarck, North Dakota, and both slightly above-average and below-average precipitation between the Rockies and the Pacific.

On the east coast, Annapolis had a per-year average deficit of 1.17 inches; New York City, .56 inches; Boston, 4.91 inches; and Portland, Maine, 5.03 inches. Strangely enough, Philadelphia had precipitation almost three inches heavier than normal.

During the opposition, most per-year precipitation averages varied from the long-term averages by less than one or two inches with the biggest deficits in New England and the biggest surplus of precipitation, 3.25 inches, at New Orleans.

Cities in the interior with below-average precipitation included Cincinnati, Nashville, Indianapolis, Sault Ste. Marie, Chicago, St. Louis, Dodge City, Oklahoma City, Fort Worth, San Antonio, Cheyenne and Moorhead, Minnesota. Conditions during the opposition will be magnified during the conjunction.

Average temperatures per year during the 1903-1914 opposition varied from the long-range average temperatures per year by tenths of a degree in most of these locations, with most locations east of the Mississippi having temperatures slightly above normal and most locations west of the Mississippi having temperatures slightly below normal.

During the coming conjunction, it appears that locations in the interior east of the Rockies will have less rainfall than normal with much less rainfall centering in New England. Temperatures in most locations east of the Mississippi will be above normal, and temperatures west of the Mississippi, a little below normal. By 1991 the effects of the conjunction should be seen plainly. A drought in New England during that year would mark a weather trend which will peak in 1993 and not be fully over until 1997.

It is tempting to note the lack of precipitation in New England during the 1903-1914 opposition and compare it to the drought there during the 1960s. The question may be asked whether conjunctions of Uranus with planets that move more slowly than itself always result in drought in this area.

A study of tree rings in Nebraska by H. E. Weakley indicates drought there between 1822-1832, overlapping the years when the last Uranus/Neptune conjunction was in effect. Was this drought related to the conjunction? If so, its effects were cumulative. It took several years for dry conditions to affect the growth of trees, and a few years following the conjunction for normal tree growth to resume.

Remember that other planets aspecting the Midheaven of local Ingress charts can completely change the weather for a season in these locations, regardless of conjunctions of slow-moving outer planets. The Saturn/Neptune conjunction, promising spectacular precipitation, was perfect in February and March of 1989, but its effect was masked in much of the Midwest by Pluto on the Midheaven of Winter Ingress charts and Jupiter on the IC in Ohio and Indiana.

The effects of the coming Uranus/Neptune conjunction are going to be cumulative. The conjunction will not result in a dramatic one-and-one-half-year drought as did the Saturn/Uranus conjunction of 1988. There is likely to be lower rainfall in the interior east of the Rockies—especially east of the Mississippi—lasting over a period of about seven years, beginning in 1991. It will be drier when the aspect is forming than when it is separating and driest in 1993 when the aspect is perfect. If the pattern of the 1903-1914 opposition is followed, New England will be the area most seriously affected. A sunspot-related drought immediately following this conjunction would have especially severe effects on the Plains, but it appears that a negative sunspot maximum is in effect now (late 1989) and the next minimum is likely about 2001.

## Sunspot Cycles of Drought

Sunspots are dark spots upon the Sun which are cooler than the rest of the Sun's surface, magnetically charged and tend to be seen in pairs. At the beginning of a sunspot cycle, the spots start to form about 30° north and south of the Sun's equator. As the sunspot cycle progresses, the number of spots grows and the spots appear closer to the Sun's equator. Sunspots reach their maximum number at about 15° north and south and then begin to disappear. The last spots fade away at around 8° north and south. This takes about 11 years.

While the formation, growth and disappearance of sunspots take 11 years, there is actually a 22-year cycle involved. During the first half of the cycle, the leading sunspot of a pair north of the equator has north magnetic polarity, and the leading sunspot of a pair south of the Sun's equator has south magnetic polarity. In the next cycle they reverse themselves with the leading sunspot of a pair north of the equator having south magnetic polarity, and the leading sunspot south of the Sun's equator having north magnetic polarity. It is after this second cycle is completed that a sunspot-related drought occurs on the plains.

Different authorities give different years for sunspot-related droughts, but they have been charted back to 1815. *Sun, Weather and Climate*, put out by the National Aeronautics and Space Administration, lists these droughts as occurring in 1815-1818, 1842-1847, 1866-1869, 1892, 1912, 1934, 1953 and 1974-1977. The early dates in these series were apparently determined by studying tree rings in the Plains area.

The 1815-1818 drought occurred during the last Uranus/Neptune conjunction, and its dates are different from those established by H. E. Weakley for the drought in Nebraska. It appears that dry conditions prevailed for a long period of time on the Plains in the early 19th century, and it is likely both the Uranus/Neptune conjunction and the sunspot cycle were involved.

*Sun, Weather and Climate* indicated that the 22-year cycle is approximate. A sunspot minimum can be identified only in retrospect.

Sunspots are due to convective cells in the Sun's interior. Attempts have been made in the past to link sunspot activity to the positions of the planets around the Sun, but this theory just doesn't bear fruit. Hard angles of the planets around the Sun coincide with radio interference, but a heliocentric ephemeris shows no consistent pattern of planetary positions during sunspot-related drought years.

No mention of sunspot-related droughts would be complete without mentioning the great drought of the mid-1930s. The experts give various dates for its beginning and end, but 1934 and 1935 saw severe drought on the Plains, and the drought peaked in 1936.

This drought coincided with the Great Depression. Problems were caused not only by a severe lack of rainfall but also by overcultivation and overgrazing of marginal lands. Crops withered, cattle died and topsoil was picked up by the winds and blown east. Insect plagues occurred in some areas. Thousands of farmers left their farms in Oklahoma and other states in the Dust Bowl and moved to California.

The May 19, 1934 edition of *Newsweek* quoted the Secretary of Agriculture as saying that this was the greatest drought in the history of the nation. At this time the country had two more years to go. Also in 1934, *Newsweek* reported drought in Canada, Great Britain, Rumania, Poland and parts of Russia.

By August of 1936, a total of 841 counties in 20 states between the Appalachians and the Rockies were located on the Emergency Drought Map of the Department of Agriculture. Every county in the Dakotas and all but ten counties in Oklahoma were on this map.

Charts set for the Summer Ingresses on the Plains during the sunspot-related drought years of 1934, 1935 and 1936 show Uranus opposing the Midheaven in 1934, squaring the Midheaven in 1935 and conjuncting the Midheaven in 1936.

All charts set for locations on the Plains for the Summer Ingresses in other sunspot-related drought years in the 20th century show some sort of testimony for dry weather. The June 21, 1953 Summer Ingress chart set for Oklahoma City is especially interesting. Jupiter is on the Midheaven—not Pluto, Mars or Uranus as one might suspect—and Saturn and Neptune are conjunct in the 2nd House, which in normal years would bring moisture. The chart indicates that sunspots have a stronger effect on drought than planetary conjunctions and also suggests that we need to know more about sunspots, conjunctions and planets aspecting the Midheaven.

Since the last sunspot-related drought on the Plains occurred in 1974 and was not fully over until 1977, the next sunspot-related drought is due anywhere between 1996-1999. If the Plains begin drying out during the Uranus/Neptune conjunction, it may make drought conditions even more severe. We should be watching not only New England but also the Plains during the coming conjunction.

*Note:* As press time approaches (mid-1990) we appear to be in a negative sunspot maximum. This means that the next sunspot maximum is due about the year 2000 or 2001. The Plains should have recovered from the effects of the Uranus/Neptune conjunction by then.

## How Does It Work?

Weather changes that accompany conjunctions of the outer planets are especially interesting phenomena. The study of these should not offend even the most rigid scientist because they are not predictive; the weather changes and the conjunctions occur simultaneously. It appears as though these planetary conjunctions affect the weather by altering the trade winds and the jet stream. Trade winds normally blow from east to west and the jet stream travels from west to east.

During the 1982 El Niño, both the Pacific trade winds and the Pacific ocean currents reversed, traveling east instead of west. The reversal was apparently caused by a strong rise in atmospheric pressure on the western edge of the Pacific and a sharp drop in pressure on its eastern edge. Nigel Calder in his book *The Weather Machine* states that areas of high pressure called blocks or, more properly, *blocking anticyclones* alter the pattern of the jet stream and are commonly associated with heat waves, record snowfalls, droughts and floods. The 1988 drought is blamed on an enormous high over the Plains and the Midwest which split the jet stream, which then carried its moisture north to northern Canada and south to Mexico.

Most dramatic weather anomalies are not isolated. Strange weather conditions in the United States usually coincide with strange weather conditions in other parts of the world. The World Meteorological Organization, a special agency of the United Nations, was founded to study weather on a global scale. Worldwide cooperation of meteorologists should result in a clear picture of global weather patterns and their causes. Then the effects of the great conjunctions will be predictable throughout the world.

We do not know why Ingress charts work in weather prediction, and we don't know how the changing aspects of the planets create weather changes on a daily basis. We can speculate that ionization or electromagnetism is involved.

### Radio Interference and Earthquakes

Not only is weather influenced by planetary positions but radio interference and earthquake timing are affected by the heavens, too.

John H. Nelson, a ham radio operator and amateur astronomer working for RCA, noted that hard angles of the planets around the Sun result in short-wave radio interference. He then went on and discovered that planetary angles in any multiple of 15 are likely to create interference. Nelson did not have an astrology background. He made his discoveries without the traditions of astrometeorology.

It also has been noted that hard angles of the planets around the Sun precede *hurricane formation* during hurricane season. A *heliocentric*, or Sun-centered, ephemeris is used to pick out likely dates for hurricane formation.

Astrologers have long noted that big earthquakes tend to occur when planets form hard angles to recent *eclipse points*. However, not all hard angles of planets to recent eclipse points result in earthquakes. It appears that *both geocentric* (Earth-centered) *and heliocentric* (Sun-centered) hard angles of planets to recent eclipse points are involved.

Earthquakes involving geocentric hard angles of planets to recent eclipse points are the easiest to predict. When such a quake occurs, other conditions conducive to earthquake triggering usually have to be in effect. These include a second planet forming a hard angle to an eclipse point along with the first; a second or third planet forming a hard angle to a second or third eclipse point at the same time; Mars in hard aspect to Neptune; or the Moon in hard aspect to its nodes. Recent eclipse points in these cases can go back about ten years, but the most spectacular quakes usually involve at least one very recent eclipse point.

It is harder to predict earthquakes which coincide

with heliocentric hard angles of the planets to recent eclipse points because it hasn't yet been determined what other factors have to be in effect before these quakes can occur. Large quakes triggered in this way usually do not depend on heliocentric hard angles of Mercury to an eclipse point because Mercury moves so quickly around the Sun that it is constantly forming such angles. Eclipse points involved in the heliocentric-type quake do not go back as far in time as eclipse points involved in geocentric-type quakes. An especially interesting study is that of heliocentric, or Sun-centered, angles of the Earth to recent eclipse points.

Earthquakes occur when the slow-moving *outer planets form hard angles to recent eclipse points*, but the faster-moving inner planets can time them to the day. Hard angles involved in earthquake triggering are the conjunction, square and opposition, but some authorities believe that trines can be involved, too.

There are a large number of quakes of a magnitude of 6.0 or more each year, but only a few of these are widely reported in the news media. These include local quakes and also those which strike in populated areas doing a great deal of damage. Earthquakes which receive wide coverage in the news media are more likely to "play by the rules" than quakes of the same magnitude which do not receive as wide a coverage.

## Astrometeorology in the Future

At the present time, astrometeorology is more useful for forecasting the weather on a west-to-east basis than it is for dealing in changes north and south. If Venus is on the Midheaven of a chart set for St. Louis at the time of an Ingress, it is also on the Midheaven for any location north or south at 90° west. This would include both Hudson Bay and Yucatán.

More study has to be done concerning priorities in astrometeorology. We know that planets on the Midheaven or IC of Ingress charts can mask the effects of the great conjunctions, but much study is necessary in regard to conflicting planets in angular houses at the time of an Ingress.

Astrometeorology is a fascinating study, on the cutting edge of both accepted science and astrology. It may be a little hard to measure a quick Aries temper, but Venus on the Midheaven of an Ingress chart can be measured in inches of rainfall. Astrometeorology is even more compelling since meteorology is now determining how weather really works. When we know why Mars on the Midheaven of a chart brings heat and drought, we will know how all astrology works.

(Instructions for finding local sidereal time follow.)

## FINDING LOCAL SIDEREAL TIME
## FOR AN INGRESS, LUNATION
## OR MOMENT AN ASPECT IS PERFECT

Local sidereal time for the moment of an Ingress, lunation (New Moon or Full Moon) or moment an aspect is perfect is necessary in order to set charts to determine how planetary positions at these times will affect the weather. The first step is to determine the *date*, *hour* and *minute* the phenomenon is perfect, Greenwich Mean Time. This information is given in the daily aspectarian of the ephemeris.

The next step is to determine your *longitude*. This may be found on a map or in an almanac or *The American Atlas* (published by ACS Publications, Inc.).

From the hour and minute the phenomenon is perfect, count back:

Five hours if you live at 75 degrees west; EST
Six hours if you live at 90 degrees west; CST
Seven hours if you live at 105 degrees west; MST
Eight hours if you live at 120 degrees west; PST
Nine hours if you live at 135 degrees west; YST
Ten hours if you live at 150 degrees west; AHST

(Note that if the phenomenon is perfect in the morning Greenwich Mean Time, it may be perfect the previous day at your location in the United States.)

Few locations in the United States are directly on an hourly meridian. This means that it is necessary to correct to local clock time by *adding four minutes per degree if your location is east* of an hourly meridian, or by *subtracting four minutes per degree if your location is west* of an hourly meridian.

**Midnight ephemeris:** Find sidereal time at midnight the day the phenomenon is perfect in your locality. Add sidereal time at midnight in hours and minutes, the time the phenomenon is perfect in hours and minutes, 12 hours if the phenomenon occurs after noon in your locality, plus one minute for each six hours after midnight in your locality the phenomenon occurs. This gives you correct local sidereal time in hours and minutes for the Ingress, lunation or aspect.

**Noon ephemeris:** For a P.M. phenomenon local time, add sidereal time at noon the day the aspect is perfect local time, the time the phenomenon is perfect in hours and minutes, and one minute for every six hours the phenomenon occurs after noon local time. For an A.M. phenomenon local time, add sidereal time in hours and minutes for noon the previous day, corrected local time in hours and minutes, 12 hours if the phenomenon occurs after midnight local time, and one minute for every six hours after the previous noon local time the phenomenon occurs. This gives you correct local sidereal time in hours and minutes for the Ingress, lunation or aspect.

After correct local sidereal time for the phenomenon is determined, the sign and degree on the Midheaven and the signs and degrees on each of the other house cusps can be determined by using a Table of Houses. It is not necessary to take daylight saving time into consideration.

## Marc Penfield

Marc became acquainted with astrology in 1964 when a coworker gave him a book in which she had outlined his planetary positions. Being an adopted child, he had absolutely no idea of his birth time, but Sagittarius or a strong Jupiter was suggested. Following years of study with George Cardinal LeGros, Marc felt qualified to teach astrology. After moving to San Francisco in 1970, he began the study of Cosmobiology and the Johndro system of Geodetic Equivalents under the tutelage of Mary Vohryzek. Soon afterwards, he began to compile *An Astrological Who's Who*, published by Arcane Books in 1972.

In 1976, Vulcan Books published his *America: An Astrological Portrait of its Cities and States*. In 1977, *The Nadi System of Rectification*, concerning Hindu astrology, was published. His fourth book was produced in 1979, *2001: The Penfield Collection*. Perhaps his most well-known book, *Horoscopes of the Western Hemisphere*, was published by ACS in 1984.

Marc also contributes articles and a column entitled "Chart Mart" to *Mercury Hour*, as well as a column to *Aspects* and *Monthly Review*, an Australian publication.

# THE MYSTERY OF THE ROMANOVS

Mundane Astrology is more than just deciphering the charts of cities or countries and infinitely more detailed than the analysis of eclipse or lunation charts. Mundane, or geopolitical, astrology may also be the study of various events in history which have affected the lives of millions. Some may call this "event-oriented" astrology, for to analyze the charts one often has to resort to techniques used in horary or electional astrology books.

One of the most enduring and fascinating mysteries of the 20th century concerns the disappearance and supposed assassination of the Russian Royal Family, the Romanovs, in the city of Ekaterinburg on the eastern slopes of the Urals in mid-July 1918 at the height of the civil war then engulfing Russia. Historians have repeatedly told us the entire family was obliterated, their bodies dismembered and burned with the remains thrown down a mineshaft. However, there are many inconsistencies in this historical version which do not bear up under closer scrutiny. No strong evidence was ever produced, and one might even presume the entire story was fabricated to occlude the truth. Using astrological techniques, I shall try to unearth the facts and investigate what probably occurred that fateful morning. Natal charts for the individuals concerned along with secondary progressions, transits and Solar Returns will be used, as well as detailed analysis of

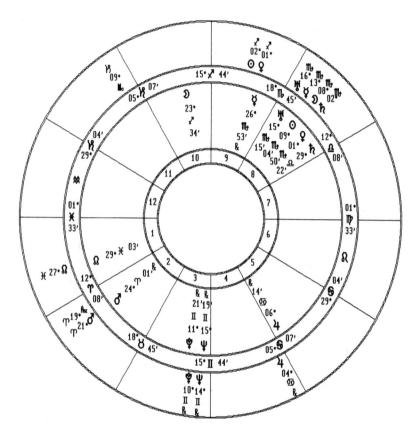

**Chart 1**
**Nicholas Becomes Czar**
**Inner Wheel: Natal**
**Outer Wheel: Progressed to 7/27/18**

the events which precipitated their disappearance. All charts are calculated with Koch houses.

## Chart 1—NICHOLAS BECOMES CZAR ON THE DEATH OF HIS FATHER, ALEXANDER III
Livadia—November 1, 1894 (NS) at 2: 15 p.m. LMT

In many respects, this chart outlines the nature and scope of Nicholas' reign. Neptune conjunct the IC certainly indicates the nature of his disappearance, while Jupiter, ruler of the MC, in the 5th House in Cancer points to his heir, Alexis, as being the source of much concern.

When Nicholas was forced to relinquish power in March 1917, the progressed Sun squared the Ascendant. He was protected from harm due to the progressed MC sextile the Sun in the 8th. By the time he arrived in Ekaterinburg, the progressed MC was approaching a quincunx to Pluto, ruler of the 9th, and the progressed Ascendant was nearing a conjunction with progressed Mars. One strong indication of survival is shown by the progressed Moon for July 1918 at 8° Scorpio conjunct the Sun, indicative of a new beginning and lease on life. But with anything Scorpionic, there's always a mystery as to how things evolve, especially when it is in the 8th House of transformation and renewal.

## Chart 2—NICHOLAS' CORONATION
Moscow—May 26, 1896 (NS) at 9 a.m. LMT

Nicholas' reign was not a happy one, either for him or for Russia. Saturn, ruler of the 6th and co-ruler of the 7th, squares the Ascendant while Pluto, ruler of the intercepted 4th, sextiles it from the 10th. By the time he was incarcerated, the progressed MC had moved to an opposition of progressed Saturn. This progressed MC was square progressed Jupiter when World War I began four years earlier, clearly indicative of overestimation of one's

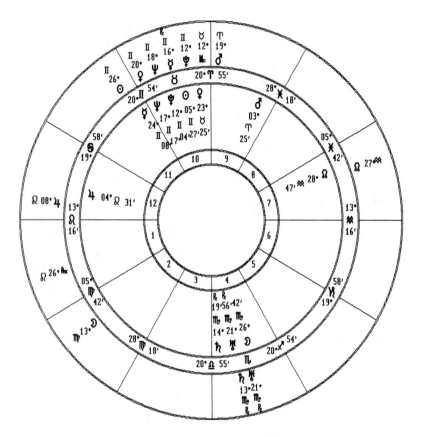

Chart 2
Nicholas' Coronation
Inner Wheel: 5/26/1896
Outer Wheel: Progressed to 8/11/88

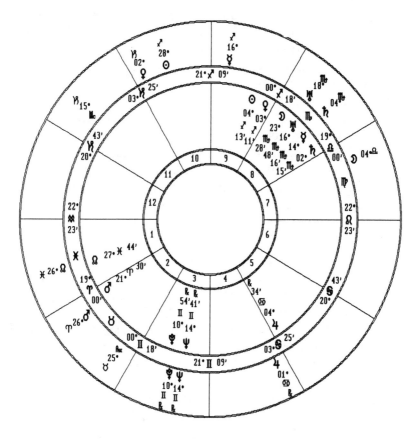

**Chart 3**
**Marriage of Nicholas and Alexandra**
**Inner Wheel: 11/26/1894**
**Outer Wheel: Progressed to 6/11/18**

ability to win a foreign war, not to mention the enormous financial cost to the nation along with the million who perished trying to save "Mother Russia" from the enemy. The progressed Ascendant for this coronation chart is about to square the Moon, ruler of the 12th, showing the 16-month period of confinement under house-arrest, indicated by the Moon in the 4th.

Transiting Saturn and Neptune were crossing the Ascendant in mid-July 1918, pointing out his depression at being forced to relocate since Saturn was also squaring its natal position. Relocating this chart to Ekaterinburg, the MC opposes Saturn while the relocated Ascendant squares the Moon, two more arguments for domestic strife and claustrophobia which we know the Czar experienced in this locale.

### Chart 3—MARRIAGE OF NICHOLAS AND ALEXANDRA
**Leningrad—November 26, 1894 (NS) at 1 p.m. LMT**

Because Nicholas was the only Czar in recent memory not to be married at the time of his becoming heir, it was deemed imperative that he and Alexandra wed as soon as possible. So just three-and-one-half weeks after the death of his father, the wedding took place, even though the court was still in mourning for the former Czar.

Jupiter, ruler of the MC, is retrograde in the 5th House of children quincunx the Sun and Venus, illustrating a source of aggravation. After four girls were born, the long-awaited son came along in 1904 just as the progressed MC at 1° Capricorn sextiled Saturn and the progressed Ascendant at 4° Aries squared Jupiter. The heir was born with hemophilia, a genetic ailment passed from the mother to her male children, which causes the absence of the ingredient which makes the blood clot. In one respect, Alexis' birth was the "enemy" of the relationship, even though it brought the couple much closer. Jupiter in the 5th is doubly important as it sesquares the Ascendant, ruled by Uranus in the 8th House of death and bereavement.

Progressing this chart to July 1918, the date of the "assassination," the progressed Sun semi-squares Mercury, ruler of the 4th House and co-ruler of the intercepted 7th House, both of which are always represented whenever a major move is undertaken. The progressed Moon at 5° Libra squares Jupiter, which governs foreign lands, and also sextiles the Sun. Did outsiders abscond with the couple to a foreign country? The progressed MC at 15° Capricorn quincunxes Neptune, so a sacrifice of some kind may have been made to keep the union from dissolving. The MC also sextiles Uranus, ruler of the Ascendant, adding an element of surprise to the scenario. Transiting Uranus was retrograding back to conjunct the Ascendant at this time, pointing to a separation of some kind. The transit Sun, ruler of the Descendant, was quincunx the Ascendant on the morning the couple was last seen alive, officially at least. But with aspects like these, one might presume that Nicholas was the one to be sacrificed as transiting Venus trined the Ascendant, indicating a certain amount of protection for the women in the family. No doubt some major trauma occurred that month due to transiting Pluto's wide sesquare (sesquiquadrate) to the Ascendant; possibly the family was forced to make a move as Pluto co-rules the intercepted 8th and is in the 3rd House of short-distance journeys. Whatever happened was kept in strictest confidence because with Pluto involved little is revealed as to plans and method.

In 1917, the Czarina was disconsolate and the Czar confused about his purpose during the war. Finally agreeing to journey to the front, he left Russia in shambles just as the Revolution began in February 1917. The war had cost

**Chart 4**
**Abdication of Nicholas II**

**Chart 5**
**Czar and Czarina Removed to Ekaterinburg**

Russia dearly. A 19th-century country trying to fight a 20th-century war against the mightiest nations in Europe, millions had already died on the battlefields, frozen or starved to death. Those who survived deserted their posts and murdered their leaders who were pressing on for victory. By the time they arrived in the cities, bread riots were erupting and strikes were paralyzing the country. Soldiers were unwilling to shoot the looters, and the government was in a state of chaos. A Provisional Government had been formed which demanded the abdication of the Czar in order to maintain a sense of law and order. After much deliberation, Nicholas abdicated, first leaving the throne to his son, then to his younger brother, Michael, who refused it. Thus did the Romanov dynasty come to an end after ruling Russia for 304 years.

### Chart 4—ABDICATION OF NICHOLAS II
### Pskov—March 15, 1917 (NS) 3 p.m. LMT

At the moment Nicholas stepped down, the Sun, ruler of the Ascendant, quincunxed the Ascendant from the 8th House. He signed his death warrant by giving up, shown by the Sun in Pisces, the sign of sacrifice and retirement. Nicholas was now simply "Citizen Romanov," no longer the absolute ruler of the largest empire on Earth. The Sun is conjunct Mars, ruler of the 9th, and both trine Saturn in the 11th. The quincunx of the Sun to the Ascendant implies that only the Czar was shot that fateful July morning, as does the Sun's semi-square to the MC.

Progressing the chart to July 1918, the void-of-course Moon was in the final minutes of Sagittarius. The MC had progressed to semi-square the Sun, while the progressed Sun quincunxed the Ascendant. With Uranus, ruler of the Ascendant, transiting the 7th House cusp, I don't see how Nicholas could have escaped danger, especially with transiting Neptune about to square the MC. True, transiting

Jupiter, which governs long-distance travel and is often prominent when miracles occur, is about to conjunct Pluto, ruler of the IC which has dominion over the "final solution." Transit Pluto also sextiled Jupiter at the MC that July morning, suggesting possible removal and escape from the grim reaper.

Contrary to what was expected, the Czar rather enjoyed retiring from life and reveled in spending time in his garden. He actually wanted to be nothing more than a country squire and hadn't desired to be Czar in the first place. But five months after his confinement began, the July revolution in Russia placed the Provisional Government in jeopardy, and it was increasingly powerless to protect the Royal Family. It was decided to move them to a much safer place, and the village of Tobolsk in Siberia was selected as it was far from the centers of unrest such as Moscow or St. Petersburg. Two days after the Czarevich's thirteenth birthday, the family began their journey of over 1300 miles.

## Chart 5—CZAR AND CZARINA REMOVED TO EKATERINBURG
### Tobolsk—April 26, 1918 (NS) 4 a.m. DST/LMT

On April 24, after a long and harsh winter of bitter winds, biting cold and rude treatment, a sailor named Yakovlev was sent to escort the Royal Family to Moscow where they were to stand trial for crimes against the people. After Yakovlev viewed the serious health condition of the Czarevich, it was decided to let him remain behind; only the Czar and his wife would make the journey at this time; the children would follow later. Marie, the third daughter would also go with her parents; the others could take care of their younger brother. Venus, ruler of the 3rd, squares the MC, showing the difficult beginning of this journey. Traveling over snow-covered fields and frozen rivers which were beginning to thaw required the royal pair to ford those rivers on foot, the rest of the time lying flat on the bottom of the wagon. When they finally reached the railhead at Tyumen, Yakovlev went to telegraph Moscow of his arrival, but after looking at the map he decided it would be safer to journey to Moscow via the Trans-Siberian Railway which ran through Omsk. When Yakovlev left Tyumen heading east, his departure was promptly wired to the Ural Soviet in Ekaterinburg which telegraphed Omsk, asking them to intercept the train. After being stopped some 40 miles from Omsk, Yakovlev went to the authorities in Omsk to plead his case, but to no avail. He was forced to turn over the Royal Couple and their daughter to the Ekaterinburg Soviets who, three days later, imprisoned them in the Ipatiev House. Pluto, ruler of the 9th, widely sesquares the Ascendant, which is ruled by unpredictable and perverse Uranus, the planet of the unexpected. Had Yakovlev passed through Omsk, thousands of miles of open track would have led him to the port of Vladivostok on the Pacific from where the Royal Couple could have journeyed to Europe or North America.

Exactly who was Yakovlev? It's known he was a sailor who deserted his post shortly after the unsuccessful 1905 revolution, traveling to Canada where he lived for the next 12 years. It's entirely possible that during his time in Canada he became a secret agent for the British who employed him to rescue the Royal Family, as the British government decided to wash their hands of the entire affair.

Nicholas was considered by many to be a despot and a tyrant, an autocrat who imperiled the outcome of the war. He had openly refused assistance from the German Kaiser Wilhelm II, who was a cousin to the Czarina, both being grandchildren of Queen Victoria. The Germans were in a strong position to dictate to the Russians after the

Treaty of Brest-Litovsk was signed in March 1918 whereby Russia was forced to cede one-third of her territory and population, over 90 per cent of her coal mines and nearly half her heavy industry. Lenin and his Bolsheviks who had overthrown the Provisional Government the previous November were in no position to say no to the Germans.

Documents relating to the English plot to kidnap the Royal Family are classified as "top secret" and are not available to the general public for viewing. It's entirely possible that King George V of England, the Czar's cousin, did try to rescue the Czar, but his plan failed when Yakovlev was stopped in Omsk. Yakovlev couldn't testify at the inquiry as he had joined the Whites (or Monarchists) and reportedly was shot or died from typhus.

The remaining children were brought to Ekaterinburg May 20, 1918 (NS).

## Chart 6—FINAL DECISION MADE ABOUT THE ROMANOVS
### Ekaterinburg—July 15, 1918 at 10 p.m. DDST/LMT

When the Royal Family arrived in Ekaterinburg, the Ipatiev House was ruled by a man named Avadeyev, a man known for his drunken tirades and brutish manner. The committee in Moscow probably decided he was not the best man to rely on during a major crisis and thus replaced him on July 4 with Yurovsky, a cold and calculating individual who had the personality of a computer and nerves of steel. He seemed to lack compassion or any remote interest in the fate of his charges. The family had no privacy as bedroom doors were torn away and soldiers allowed to mill about at will. The girls had to be escorted to the bathroom where they were forced to look at pornographic cartoons of the Czarina and Rasputin cavorting together.

Because the White Army was fast closing in on

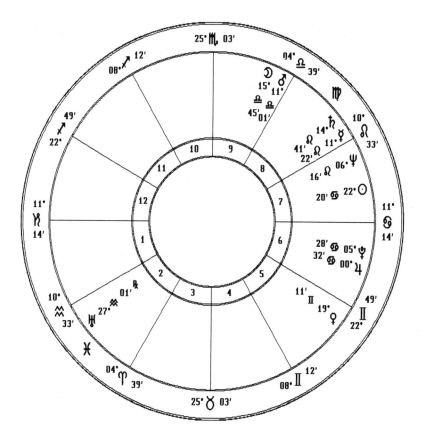

**Chart 6**
**Final Decision About the Romanovs**

Ekaterinburg, the situation became perilous for the family. The Ural Soviet had to decide whether to remove the Romanovs to a safer place or to get rid of them once and for all. History tells us the latter option was taken, but the former was probably closer to the truth. The decision was made one day before the Royal Family spent their last night on Earth (so they say), just as Mercury and Saturn quincunxed the Capricorn Ascendant. The ruler of the Ascendant in the 8th House is generally a clear-cut indication that some form of transformation was about to take place; death is a distinct possibility, but not the only one.

The ruler of the 8th, the Sun, trined the MC and was in the house of associates and outside interests. Mercury and Saturn in the 8th had no stressful aspects. Saturn's semisquare to Jupiter implies a change of residence (per Ebertin), doubly so since the Sun was at the midpoint of these two planets. The Moon had just sextiled Saturn, thus the ruler of the Ascendant had recently come into some form of agreement with the ruler of the Descendant. The Moon was moving to trine Venus, ruler of the 4th as well as the 9th, and its last aspect would be a trine to Uranus in the 2nd House which governs the future.

Mars squared the Ascendant and ruled the 3rd, but it's in the 9th disposed of by Venus, ruler of the 4th, which will be trined by the Moon. Mars semi-squared the MC, thus sesquared the IC, indicative of the preparations for violence we know to have occurred, according to the history books. To make it look convincing, soldiers were sent to obtain gallons of sulphuric acid and petrol, a lorry was rented, and firearms gathered. When Yurovsky became Commandant of the Ipatiev House, he subsequently replaced the old guards with his own men, thus leaving little question of their loyalty to the man designed to carry out orders from above.

It's rumored that the Bolsheviks under Lenin were offered a cache of money, or a bribe if you prefer, to let the Royal Family go free, and this is entirely possible. Lenin needed cash to run the crumbling government, which was trying to hold the country together during a civil war that was devastating the countryside. Russia was at the mercy of a Germany still in the position to demand favors from Lenin, who was trying to get Russian political prisoners, like Karl Liebknecht, out of German jails. Lenin was not the butcher or tyrant as he has been portrayed in Western literature—far from it. That title fell to his successor, Stalin, whose reign of terror was worse than anything under the Czars. As Yurovsky disappeared before the investigating committee could subpoena him, we'll never know his connection to Lenin and Trotsky, who probably told him to stage a "fake assassination" and to cover their tracks as best they could. After all, if the Whites did win the civil war, Lenin and his cohorts would have fared considerably better if they spared Nicholas and his family, should the victors demand a renewal of Czardom. Lenin's thirst for power was one thing; his ability to get it, another. Uranus in this chart implies that a monetary deal may have been finalized with that fact relayed to the Ural Soviets in Ekaterinburg, thus setting the stage for the greatest mystery in Russian history up to that time.

The family had gone to bed at 10:30 p.m., July 17, 1918, and were awakened when heavy footsteps on the stairs ended with a knock on the door and the order to get dressed as quickly as possible and come downstairs. They were being taken to a safer place as the Whites were fast approaching the city. A curfew had been imposed on Ekaterinburg that night, an odd fact seeing as how none had been imposed before. Confusing testimony was given with respect to the time events took place because the government had instituted Double Summer Time at the end of May, thus advancing the clock two hours from normal.

Some kept the old time, some the new. All agree that the family was awakened about midnight and the entire thing was over two hours later. The Russians had also advanced the calendar 13 days earlier that year, bringing Russia into step with the rest of the Western world. Some people, obviously, didn't know the right day, much less the correct time, with these changes.

Were members of the royal family drugged to keep them quiet while they were taken out of the Ipatiev House into the van which then drove off into the night?

About this time, witnesses report the sound of shots being fired inside the house. The assassination theory has as many adherents as does the theory that the entire family survived. Lenin and Trotsky probably ordered the fake shooting to show the world that there was no returning to the old ways and that the Russians were stuck with the Bolsheviks. Lenin probably cared little what happened afterward; he just didn't want to be held responsible for the Royal Family's deaths, which might anger their German conquerors. Even if the truth were told at a later date, who would have believed it after years of lies, which snowballed into historical truth?

### Chart 7—MASSACRE OR ESCAPE?
### Ekaterinburg—July 17, 1918 (NS) at 4 a.m. DDST/LMT

The dastardly deed or the faked assassination was over by 4 a.m. July 17, 1918 (NS), according to all sources consulted. Pluto rising cloaks the previous half-hour in mystery, but its trine to and mutual reception with the Moon suggest that "an escape" was indeed made at this time, doubly reinforced by Jupiter rising above the Ascendant. Jupiter also trined the Moon and Uranus, ruler of the MC. If the MC represents the government under Lenin and his cohorts, the Ascendant depicts the Romanov family, the Descendant shows those who helped them to es-

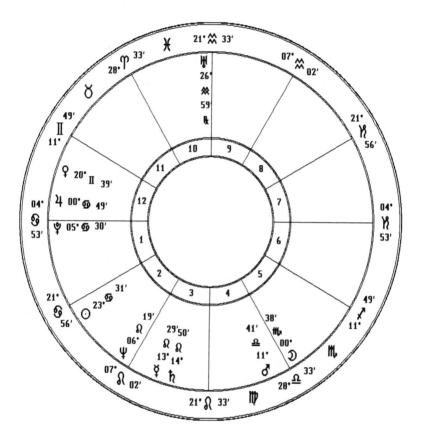

Chart 7
Massacre or Escape?

cape or murdered them, and the IC connotes their "final destination," be it the grave or a foreign country. One must realize that with the ruler of the MC trine the ruler of the Ascendant there was little reason to harm the family from the viewpoint of the government. Saturn in the 3rd House, ruler of the 7th as well as the 8th, illustrates the telling of half-truths, especially since Mercury last passed over Neptune. The Sun, ruler of the IC, quincunxed the MC, implying that the Romanovs were beginning to get on the nerves of the Bolsheviks and something had to be done, and quickly, in order to set the situation right.

Exactly what does history and various evidence tell us about the events that morning? The first telegram sent from Ekaterinburg that night at 9 p.m. said that the "family suffered same fate as head officially family will die in evacuation." The key word here is *officially*, which implies a  cover-up at the behest of the government, giving the Romanovs time to get to their destination before the truth could be uncovered and their safety imperiled. With Saturn in the 3rd House, this could be the "official" version straight from the top. Ironically, this telegram may be a fake, as there is no record of it being sent in the logbook and its signature differs from other signature samples of the individual who signed it. Was this telegram placed into evidence at some later time? Saturn governs delays, so this is a distinct possibility.

The first public notice in Ekaterinburg two days later said that the Czar had been shot, the remaining family members sent elsewhere. Insiders felt it was Perm, a city 200 miles to the northwest, the next stronghold of the Bolsheviks, who were about to lose their hold on Ekaterinburg. Even the newspaper *Pravda*, which means "truth," said only the Czar had been shot, and for once they may have been telling the truth, even if they didn't know it.

The first investigation into the Romanov disappearance began at the end of July 1918, shortly after the Whites captured Ekaterinburg. Judge Sergeyev arrived on the scene a few weeks later and began to amass evidence. After viewing what was available and talking to several witnesses, all but one of whom had heard the events second-hand, Sergeyev believed that somewhere between July 16-22 violence of some kind had occurred in the basement room of the Ipatiev House, but exactly what he couldn't say since there was an absence of bones or skeletal remains. Investigations come under the aegis of Pluto, and with its mutual reception to the Moon, the suppositions went from one extreme to the other, never fully revealing the extent of the "massacre" to anyone outside the house that fateful morning. Supposedly, 11 people died in that room, but the amount of blood found on the floor and walls did not account for this number of people being murdered. The bones which were later found at the Four Brothers mine outside town weren't enough to account for one body, let alone 11. And there was serious doubt as to whether those bones that were found were entirely human; some appeared to be animal fragments. Forensics experts viewing photographs came to the same conclusion.

Blood samples from the floorboards and wallpaper revealed that not enough was in evidence to suggest that more than five perished in that room. The room had been washed and sanded over and over, but what little blood was found was human in origin. By the time the third investigation was underway, the amount of blood on the floor had increased measurably. Clearly by that time someone had tampered with the original evidence to lend support to the historical version.

Thirty bullet holes were found in the wall or the floor. Most of them were only two-and-one-half feet above the floor, an odd fact unless those murdered were kneeling at the time of their demise. Sergeyev felt, again, with this evidence that probably only five had perished that morning: Dr. Botkin, the royal physician, the maid Demidova, two manservants, and probably the Czar himself.

The upstairs rooms produced even stranger findings. The closets were completely empty, an odd fact considering the Royal Family was given little time to get dressed that morning and no trunks were reported to have been carried down the stairs or loaded into the van. Exactly what happened to those garments is cleared up when one views the number of personal articles which were found the following spring at the mine outside town. More than likely, the clothes were removed from the closets and taken to the mine where they were torn apart (thus revealing the jewels hidden inside) before being tossed down the mineshaft and destroyed by acid or gasoline.

Other evidence found at the mine is also misleading. The corset stays were burned a bit but completely undamaged by bullet holes. It would be a miracle if none of the bullets pierced one of the corset stays as it made its way through the body of the Czarina or her daughters. This evidence was probably planted later to corroborate the assassination theory then taking shape.

For those versed in chemistry and forensics, it seems odd that one would try to destroy the chief evidence (bones) by resorting to acid. Any third-rate chemistry student knows that it's almost impossible to destroy bones this way in only a few days. Even if the bones could be destroyed, one cannot destroy teeth, and none were found at the mine, with the exception of dentures probably belonging to Dr. Botkin. Since most people do not go without their teeth, one can suppose that Dr. Botkin was a victim. No other teeth were found at the mine. Pouring petrol over the bodies along with sulphuric acid is counterproductive; the fumes from the acid would be extremely dangerous to those involved in planting the evidence.

The corpse of a female dog was found at the mine in the spring of 1919, supposedly having been underwater for over half a year. Had it indeed perished with the rest of the family it would not have been so well-preserved; little hair was missing and its internal organs were those of an animal which had been dead for only a week at the most. All mammals begin to lose their hair or fur within a few days of being submerged in water, but Sokolov ignored the facts in his effort to produce the official version of the assassination. Clearly, this dog, like so much other evidence at the mine and the house, was designed to throw the investigators off guard. If this were a courtroom drama with the evidence able to talk, the request for the truth, the whole truth and nothing but the truth came out as everything but the truth. Why was this so important?

One theory has it that Nicolai Sokolov's investigation, which began in February 1919, seven months after the crime, was designed to protect the Romanovs whom the authorities knew to be safe. An official version was needed to quell the persistent rumors around the country that the Romanovs did indeed escape; after all, there was no hard evidence to back up either side. This probability is amplified when one notes that the ex-Czarina Maria, mother of the Czar, paid $5,000 for the publication of Sokolov's book. She knew the Royal Family was safe and it was imperative that others believe the opposite in order to protect them. She said as much while in Malta in April 1919, but she refused to divulge their hiding place. Even the German secret agents in the Urals, who were in a position to know, believed the Royal Family escaped; some obviously knew where they were living.

A prediction was made by a German emissary in Kiev on July 6, a full ten days before the Romanovs officially disappeared, that between July 16-20 news of the assassination of the Czar would be made public. This was even before the Ural Soviet had decided the final solution, or was Moscow just stringing them along as well, not revealing their own decision until the last minute when the plan was fully hatched and the individuals and materials needed for the Romanov escape were available? Sergeyev believed that "stand-ins" might have been used in place of the Czar and his family. After all, witnesses saw sacks being loaded into the van, but exactly who or what was inside remains a mystery. If the Germans were indeed the source of the escape plan, then only they were in a position to know exactly when the plans were to be put into operation.

Sergeyev felt, as did the English consul for Siberia, Charles Eliot, that the Romanovs were taken away by train to a safer locale. A train, ready for departure, was seen at Station #2 outside Ekaterinburg the following morning. The blinds were drawn so witnesses could not see who was inside, but most believed it to be the Romanovs. Looking at the chart, trains were ruled by the 3rd House. Saturn there indicates something well-planned in advance, not an afterthought as might be the case with Uranus or Neptune. Pluto rising indicates the need for secrecy as well as the elimination of strong evidence.

But Sokolov ignored all the foregoing when it pointed in a direction away from the "facts" he was supposed to record. His reputation as a superior investigator was severely threatened if evidence to the contrary was revealed or made public. So evidence was planted which supported his preconceived notion of what happened that fateful July morning, and leads which pointed in the opposite direction were disregarded. Testimony from witnesses was ruthlessly suppressed if it did not conform to the final scenario. Pluto rising points to the need for utmost secrecy, and there's a possibility that Sokolov had been told the truth and was told to print otherwise.

Enough inconsistencies in his version, published in 1924, exist to suggest he knowingly suppressed evidence which would lead other investigators to uncover the whereabouts of the Romanovs. Sokolov died in 1924, shortly before the official version of his investigation (which differs in content between those written for Russian and French audiences) was made public.

According to his investigation, the Czarina and her daughters were known to be alive, if not well, in Perm until the end of 1918. When they first arrived in that small town on the west side of the Urals 200 miles northwest of Ekaterinburg, they were housed in the Excise Office and later moved to the Berezin house down the street. After one of the Grand Duchesses, probably Anastasia, escaped briefly in mid-September 1918, they were moved to a convent outside Perm on the road to Glazov. A doctor who examined the escaped girl on September 21, 1918 lists her as being the Grand Duchess Anastasia, but it could have been one of the other daughters. Perm fell to the White Army on Christmas Day, 1918, and soon after the family was moved from Glazov through Perm on their way westward. History loses track of them in the early months of 1919 after the train on which they were known to be riding passed through the city of Kazan. The final destination was thought to be Moscow. No mention is made in Solokov's notes (not printed in his book) of the Czar or the Czarevich. It's entirely possible they were kept in another place, or that they perished that morning in Ekaterinburg. It was also noted that only three daughters left the convent in Glazov, one of them, probably Anastasia, having escaped again.

With Germany defeated, Lenin no longer had to fear reprisals from the Kaiser. Having no direct use for the Royal Family anymore, he washed his hands of them, leaving them to their fate. It's known that Lenin was still using the Royal Family as pawns as late as September 1918, so if they weren't alive, why bother to use them as bargaining tools? The deception could easily be uncovered by any German secret agent then operating in the Urals, and Lenin knew better than to try and fool them.

The Czarina's brother, the Grand Duke Ernest of Hesse, knew the family was safe and relayed that fact to the Marchioness of Milford Haven at the end of September 1918. But where they went after the beginning of 1919 remains speculative and goes beyond the scope of this astrological investigation.

A defector from the Soviet bloc, Michal Goleniewski, later claiming to be the former Czarevich Alexis, said his sisters Olga and Tatiana went to Germany while he and his sister lived in Poland. Anastasia went to America in 1922, two years before Alexandra died. Nicholas passed away, according to this defector, on his birthday in 1952 at the age of 84 in the small Polish town of Ciosaniec.

Four long strands of hair of varying color found in the upstairs rooms of the Ipatiev House give a strong indication that the family survived and escaped by disguising themselves. Beard clippings, obviously belonging to Nicholas, were found in the fireplace. Without his famous beard, Nicholas would have been totally unrecognizable. A priest who said Mass for the Romanovs two days before they disappeared said that the family looked "somehow different" but he couldn't put his finger on it until the hair strands were found. He then remembered that the girls had short hair and the Czar had trimmed off part of his beard. Combine this with the torn calendar, revealing the date June 23, on the wall of the Czarina's bedchamber, and the mystery deepens as to whether it was possible the Romanovs could have been spirited away from Ekaterinburg before their "official disappearance." The date of June 23 was obviously Old Style, as the calendars printed in 1917 did not anticipate the Russian government adding 13 days to the calendar in early 1918. The New Style date thus becomes July 6, the same date the German emissary in Kiev made his famous prediction that news about the Czar's death would be made public between July 16-20. Coincidence? I don't think so.

It's entirely possible that the Romanovs did perish that summer morning as history states. The Russians murdered the Czar's younger brother, Michael, in Perm on July 10, and the Czarina's elder sister, the Grand Duchess Elizabeth, was thrown down a mineshaft, screaming all the way, the same day her sister disappeared. The Russians weren't averse to killing off royalty, so bear this in mind while examining the following charts.

## Chart 8—NICHOLAS II
## Tsarskoe Selo (Pushkin)—May 18, 1868 (NS), 12:02 p.m. LMT

Progressing this chart to Nicholas' abdication, we find Jupiter, co-ruler of the IC, at 13° Aries semi-square the Sun, ruler of the 12th House, indicative of his imprisonment for the next 16 months. Venus, ruler of the progressed Ascendant, trined Saturn, ruler of the progressed IC. During 1918, the progressed Sun squared Neptune in the 8th, but sextiled Pluto, ruler of the 3rd, in the 9th. The progressed Ascendant at 11° Libra was transited by Mars on the day of his "assassination." All of the above indicate the possibility of a long trip combined with violence and danger, not to mention intrigue and sinister activities.

Nicholas' Solar Return (Ekaterinburg—May 19, 1918 at 4:05 p.m. LMT) shows natal Mars square the SR MC and natal Saturn semi-square the SR Ascendant. Both rule angles, and this does not bode well for survival. The Sun squares Uranus within three minutes from the 5th to the 8th, showing the distinct possibility of his own demise as

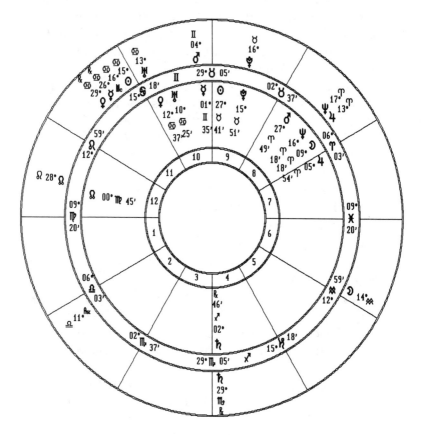

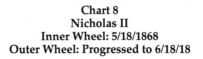

**Chart 8**
**Nicholas II**
**Inner Wheel: 5/18/1868**
**Outer Wheel: Progressed to 6/18/18**

well as his son's; natal Neptune opposes the SR Ascendant, adding further complications. Progressing the Moon to July 1918, it conjuncts Mars and squares Jupiter in the SR 9th. Jupiter rules the SR 3rd of short-distance journeys, while Mars rules the house of open enemies or supporters, so possibly Nicholas was indeed saved at the last minute by his "enemies," or those he thought were hostile to his position. The square of the Sun to Uranus says otherwise, however, and no mention was made of him being in Perm with his wife and daughters.

## Chart 9—ALEXANDRA
### Darmstadt, Germany—June 6, 1872, 3:45 a.m. LMT

Throughout 1918, Alexandra's progressed Sun at 29° Cancer was still within orb of Jupiter and Uranus in her natal 3rd, and progressed Jupiter had moved to an opposition of the natal MC. Both illustrate the strong possibility of escape to a foreign land, but not without complications, shown by the progressed Ascendant opposing natal Saturn, ruler of her 8th and 9th Houses. This Saturn aspect promises that some strong male figure in her life could have perished that year, possibly her son as well.

The progressed Moon in July 1918 quincunxed the progressed Ascendant, showing the likelihood of domestic strife and adjustment, which was doubly probable as it also squared Pluto. On the day of her disappearance, Mars was transiting trine its own position as well as the natal Ascendant. Ascendant ruler Mercury was sesquare transiting Mars. Transit Saturn was sextile the luminaries, and Pluto semi-squared its natal position. Clearly, the summer of 1918 was not easy for the Czarina, yet from the above aspects I believe she survived, but at great cost to her health. A major indication of the change in her status is shown by transit Uranus (ruler of her MC) square natal Mercury (ruler of her Ascendant).

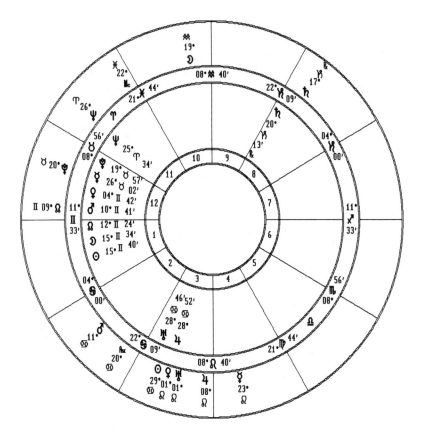

**Chart 9**
**Alexandra**
**Inner Wheel: 6/6/1872**
**Outer Wheel: Progressed to 4/25/18**

Her Solar Return (Ekaterinburg—June 7, 1918 at 9:23 a.m. LMT) has similar aspects. Venus is at the SR MC and Uranus opposes the SR Ascendant. In this chart, Venus rules not only the Taurus MC but also the 3rd House; Uranus rules the 7th. Alexandra could have been saved, and probably was, even though the cost was steep as Neptune and Saturn are square the MC from the 12th. In July 1918, the progressed Moon conjuncted Mercury (nominal ruler of travel), and three months later it squared Uranus. This was about the time one of her daughters escaped and the family was moved to the convent. Protection seems to be assured with the Sun conjunct Jupiter, co-ruler of the 4th, which widely trines Uranus.

## Chart 10—OLGA
## Tsarskoe Selo (Pushkin)—November 15, 1895 (NS), 8:56 p.m. LMT

Olga's progressed Ascendant squared the natal Sun, ruler of the natal and progressed Ascendant. The natal Sun conjuncts natal Uranus in the 4th, and Uranus rules the 7th House. Even if she managed to survive, some male figure in her life would come under severe emotional or physical stress with aspects like these. The progressed Sun opposed progressed Neptune in the 10th, ruler of her 8th. The progressed MC semi-squared natal Neptune about the time she and her family began their imprisonment. In July 1918, the progressed Moon sextiled natal Mercury, ruler of her 3rd, as transiting Uranus semi-squared the natal MC.

Olga's Solar Return (Tobolsk—November 16, 1917 at 7 a.m. LMT) shows Mars conjunct the SR MC square Jupiter in the 8th, which opposes the Moon in the 2nd. A tight T-square involving the ruler of the 9th with the planet which rules the nominal 9th and a planet in the 9th implies that a long journey was made that year, which we know to be certain as she moved from Tobolsk to Ekaterinburg six

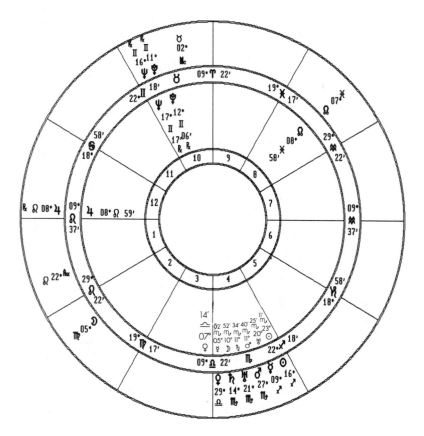

**Chart 10**
**Olga**
**Inner Wheel: 11/15/1895**
**Outer Wheel: Progressed to 8/1/18**

months later. Venus, ruler of the 7th, trines the MC from the 3rd. The Sun receives only a semi-square from Venus, but as it is in the 1st House, there's a good possibility of personal survival. In July 1918, the Moon moved to a sextile of Uranus in the 3rd.

Assuming that Olga survived the massacre, we will look at her Solar Return for 1918 (Perm [Molotov]—November 16, 1918 at 12:48 p.m. LMT). The Sun is in the 9th conjunct Venus, ruler of the 3rd, but it squares Saturn, ruler of the Ascendant, and Uranus in the 1st. Saturn is quincunx the Ascendant, which is squared by the Moon, ruler of the SR 7th. Mercury, natural ruler of the 3rd, is at the SR MC trine Neptune but quincunx Pluto, ruler of the 9th. As the progressed Moon trined Saturn, ruler of the Ascendant, and squared the Ascendant in December 1918, she disappeared from view, on the way from Perm to Moscow, more than likely. Something went wrong, I feel, at this time due to the square of the Moon and the Sun's square to Uranus, co-ruler of the Ascendant.

## Chart 11—TATIANA
**Peterhof—June 10, 1897 (NS), 10:59 a.m. LMT**

The progressed MC for 1918 quincunxed Saturn and Uranus in Tatiana's 3rd House, but the progressed Ascendant sextiled those two planets, softening the adjustments required of her that year. The progressed Moon trined Saturn and Uranus just as Mars, ruler of her 8th, squared them. The Sun sesquared progressed Saturn, an indication of the probable loss of a strong male figure, at the same time Mercury from the 9th trined the progressed Ascendant. During July 1918, Mars transited semi-square natal Saturn and Uranus while Uranus squared its own position.

The Solar Return chart (Ekaterinburg—June 11, 1918 at 2:43 p.m. LMT) shows Uranus quincunx the SR MC with

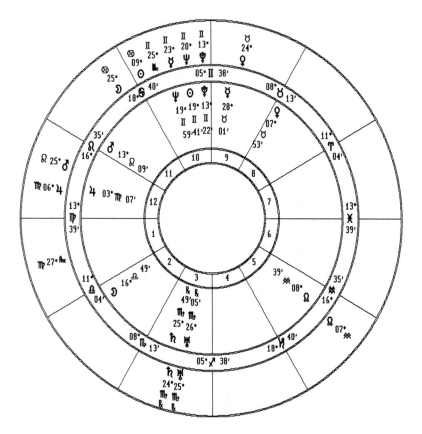

**Chart 11**
**Tatiana**
**Inner Wheel: 6/10/1897**
**Outer Wheel: Progressed to 7/25/18**

the Sun and Jupiter trining Uranus from the 9th. No progressed lunar aspects were operating at the time of her disappearance, but in October 1918, the Moon sextiled Mars in the 12th about the time she was moved from Perm to a convent near Glazov. One word of caution, however: Venus, ruler of the SR Ascendant, was in the 7th House of open enemies and squared Saturn, ruler of the SR IC, so depending on whether you view the Descendant as salvation or nemesis, the prognosis can tilt either way.

### Chart 12—MARIE
### Peterhof—June 26, 1899 (NS), Noon LMT

During 1918, Marie's progressed Sun received no aspects at all, but the progressed Ascendant trined Pluto from her 9th and was about to be crossed by the progressed Moon, a double indication of a change of residence to a foreign country. Transiting Mars trined natal Venus the night she disappeared, and Venus ruled her Ascendant as well as the 8th. Transit Pluto was crossing her MC, showing a deep and lingering loss of a strong male figure, reinforced by transiting Mercury and Saturn opposing her Moon, ruler of the MC.

The Solar Return (Ekaterinburg—June 27, 1918 at 4:13 a.m. LMT) shows a triple conjunction of the Sun, Mercury and Pluto in Cancer in the 12th trine the SR MC but quincunx their ruler, the Moon, in the 8th. No progressed lunar aspects were in operation during July 1918, but in November the Moon opposed Saturn, showing another removal with consequent depression.

### Chart 13—ALEXIS
### Peterhof—August 12, 1904, 1 p.m. LMT

Alexis was the youngest child and only son of Nicholas and Alexandra, a hemophiliac from birth due to the defective gene passed from Queen Victoria to her granddaughter Alexandra. This disease might be shown

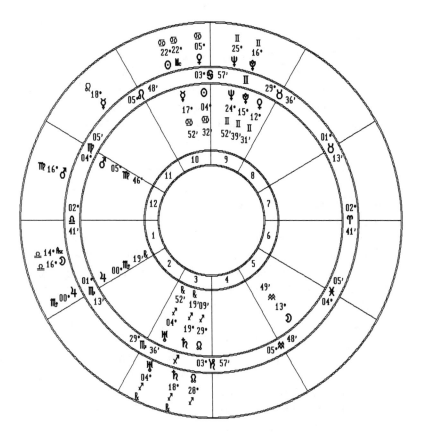

**Chart 12**
**Marie**
**Inner Wheel: 6/26/1899**
**Outer Wheel: Progressed to 7/26/18**

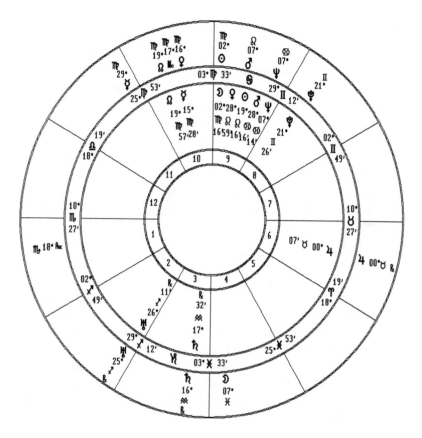

**Chart 13**
**Alexis**
**Inner Wheel: 8/12/04**
**Outer Wheel: Progressed to 8/27/18**

by Jupiter in his 6th House square Mars—one, the ruler of the 6th, the other, the co-ruler of the Ascendant. The Moon semi-squared the Mars/Neptune midpoint for further confirmation of a wasting disease.

During 1918, Alexis' progressed Sun was squaring his father's natal Saturn, illustrating the distinct possibility he might have suffered the same fate as his father. The progressed MC quincunx natal Saturn and the progressed Ascendant square the same planet doesn't augur well for survival or good health, especially if a change of residence or a long journey is needed. The Moon in July 1918 had just opposed his natal MC; two months later, it trined Neptune, ruler of the IC, and quincunxed progressed Mars, ruler of the 6th. Mars was completing the semi-square to Pluto in the 8th, ruler of the Ascendant. To add aggravation to an already negative picture, transiting Neptune was conjunct progressed Mars and semi-square Pluto, showing further emphasis on the rulers of the Ascendant IC and a planet in the 8th. But a miracle may have happened as transiting Jupiter and Uranus were sextile their own positions, but their midpoint squared Mars.

Alexis' Solar Return (Tsarskoe Selo—August 12, 1917 at 4:20 p.m. LMT) is almost as portentous of doom as his father's. The Sun opposes Uranus from the 3rd to the 9th, indicating the long journey to Tobolsk two days after his birthday. As both planets are in their own signs, their negative impact, I believe, is strengthened. Jupiter, ruler of the SR Ascendant, sextiles Saturn and Neptune in the 9th, but Pluto semi-squares the Sun from the 8th. Mars, ruler of the IC, quincunxes the SR Ascendant from the 8th while Mercury, co-ruler of the 9th, squares it from the 9th. The progressed Moon void-of-course made no aspects at all during this year.

Operating on the slim premise that Alexis survived Ekaterinburg, we should investigate the Solar Return for

1918 (Perm—August 12, 1918 at 11:55 p.m. LMT). The Sun, ruler of the SR IC, conjuncts Saturn, ruler of the 8th House of death, in the 4th. Both planets also semi-square the SR Ascendant. Since the rulers of the 4th and 8th Houses are involved, it doesn't bode well for Alexis' survival. Even if he did survive, his health would not have been up to par, especially if he had lost his father the previous month. Jupiter on the SR Ascendant also semi-squares the Sun, but its dispositor, the Moon, conjuncts Mars. Two months after his 14th birthday, the progressed Moon conjuncted Mars and trined Uranus, showing possible severe bleeding as well as nervous irritation within the family. I find it quite interesting to note that all members of the Royal Family had progressed lunar aspects in their Solar Return charts which vanish at the end of 1918 or the beginning of 1919, with the exception of Anastasia, whose chart we shall look at now.

### Chart 14—ANASTASIA
### Peterhof—June 17, 1901 (NS), 10:55 p.m. LMT

I've saved Anastasia for last, as one could write an entire book about this woman and the pretenders who claimed to have survived the massacre in Ekaterinburg. Her progressed MC during 1918 shows no threatening aspects, having already opposed the Sun at the time her father abdicated the throne 16 months earlier. The only negative aspect coming up was an opposition to natal Neptune, which occurred one-and-one-half years after she disappeared from Ekaterinburg. The progressed Ascendant had already opposed natal Mars in the 8th, and before the year closed, it trined Mercury, ruler of her IC as well as the 8th House of transformation and renewals. Two long-lasting aspects occurred in Anastasia's natal chart—the opposition of Saturn and the quincunx of Uranus to the Moon, situated in and ruling the 6th House.

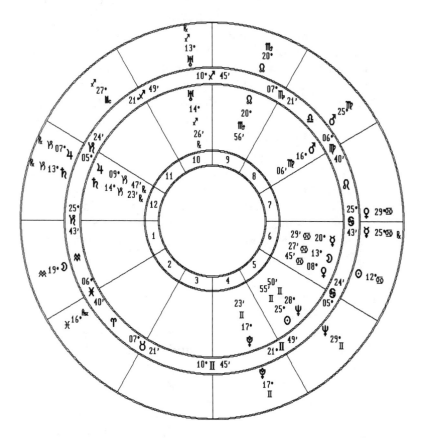

**Chart 14**
**Anastasia**
**Inner Wheel: 6/17/01**
**Outer Wheel: Progressed to 8/3/18**

Looking at Anastasia's Solar Return chart (Ekaterinburg—June 18, 1918 at 3:30 a.m. LMT), the SR Ascendant conjuncts natal Neptune while natal Mars quincunxes the SR MC. The Sun conjuncts Jupiter just above the SR Ascendant and both trine Uranus, ruler of the MC, in the 10th. Mars squares the Sun and SR Ascendant from the 4th the same time it quincunxes Uranus, so while violence was a distinct probability in the home that year, Anastasia would have been protected from harm. On the morning of her disappearance in July 1918, Mars was transiting the Moon at the same moment that Jupiter was crossing the SR Ascendant. In October 1918, a few weeks after she escaped from her captors in the field outside Perm, the progressed Moon sextiled Saturn, ruler of the 8th, then trined Mercury, ruler of the Ascendant and 4th House of relocation. By the time the next Solar Return took place, the Moon trined Jupiter, so by then it's presumed she was in the protection of her rescuer with whom she was cohabiting as Jupiter rules the house of close relationships.

Officially, according to the information gleaned by Sokolov, this is where the story stops, at the beginning of 1919. But according to his data, there were only three girls on the train out of Glazov on the way to Moscow, so where was Anastasia? For these answers or speculations, we must turn to the biography by Peter Kurth entitled *Anastasia: The Riddle of Anna Anderson* (Little, Brown & Co., 1983). According to Kurth, Anastasia escaped from Russia with a man named Tchaikovsky, who took her to Romania where the couple lived for the next year and a half or so. On February 17, 1920, a woman later called Anna Anderson tried to commit suicide by jumping off a bridge over the Landwehr Canal in Berlin. If the two women were identical, then the relocation chart should show the propensity for such an activity taking place in Berlin, and it does. The relocated MC quincunxed the Sun and Neptune, indicative of emotional depression and a tendency to escape from reality, possibly through suicide. The MC also sesquared Venus, ruler of the relocated IC. Adding more spice to the already depressing environment is Pluto quincunx the relocated Ascendant and Mars trining from the 8th. Clearly, life for Anastasia would be no bed of roses in Berlin as psychological problems relating to the "massacre" in Ekaterinburg would surface, causing extreme feelings of guilt.

Operating on the premise that the woman who jumped into the canal was indeed Anastasia, her Solar Return chart for that year should indicate such an event. As she was probably living in Bucharest, the chart must be located there for June 18, 1919 at 7:25 a.m. LMT. The SR MC squares the natal Moon and Saturn, a fine augury of emotional depression, but natal Uranus trines the same point. The Sun in the 11th sextile Saturn in the 1st implies she was searching for relatives or friends of her family that year but couldn't make contact since the Sun semi-squares Venus, ruler of the IC, and Neptune. Disillusioned, she tried to end it all, also shown by Uranus quincunx the SR Ascendant from the 8th. Progressing the Moon to the early months of 1920, it opposed Saturn in January but trined the Sun two months later. Between those two dates, she came to the attention of the world just at the moment transiting Jupiter was conjuncting the SR Venus, ruler of the IC, and trining her natal MC. Combine the above with her progressed natal chart containing the MC opposing Neptune and the Ascendant squaring the Sun and Neptune and you have the beginnings of a great mystery about this woman's true identity. By the time Anastasia's progressed MC moved into Capricorn and the Ascendant progressed into Aries, the woman in the hospital had been recognized by a patient as the Grand Duchess Anastasia, thus beginning a "new lease on life" for Anastasia, if she was indeed still alive at this time.

If we conclude that the two women were identical, then those interested in her story should progress the chart for Anastasia over the next six decades to the dates mentioned in Peter Kurth's book. Accordingly, the moment that Anna Tchaikovsky Anderson Manahan passed from this plane of existence on February 12, 1984 should be quite revealing, and it is. Her progressed Sun at 15° Virgo was in the 8th House about to conjunct natal Mars and square Uranus, co-ruler of the natal Ascendant. Mercury, ruler of the 4th and 8th, squared the natal Sun, giver of life. Natal Mercury was also squared by progressed Venus, while the progressed Ascendant sextiled Mars in her 8th.

A number of similarities between the two women were brought to light over the years. Despite the fact that there were no fingerprints for a positive identification and dental records could not be obtained, ear measurements were taken and the correspondences matched completely. Anthropomorphic (or head) measurements were taken, which were also identical. The real Anastasia was known to have a deformed big toe, as did Anna Anderson. This anomaly is known as *Hallux Valgus*, which enlarges the joints around the toe. Anastasia was known to have had a mole cauterized on her right shoulder some years earlier while in her teens, and Anna Anderson also had a scar in the same spot. A groove above the right ear implied a bullet wound, while the triangular scar on her foot indicated an attempt to crush that foot with a firearm. Both women had regular finger length, the middle one not noticeably longer than the others. Samples of their handwriting revealed 137 identical characteristics, a feat impossible even for the best of forgers. Some investigators thought it odd that Anna Anderson refused to speak Russian, but it is not such a mystery when one realizes that English, not Russian, was the usual language of the royal household. Anastasia had been tutored in French and German and used Russian only on occasion. But when in the company of a trusted friend or ally, she seemed to understand the language quite well.

Whenever someone tries to pass him/herself off as someone else, it's imperative to know intimate details about that individual's family life that only those involved could know. One of the most startling and intriguing episodes concerns the mention of Uncle Ernest's trip to Russia in late 1916 where he tried to arrange a peace treaty between Germany and Russia. The mission was "top secret" and known only to the bigwigs, for to reveal the true purpose of his journey would have placed the Grand Duke of Hesse's life in jeopardy, as he was a traitor for consorting with the enemy. Anna Anderson knew of this visit about which history books are silent, so unless she was there, how could she have known about it?

Monetary gain couldn't have been the reason behind Anna Anderson's quest for her identity. The hundreds of millions of dollars deposited by the Czar in banks around the world had largely been withdrawn before his abdication to pay for ammunition and hospital expenses, and there was little, if anything, left in those vaults. Besides, if the family had survived, including the Czar, then no one could safely come forward claiming the inheritance of the Romanovs, for to do so would reveal their identity and whereabouts to the Bolsheviks, who kept insisting they had all been eliminated. The real reason relatives of the Grand Duchess Anastasia branded her as a "fraud" was because they knew she had survived and feared for their own lives under Stalin's reign of terror. Living under aliases while in exile is not all that unusual: Josef Mengele spent 34 years in hiding, his identity and whereabouts known only to his family and trusted associates.

The final *coup de grâce* comes from Mary Frances

Wood, an astrologer who visited with Mrs. Manahan in Virginia shortly before her death. Stating there was little, if any, trace of her royal upbringing or regal bearing, this could be accounted for by the years of attempting to establish her identity as well as time spent in various hospitals and asylums, not to mention trying to forget that traumatic event in Ekaterinburg when she was a teenager. But Mary Frances Wood had a friend who wanted to visit with Mrs. Manahan to see whether this woman was an impostor or not. The test was to be quite simple—the royal children had been taught a secret language or esoteric code almost from birth, similar to the one used by the Knights Templar or Masons. The reason for this secret language or code is buried in obscurity, and possibly nothing more than superstition. When this woman met Mrs. Manahan, she immediately began babbling in this secret language, and Mrs. Manahan replied in kind, proving to this woman, once and for all, that Mrs. Manahan was of royal birth and the woman she claimed to be.

It has recently come to light that a Russian writer, Geli Ryabov, claims to have found the remains of the Romanovs over a decade ago in an unmarked burial mound outside Sverdlovsk, then called Ekaterinburg. The site was kept hidden as the Bolsheviks wanted to avoid it becoming a place for pilgrimage by those who wished to return to Czarist rule. He also notes that the Ipatiev House where the Romanovs spent their final days had become a popular site for tourists and was blown up in 1977. After perusing closed state archives and talking with relatives of Yurovsky, the Commandant of the Ipatiev House, he believes that it was the Central Committee in Moscow, not the Ural Soviet in Ekaterinburg, which ordered the murder of the Romanovs. His scenario is as follows: The truck containing the bodies of the Czar and his family and four servants arrived at the mine where they were to be disfigured by acid, their bones chopped up and thrown down a shaft to conceal the crime. After some consideration, the squad commander deemed the site unsuitable, so articles of clothing and other artifacts were deposited at the mine as a decoy to throw off any investigation. The bodies were placed back on the truck, which a short while later became mired in the mud. The bodies were then dumped at the side of the road and acid poured over them to hasten decomposition, the skulls already smashed in to prevent identification. Ryabov says he will reveal the exact site only when a Christian burial is guaranteed by the authorities and not before. He made the discovery on May 30, 1979 and revealed it to the world on April 12, 1989.

Does it really matter if the Romanovs were assassinated, as history says they were, or if they managed to escape, as the evidence indicates? What does an event which occurred over seven decades ago have to do with anything today?

The Sokolov investigation on the Romanovs was a whitewash and cover-up to protect the Romanovs, for to reveal otherwise would have placed the Bolsheviks in an embarrassing and dangerous situation. Too many rumors were circulating about the survival of the Romanovs to sit well with the government which was trying to hold the country together in the midst of a civil war. The Warren Report also tried to quell rumors about a conspiracy in the John Kennedy assassination, not to protect the guilty if they were found, but to allow the government to get back to the business of running the country.

But the public deserves to be told the truth. With *glasnost*, or "openness," now the norm in Russia, we may one day know the truth behind the Romanov assassination and disappearance. The Russians are in an embarrassing predicament, for to reveal the truth implies that other events in their history have also been falsified, designed to protect the guilty and the mission of their state. To continue the lie serves no purpose at this point in time, as most of the participants have long since passed from the scene.

Even if Ryabov's "discovery" proves correct and the history books are vindicated, the final days of the Romanovs is one of the great tales of this century, and one of the most intriguing stories of all time. The final clues may never come in, so like many mystery novels, you will have to draw your own conclusions about what happened that July morning back in Ekaterinburg when the most powerful family in the world passed into oblivion and into the realm of speculation.

## Sources for Charts

1. Nicholas becomes Czar—Livadia (34E10, 44N30), November 1, 1894 (NS) at 2:15 p.m. LMT, from *The Romanovs* by W. Bruce Lincoln (Doubleday, 1983).
2. Nicholas' Coronation—Moscow (37E35, 55N45), May 26, 1896 (NS) at 9 a.m. LMT, from *The Romanovs* by W. Bruce Lincoln.
3. Marriage of Nicholas and Alexandra—St. Petersburg (Leningrad) [30E15, 59N55], November 26, 1894 (NS) at 1 p.m. LMT, from *Nicholas & Alexandra* by Robert K. Massie (Dell, 1978).
4. Abdication of Nicholas II—Pskov (28E20, 57N50), March 15, 1917 (NS) at 3 p.m. LMT, from *Nicholas & Alexandra* by Robert K. Massie.
5. Czar and Czarina removed to Ekaterinburg—Tobolsk (68E16, 58N12), April 26, 1918 at 4 a.m. DST/LMT, from *Nicholas & Alexandra* by Robert K. Massie.
6. Final Decision made about the Romanovs—Ekaterinburg (Sverdlovsk) [60E36, 56N51], July 15, 1918 at 10 p.m. DDST/LMT, from *Last Days of the Romanovs* by Alexandrov, who says the clock on the wall said 8 p.m., presumably the Old Time as the Bolsheviks upped the clock two hours on May 31, 1918.
7. Massacre or Escape?—Ekaterinburg (Sverdlovsk) [60E36, 56N51], July 17, 1918 (NS) at 4 a.m. DDST/LMT, from *Last Days of the Romanovs* by Alexandrov, who says 2 a.m., again using the Old Time.
8. Nicholas II—Tsarskoe Selo (Pushkin) [30E25, 59N42], May 18, 1868 (NS) at 12:02 p.m. LMT, from *Sabian Symbols*.
9. Alexandra—Darmstadt, Germany (8E40, 49N52), June 6, 1872 at 3:45 a.m. LMT, from State Archives of Hesse. *Sabian Symbols* gives the time of 3:15 a.m.
10. Olga—Tsarskoe Selo (Pushkin) [30E25, 59N42], November 15, 1895 (NS) at 8:56 p.m., from *Sabian Sym-*

*bols,* which computes to 9 p.m.

11. Tatiana—Peterhof (Petrodvorets) [29E54, 59N53], June 10, 1897 (NS) at 10:59 a.m.; 11 a.m. per the *London Times.*

12. Marie—Peterhof (Petrodvorets) [29E54, 59N53], June 26, 1899 (NS) at Noon per the *London Times.*

13. Alexis—Peterhof (Petrodvorets) [29E54, 59N53], August 12, 1904 at 1 p.m. LMT, from *Nicholas & Alexandra* by Robert K. Massie. The diary of Nicholas gives the same time. *Sabian Symbols* and the *London Times* give the time of 12:30 p.m.

14. Anastasia—Peterhof (Petrodvorets) [29E54, 59N53], June 17, 1901 (NS) at 10:55 p.m. LMT. The *London Times* of June 18 (which is printed shortly after midnight) says "late at night," while *Sabian Symbols* gives no time, but the chart computes to 11:04 p.m. Russian Royal Archives reportedly give 11 p.m. as well. I've rectified the chart by five minutes from this time.

### Steve Cozzi

Steve Cozzi began his study of astrology in 1968. He began teaching astrology in 1970. He is a member of all the major astrological groups in the United States and abroad and has lectured at several conventions. As the co-chairperson for programs of the Colorado Fellowship of Astrologers, he has obtained many of the best astrologers as speakers.

He has been active in the area of Locality Astrology since 1979. His research into the practical methods of Local Space astrology and his invention of the first geomantic compass in the West qualify him as one of a handful of practicing geomancers.

Steve has been a sincere student of Yoga for many years and has a wide-ranging interest in the field of metaphysics. He is the author of *Planets in Locality* and *Generations and Outer Planet Cycles*. Along with his writing and teaching activities, he also works in the areas of business management and the travel industry. He lives in Lakewood, Colorado with his wife Janet and their two children, Anthony and Nicholas.

# THE ASTROLOGICAL QUATRAINS
# OF MICHEL NOSTRADAMUS

Nostradamus, the 16th-century prophet, is without a doubt the world's most famous psychic of the last 500 years. There are many reasons for this title, not the least of which is that he simply wrote more predictions than anyone else to date. To his credit are over 1000 *Quatrains* (cryptic paragraphs), arranged in ten groups of 100 each, which he calls *Centuries*. There are also fragments of the speculated other centuries and the *Sixains* and *Presages*, which are labels for parts of his other writings.

All of his quatrains are attempts to describe future events. Most authorities feel that over 90 per cent of his predictions have already transpired.

This immediately generates the question: To what degree was Nostradamus accurate? It is a matter of opinion, depending on which authority you consult. Although the percentages are hard to pin down, the lowest would be 50 per cent with the highest perhaps about 90 per cent. His writings have received much criticism, but no one has systematically shown that his prophecies are just a work of his imagination. There are too many exact dates, names, and descriptions of events.

The quatrains have been in print since 1555, and they have certainly withstood many critical assaults. Although it takes skill, patience and intuition to make sense of most of the quatrains, they invariably have an uncanny descriptive quality. Often they don't seem to fit the event until after it occurs. There are some remarkable depictions, like the exact spelling of De Gaulle, or Hister instead of Hitler, with Hister a variation on the name of the river in close proximity to where Hitler was born. He also mentions satellites, newspapers, missiles, aeroplanes, tanks, gas masks and many other objects which were unknown in his time.

Nostradamus had a medallion made for his own funeral, and some 150 years later (in the year 1700) when government researchers opened his grave in the hopes of finding his secret code, they found the medallion with just one inscription on it—1700! The code was never found.

Nostradamus was a complex, deeply searching individual with a tremendous amount of practical experience. His major vocation was medicine; in fact, he may have been almost as good a doctor as he was a prophet. Evidence shows that he knew a great deal about herbs. He used them extensively in the treatment of the Black Plague. He also employed a number of new treatment procedures which caused resentment and anger in the medical community. The major part of his unique treatment consisted of daily baths, healthy fresh foods and good ventilation! Nostradamus had a high success rate concerning the plague, and this was, perhaps, the real reason that other doctors were upset.

He also aroused the suspicions of the Inquisition. He was a Catholic by birth, but his parents were among a group of European Jews who were forced to convert to Catholicism. This background, along with his supposed unconventional medical practices, certainly made him suspect. Of course, this bias intensified when his predictions were released. He certainly had his share of enemies, but he also had many powerful friends. Kings, queens and people with influence sought his wise counsel.

The greatest tragedy in his lifetime was the loss of his

wife and children to the plague. (He had one son who survived, but he was not from the same marriage.)

He spent most of his life traveling, healing, counseling, studying and, of course, writing. His writings have lasted for over 450 years and have never been out of print since they were written! The big question has always been: How did he do it? This has puzzled many researchers for the past four centuries. Perhaps the most honest answer is that nobody really knows "in detail" how it was done. All we have to go on is what he has told us and his life history, which describes his character. Knowing something about his lifestyle and personality, we can determine his behavior. Understanding why he would write something one way and not another often serves as a key to interpreting his quatrains.

In order to reach the state of consciousness where he could see future events, he went through some process, ceremony, or ritual. He tells us part of this process in the very beginning of his prophecies (Century I, Quatrains 1 and 2):

1. *Being seated by night in secret study,*
   *Alone resting on the brass stool:*
   *A slight flame coming from the solitude,*
   *That which is not believed in vain is made to succeed.*

2. *With rod in hand set in the midst of the stool legs*
   *With the water he wets both limb and foot:*
   *Fearful, voice trembling through his sleeves:*
   *Divine splendor. The divine seats himself nearby.*

Some researchers strongly feel that he is describing the use of a magic mirror. This is an apparatus wherein, using a flame and water, one can perceive the future as a reflection, much the same way as in a crystal ball. It certainly seems possible that he invoked some higher form of angelic intelligence while reaching a level of deep meditation.

Although he never states it directly, it seems apparent that he was shown the future on the condition that he would present the information in an occult and symbolic manner. Nostradamus mentions that he submitted information in a cryptic way to avoid political and religious vendettas. When he saw something in the future that was quite clear and understandable, he purposely disguised its meaning. He also may have seen events and circumstances that he did not fully understand, and these were written in a cryptic fashion. Very rarely are the quatrains in any order: You may find the same story continued in two or three different centuries and quatrains.

He generally wrote in 16th-century French, the French of an educated man; he also knew Latin, some Greek and other European dialects. At times he uses slang words, words that have two actual meanings, words that are reversed, and words that rhyme with another word which is not mentioned. Latin and Greek words are used along with words used only in metaphysical circles. He also invented his own words—this has really challenged researchers.

He really didn't make it easy for us. However, when the homework is done and a quatrain is thoroughly contemplated, an insight often breaks through. He seems to be telling us that knowledge alone will not give the full meaning, only *intuition* will take you the final step in understanding.

Nostradamus says in his *Preface to Cesar Nostradamus* that ". . . the incomprehensible secrets of God . . . come from a sphere very remote from human knowledge" and that they are ". . . made known by celestial movements." In his *Epistle to Henry the II of France* he states that poetry has been ". . . integrated with astronomical calculations corresponding to the years, months and weeks of the regions, countries and most of the towns and cities of Europe. . . ." A few paragraphs later, "I have calculated and composed during choice hours of well-disposed days. . . ." Again in the *Preface:* ". . . judgment [is] obtained through the calculations of the heavens. By this one has knowledge of future events while rejecting completely all fantastic things one may imagine. With divine and supernatural inspiration integrated with astronomical computations, one can name places and periods of time accurately, an occult property obtained through divine virtue, power and ability."

In looking over the works of Nostradamus, I found about 60 quatrains and/or passages that had obvious astrological references. Key words were mentioned, words that all astrologers know. There are also a few quatrains with hidden astrological meaning that have been overlooked. Yet, the amazing fact is that although all of the quatrains relate to the movements in the heavens, Nostradamus selected only 60 places where he used *direct* astrological quatrains. An even more significant point is that only about 15 of the astrological quatrains have already occurred! Since there are less than 200 quatrains which have not transpired, this makes the astrological quatrains extremely important. These facts also raise a very important point: Why did Nostradamus include almost all of his astrological quatrains toward the end of his forecasting period? (Most researchers think that 99 per cent of his predictions will have happened by about 2005.) The only answer I can come up with is that he perceived the wider use of astrology in the last half of the 20th century.

This was not my only motivation for investigating these quatrains. While reading the various interpretations, I saw how poorly the astrological quatrains were treated. Wrong dates and naive mistakes were frequent. In one case, Neptune was thought to be a substitute for the sign Aquarius. In another book, wrong dates were given for planetary configurations, and, even worse, in some books no dates were given at all for supposed astrological aspects. It is quite obvious that of all the authors none claimed to be astrologers, and it was apparent that they had only the most basic knowledge of the subject. When they did consult an astrologer for help, they rarely asked for a second opinion.

When Nostradamus wrote an astrological quatrain, he did it in a most unusual way. He often used the sidereal constellations. Sometimes he used them in the same quatrain with the tropical zodiac. His planetary positions could also be in zodiacal longitude and/or right ascension. He relied on the fixed stars, again using a mix of systems. He mentions eclipses, comets, and meteors, and it is also possible that he used a Kabalistic and/or Hermetic system(s) of planetary cycles.

I took up the challenge to see if I could decode some of these important quatrains pertaining to the immediate future. Only time will tell whether I am right in my interpretations and timing, and also whether Nostradamus was correct in what he saw.

Of the probable 45 remaining Astro-Quatrains, about 20 contain a minimal amount of information, which leaves us stranded and unable to go further. About 25 quatrains remain, six of which tell a symbolic story not involving actual aspects. Thirteen of the remaining 19 had enough clues to be worthy of investigation.

A word of caution before reading what follows: There is, and perhaps always will be, an element of chance involved in the future. Unexpected events or "wild cards" in the game of life seem to suddenly alter what seemed to be predictable. In the world today, terrorist activity is perhaps the biggest wild card. Certainly natural cataclysms are another. Aliens, physical and non-physical, cannot be disregarded. Last, but not least, stellar events, such as the discovery of a new planet (Transpluto), meteors, supernovas, etc., all have a chance of changing our future history irrespective of what would seem inevitable.

## Setting the Stage

### C2 Q10

> *Before long everything will be organized*
> *We await a very evil century:*
> *The lot of the masked and solitary ones greatly changed*
> *Few will be found who wish to stay in their places.*

### C1 Q63

> *Pestilences extinguished, the world becomes small.*
> *For a long time the lands will be inhabited in peace:*
> *People will travel safely by air, land, sea and wave,*
> *Then wars will start again.*

The first quatrain is one of the attempts to describe the 20th century—everything categorized, labeled, filed; scientists becoming the new priesthood. There's a general rebellious attitude and restless energy amongst people. The second quatrain reveals where we are now, the last decade of this century.

I mentioned that there were about 200 quatrains remaining. The great majority of these speak of a time of transformation—not the end of the world, but certainly the end of the world as we know it. Many war quatrains describe numerous battles in Asia, the Middle East, Europe and America. Wars where whole fleets and complete armies are annihilated. Wars so fierce that fish are boiled in the sea and people beg to die. He speaks of a day when more people will die than have perished in all the wars of recorded history.

These are not pleasant thoughts, certainly not very comforting for those who feel we are somehow going to all hold hands and merrily dance into the Aquarian Age. We will get there, but not until the old ways are transformed. He also says that fields will not be tilled for almost as long as they have been. Asian and Arab powers assume key positions in this last great war. The person who stands out the most is the anti-Christ, the third one, according to Nostradamus. The first two were Napoleon and Hitler. (Some authorities say Stalin and Hitler.) Natural cataclysms are also mentioned along with AIDS.

We all hope that Nostradamus or his interpreters are wrong, but what if he is right? Even if he is only partly right, can we ignore these probable events? Astrology, after all, is a way of seeing the future so that *something can be done to change it* for the better.

In looking at positions of planets and fixed stars, I use the rule that *both* the conjunction and the opposition should be used. Some say that it is easy to relate terrible interpretations with the fixed stars because so many of them have a bad reputation. The disharmony of the fixed stars may or may not be true, but the exact descriptions are confirmed over and over with the use of words that are amazingly similar to the words in the quatrains.

I had my doubts when I started this project. I felt I was going to be some sort of "Chicken Little," bitten by the prophecy bug. As my research proceeded, I slowly found the pieces falling into place. Quatrain after quatrain made a "helluva lot of astrological horse sense." The pieces fit to the point where I knew I was onto something very significant and powerful. Let's see what you think.

## C1 Q16

*The scythe joined with the pond toward Sagittarius*
*At the high point of its ascendant,*
*Plague, famine, death by military hand,*
*The century approaches its renewal.*

This quatrain tells what is going to happen and approximately when; the first two lines reveal the pertinent century. The scythe is what the reaper carries, so it probably represents Saturn. Joined in a pond may mean a Water sign or Aquarius the Water Bearer. In early March 1995, Saturn will reach 15° of the Water sign Pisces. Pisces' co-ruler is Jupiter, also ruler of Sagittarius. While Saturn is in watery, tropical Pisces, it is also in sidereal Aquarius; this also places it near the Milky Way (a pond of stars), so any way you look at it, the pond has Saturn in it. The term "high point of its ascendant" also has been translated as "increasing exaltation" (E.L.). Saturn squares Jupiter, which is at approximately 15° Sagittarius, a good placement. Saturn also conjuncts the fixed star *Achernar*, which is called the "end of river Eridamus," so again we have water indicated. Saturn quincunxes Mars, which corresponds with iron, the metal of the scythe's blade; this instrument is used by the Saturnian reaper. The 150-degree aspect (inconjunct/quincunx) is a separating type, which is how the scythe is symbolically used, i.e., separation of the spirit from the physical body at the time of death. In June 1993, there is a Total Lunar (water) Eclipse at 14° Sagittarius. The Babylonians said a Lunar Eclipse in the second decan of Sagittarius "Causes pestilence and many evils among mankind." Mars' position at 15° Leo is conjunct the fixed star *Mizar*, which has a Martian nature and is connected with mass catastrophes. The Sabian symbol for 15° Pisces says: "An officer instructing his men before a (simulated?) assault under a barrage of live shells."

## C2 Q5

*When iron and documents are enclosed in a fish*
*Out will come one who will make war.*
*His fleet will have traveled far across the sea*
*To appear near the Latin shore.*

Almost immediately one can see a submarine that carries a commander to a battle area. But this is only one of the quatrain's meanings. It also could imply Mars and Mercury conjunct in Pisces. Mercury conjunct Mars is quite common, but on March 23, 1996 it is conjunct in the 29th degree of Pisces. Saturn is at 28° Pisces, and all three are conjunct the star *Scheat*. This fixed star has a Saturnian nature and is linked to shipwrecks, suffering through water, and extreme misfortune! There are no eclipses, but the Sabian symbol says: "The power of Archetypes." Great leaders, like the commander of a fleet, have this power.

## C2 Q35

*The fire by night will take hold in two lodgings,*
*Several within suffocated and roasted.*
*It will happen near the two rivers surely*
*When the Sun, Sagittarius and Capricorn are all*
    *diminished.*

There's not very much to go on in this quatrain. It could be a symbolic story or an astrological configuration. Most authorities think that it has to do with the Sun leaving Sagittarius and entering Capricorn. This is much too general since this happens every year. Some say the events already happened about 100 years ago in Lyon, France; others say it is yet to happen when the Pope visits Lyon. I really can't buy either of these explanations based on a French obsession. All the French writers as well as others think that because Nostradamus was French the majority of his prophecies must happen in or be connected in some way to France. Nostradamus' vision was a world view, far-reaching and, at times, galactic in its scope. No doubt he had natural sentiment for his native soil, but when he was in trance I don't think patriotism was the dominant feeling. If it had been, he couldn't have seen so far and wide. I would agree, however, on a concentration on future history in the Western world, and to some degree, Asia.

If this quatrain is just symbolic, then it could mean that the duality of life will somehow cause death when religions (Sagittarius), governments (Capricorn) and man's spirit (Sun) are reduced in power.

In January 1996, the Sun, Mars, and Uranus all leave Capricorn while Jupiter enters this sign. Yet this occurrence is just not solid enough. On December 25, 2000, there is a Solar Eclipse at 4° Capricorn, which includes Mercury. The fixed star *Dirah* at 4° Cancer is opposing the eclipse and is connected with floods and drowning. Sabian talks about "A group of people outfitting a large canoe at the start of a journey by water" and emphasizes using natural resources and skills. Are these the two mentioned in the quatrain? Certainly at the turn of the century mankind will need both to survive.

## C2 Q48

> *The great army will pass the mountains.*
> *Saturn in Sagittarius and Mars turning from the*
> *  Fish:*
> *Poison hidden under the heads of salmon,*
> *Their war chief hung with a cord.*

This quatrain may be the first to be fulfilled, assuming that I'm right in my following interpretation. The Russian army leaves Afghanistan. The puppet government they leave in place is losing the war to the Moslem guerrilla fighters. They use poison gas to stop the attacks, but finally they lose anyway. Their leader is hung with a cord, or hangs himself. It may have nothing to do with Afghanistan, yet it seems the best choice at present.

Think of how the head of a salmon looks, and then picture a gas mask. A salmon is a fish that swims against the current. The Russian ideology is against the current of the Islamic revival.

On May 30, 1990 Saturn is at 24° Capricorn, but about 29° Sagittarius sidereal. Mars at 29° Pisces is turning from the Fish and is conjunct the fixed star *Scheat*, a Saturn-type star associated with loss of life. The fixed star *Pollux*, the wicked boy, is opposing Saturn. This star indicates deception and cruel tricks that can be played on gullible people. The Russians telling the Afghan leaders they leave behind that everything will be all right seems to be deceptive as well as a cruel trick. Not only are the present leaders wicked boys, the star *Procyon* (Mars/Mercury nature) describes these natives as "pig-headed, hot-tempered, imprudent, and liable to fall from high places"! On March 18, 1988 a Solar Eclipse occurred at 28° Pisces. This may have been when the Russians first decided to pull out their troops from Afghanistan. According to the Babylonians, the third decan of Pisces receiving a Solar Eclipse means "fierceness and the inhumanity of soldiers." Sabian symbol: "A store filled with precious Oriental rugs, and reliance on tradition."

## C3 Q5

*Near, far the failure of the two great luminaries*
*Which will occur between April and March.*
*Oh, what a loss! But two great good-natured ones*
*By land and sea will relieve all parts.*

This is a hard one to figure out. We know there will be a great loss and that it will be triggered by an eclipse. When Nostradamus mentions March and April, it's not clear if he means from 10° Pisces to 10° Taurus (i.e., March through April) or an 11-month period (April through March). There is something unusual about the eclipse cycles in the near future, but I can't figure out what. The longest eclipse of the last 1200 years was on June 8, 1937 at 18° Gemini, 7m 13s. Some lengthy eclipses also occurred from 1955 to 1973. Was this the time of the most destruction to the biosphere? From July of 1999 to July 2000, there is a total of seven eclipses, three lunar and four solar. This is the maximum amount that can occur in a 12-month period, which makes it somewhat unusual.

The only eclipse that seems to stand out is the Total Solar Eclipse of August 11, 1999. It is a powerhouse of a chart with a Fixed Grand Square (see Chart 1). The Sun and Moon in Leo are square Saturn in Taurus, which is square Uranus in Aquarius, which in turn is square Mars in Scorpio. Its path of totality begins northeast of America and runs through Europe, the Middle East, and ends in Southeast Asia. The shadow will cover most of the Northern Hemisphere, and it will be seen by more people than almost any other eclipse occurring in the last 50 years.

Are Jupiter and Venus the two great benefics? Does it mean that love and peace (Venus), knowledge and laws (Jupiter) will help soften the loss?

## C3 Q92

*The world near the last period,*
*Saturn will come back again late:*
*Empire transferred towards the brode nation,*
*The eye plucked out by the Goshawk at Narbonne.*

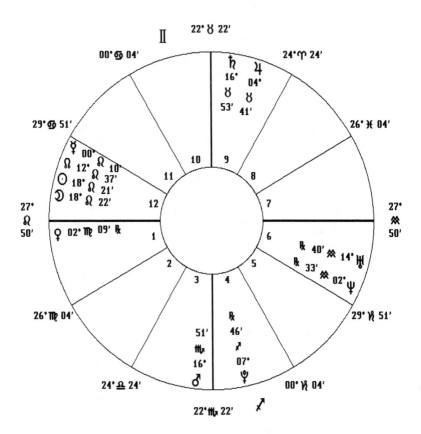

Chart 1
Total Eclipse
Aug. 11, 1999   7:10 A.M. EDT
77W01   38N53
Washington, D.C.
Koch Houses

I believe we are in this last period now, the last decade of this century. It seems that Nostradamus viewed it as such because he concentrates on the 1990s, especially 1999. This could pertain to the new age which was related to Saturn, the secondary or ancient ruler of Aquarius. (In his time, Uranus was not (re)discovered.)

Saturn being late may mean that the difficult time is not yet over, when the hawk takes the eye. In the Kabalistic cycles, the solar period we are now in has two Saturn subcycle years in the 1990s: 1992 and 1999.

Some say that *brode* (dark or decadent) means the nation of boots and/or primitive people (A.P.), namely northern European, perhaps Russian or German. What empire we do not know—maybe the common market countries?

The Goshawk has been related to the Warsaw Pact (J.F.) or air raids (A.P.). The Goshawk or Goosehawk is a small winged bird that may attack other larger birds. Very powerful for their size, they have been trained in falconry. This sounds to me like small fighter jets with highly trained pilots. Perhaps it means cruise missiles. My first impression of the word *Goshawk* was a Uranus/Pluto meaning—Uranus with its correspondence to aviation and Pluto as a hidden and powerful force. Uranus will be in its own sign, Aquarius, an Air sign (aviation), sextile Pluto in Sagittarius (long distances) most of 1998 and 1999. When Uranus was last in an Air sign (Gemini) sextile Pluto in a Fire sign (Leo), the "Battle for Britain" took place and was subsequently won by the English. Small fighter aircraft were the key to this battle. V-1 rockets were directed at London, but on the Pacific front General Jimmie Doolittle bombed Tokyo, a daring raid where none of the planes returned although many managed to land in China.

The plucking out of an eye could simply mean taking

or destroying half (one eye) of a force or city. In more modern terms, this phrase may refer to radar.

Narbonne was an important port city in Roman times. Does Nostradamus really mean this city in southern France, or is it a generic term for a very important port, somewhere to the south?

In Century IV, quatrains 28-32, Nostradamus takes off on a flight of mystical, astrological and deeply symbolic poetry. My guess is they describe this century. He may also be talking about actual configurations, but the occurrences are all very common.

## C4 Q28

> *When Venus will be covered by the Sun,*
> *Under the splendor will be a hidden form:*
> *Mercury will have exposed them to fire,*
> *Through warlike noise it is insulted.*

When desire is covered by our spiritual consciousness, another planet will be found. Wrong thinking will be destructive, the stress of modern life insulting to our spirit.

## C4 Q29

> *The Sun hidden eclipsed by Mercury*
> *Will be placed only second in the sky:*
> *By Vulcan Hermes will be made into food,*
> *The Sun will be seen pure, glowing red and golden.*

The way we think will take a leading role, placing our spirit as second. When our vast knowledge is used in a wise way, then our spiritual essence will shine forth.

## C4 Q30

*More than eleven times the Moon will not want the*
*    Sun,*
*All raised and lowered by degree:*
*And put so low one will sew little gold:*
*Such that after famine and plague, the secret*
*    uncovered.*

For eleven cycles, women (nature) and men will not agree; this fluctuation will cause little wisdom to develop. After famine and plague, the secrets behind the socio-sexual and ecological problems are uncovered.

## C4 Q31

*The Moon in the full of night over the high mountain,*
*The new wise man with a lone brain has seen it:*
*By his disciples invited to be immortal,*
*Eyes to the south. Hands in the marks of holy relics,*
*    body in the fire.*

The wise man in deep meditation sees the great secret (unified forces of physics) and his disciples proclaim him immortal, his inner mind on the source of all life, his spinal centers balanced, energized. [1]

## C4 Q32

*In the places and times of flesh giving way to fish,*
*The communal law will be made in opposition:*
*It will hold strongly the old ones, then removed from*
*    the midst,*
*Communism put far behind.*

---

[1] Self-realization/cosmic consciousness.

This quatrain is almost completely clear. Flesh means humanity and the fish as a Neptune symbol represents Communism (like Pluto with Fascism and Uranus with Democracy).

## C4 Q33

> *Jupiter joined more to Venus than to the Moon*
> *Appearing with white fullness:*
> *Venus hidden under the whiteness of Neptune*
> *Struck by Mars through the white stew.*

This quatrain seems a bit too specific to be considered just poetry. The configuration certainly involves the four mentioned planets. Jupiter conjuncts Neptune every 13 years. At that time, Venus and the Moon must be involved with a (hard?) aspect from Mars. We simply don't know the nature of the event. (Try early January 1997.) There are many translations of the last line. "White stew" is thought to mean the Milky Way. However, it has also been translated as "engraved wand," "heavy branch," and "weighty extension."

In the poetic sense, could it mean that the true expression of love (Venus) this century is somehow linked to education, religion, decadence? Hidden under the illusionary Neptune is the love and beauty of Venus. Venus should be with the Moon, and none should be struck by the harshness of Mars.

## C4 Q67

> *The year that Saturn and Mars are equally combust,*
> *The dry air is very parched, a long meteor:*
> *Through secret fires a great place blazing from*
> *    burning heat,*
> *Little rain, warm wind, wars, incursions.*

In this quatrain we know what will happen and that Saturn and Mars will be the cause. Between March 17 and 21, 1996, the Sun, Saturn and Mars are in conjunction and combust. The world point of 0° Aries/Cardinal is involved, perhaps indicating the significance of the events. The New Moon on March 19 is at 29° Pisces, another tie-in to the whole picture. The fixed star *Scheat* is involved here, as it has been for many of the astrological quatrains. Since this star is noted for catastrophes by water, this introduces a paradox of sorts. The quatrain specifically states "dry air" and "little rain." Could this mean a disaster due to the lack of water? The conjunction of Mars and Saturn takes place March 21 at 28° Pisces and opposes the fixed star *Benetnash*, which has a Mars/Saturn/Uranus flavor and is noted for claiming many human lives. It is associated with the realm of the dead, and one of the ways it takes lives is through catastrophes caused by weather!

Does this dryness have something to do with the ozone layer? What is its association with the long meteor shower and/or the northern lights? The "secret fires" certainly seem to suggest volcanic activity or radiation, i.e., something that burns but is not readily seen.

Another period to look at is mid-October of 1997 when Saturn and Mars are in Aries and Sagittarius, respectively. These planets would be equally "combust" or fiery since Mars and Saturn are exactly in the middle of these Fire signs and trine each other while the Sun opposes Mars. On April 1, 1998, Mars and Saturn are conjunct again in Aries (21-22°), and the Sun is 11° away at 11-12° Aries. Their midpoint is about 15-16° Aries, halfway through the sign, i.e., equal in Fire.

## C4 Q84

*A great one of Auxerre will die very miserable,*
*Driven out by those who had been under him:*
*Put in chains, behind a strong cable,*
*In the year that Mars, Venus and Sun are conjunct*
  *in the summer.*

No one seems to know what Nostradamus meant by using the town of Auxerre, which is 100 miles east of Orleans in the Burgundy region of France. It could be a symbol for Neptune because of its association with alcohol. On June 24, 2000 the Sun, Mars and Venus are conjunct at 3°, 5°, and 6° Cancer, respectively. *Alhena*, a fixed star at 8° Cancer, is said to confer a spiritual orientation as well as a loss of military honors. This may describe the character of the person in the quatrain. In opposition at 7° Capricorn is *Facies*, a fixed star noted for leadership but also for severe falls from power. People with these placements can get involved with intrigues and unpopular ideas that are ahead of their time. All this seems to fit very well with this quatrain. The Sabian Symbols are also quite descriptive. At 5° Cancer (the midpoint of this conjunction) it says: "The tragic results which are likely to occur when the individual's will pits itself carelessly against the power of the collective will of society" and "karmic readjustment." In opposition at 8° Capricorn: "Indian Chief," "Indians on the warpath" and "aggressiveness."

## C4 Q86

*The year that Saturn will be conjunct in Aquarius*
*With the Sun, the very powerful King*
*Will be received and anointed at Reims and Aix,*
*After conquests he will murder the innocent.*

Saturn conjunct the Sun in tropical or sidereal Aquarius, sounds easy enough. Aix is an old coronation site for emperors. Although this seems like a French leader, Nostradamus could be referring to a powerful and ruthless leader in some other region where coronations take place. This conjunction happens four times in the coming years. Two are tropical: January 30, 1992 and February 9, 1993. Two are sidereal: February 21, 1994 and March 5, 1995. February 21, 1994 seems to be the best prospect. The conjunction is at 2° 53' tropical Pisces. This is very near the fixed star *Fomalhaut*, which is considered one of the four royal stars. It has a rather strong connection with magic and alchemy. It shows fame and/or infamy, a character who is very good or very bad. It also describes a person who could commit crimes, has bad acquaintances, and is easily influenced, etc. This all fits quite well with the person of the quatrain who is crowned. In the Kabalistic cycle, 1994 is a Sun/Mars year, a time when a powerful leader becomes prominent. The Sabian symbol says that this "sequence brings the promise of social immortality" and that it is a symbol of "indestructibility." This, after all, is what a coronation is all about—the decree from on high that God and man recognize the rightful heir to a throne.

## C5 Q25

*The Arab Prince Mars, Sun, Venus, Leo,*
*The rule of the Church will succumb by sea:*
*Towards Persia very nearly a million men,*
*The true serpent will invade Turkey and Egypt.*

In early August of 1987 the above planets were conjunct in Leo. Around that time it was reported that the Iranians were amassing close to a million men at the front for a massive push into Iraq. It never happened. Maybe the reason was disorganization in the military and/or conflict in decisions at a high level. Maybe the million men are not from Persia/Iran at all, but farther east.

Unfortunately, there is another date. August 22, 1998 the Sun, Venus, and Mars, along with Mercury and the Moon, are in Leo. They are not all conjunct, nor do they have to be; they just need to be in Leo in accordance with the quatrain.

On August 21-22, there is a Solar Eclipse at 29° Leo. This is the location of the royal star *Regulus*, often called the little King, which may be another way of saying Prince. According to the Babylonians, an eclipse in the third part (decanate) of Leo denotes motions of armies, death of kings, and danger of war.

Venus is at 11° Leo conjunct *Kochab*, a star known for its cold, violent and malicious energies. It is also noted for military gains.

The third planet, Mars, at 0° Leo opposes *Altair*. This star is Martian and is noted for its boldness and its nonstop pursuit of aims.

The opposing Sabian symbol to the Sun at 29° Leo says: "Deeply rooted in the past of a very ancient culture, a spiritual brotherhood in which many individual minds are merged into the glowing light of a unanimous consciousness is revealed to one who has emerged successfully from his metamorphosis." Looking at the sinister side of this picture, it is not difficult to envision an anti-Christ-type figure leading an army. As if all this weren't enough, Mars at the 1° Leo Sabian symbol says: "Blood rushes to a man's head as his vital energies are mobilized under the spur of ambition."

In order to understand this quatrain, you should view it as part of a larger story. This story is a sequence of quatrains starting with Q22 and ending with Q27, all of which are in Century 5. All things considered, the astrological correspondences seem solidly behind the date and the quatrain theme.

## C6 Q35

> *Near the Bear and close to the white wool,*
> *Aries, Taurus, Cancer, Leo, Virgo,*
> *Mars, Jupiter, the Sun will burn a great plain,*
> *Woods and cities letters hidden in the candle.*

This one is a great little astrological puzzle. The Bear probably refers to the Bears of the Ursa Major and Minor constellations. The "white wool" may mean the Milky Way. We will come back to this. The signs seem to indicate the time of year when the drought will occur. For some reason, Gemini is not included, but he does mention "letters," a strong Gemini correspondence and a possible indication that communications will break down (from Sun spots?). The three planets involved are the Fire planets, those that produce heat and decrease reproductivity. Jupiter and Mars conjunct on June 14, 1991 in 11° Leo. (This happens while the Sun is in Gemini. Is this the reason Gemini is not mentioned?) The Sun and Jupiter are conjunct August 17 of the same year at 24° Leo. No contacts to fixed stars that are noted for droughts occur. The Sabian symbol for 10° Leo (when the conjunction is forming) says: "Early morning dew sparkles as SUNLIGHT floods the field." At 24° Leo, a striking image: "A large camel is seen crossing a vast and forbidding desert."

There is a Solar Eclipse at 19° Cancer on July 11, 1991. The Babylonian meaning for the second decan of Cancer says that "rivers dry up." The Galactic Equator, i.e., the Milky Way, is "close" to 19° degrees of Cancer. The conjunctions in Leo are "near" the Bears (Ursa Major and Minor) in zodiacal longitude and also in geographical latitude. The latitude is approximately 34 to 64 North Latitude, where many of the great plains and deserts of the Northern Hemisphere exist. The Kabalistic cycle is of the Sun with a Moon sub-cycle. The Sun, of course, is the heat in the atmosphere, and the Moon is the biosphere receiving the excessive heat.

## C10 Q67

> *A very mighty <u>trembling</u>[2] in the month of May,*
> *Saturn, goat, Jupiter, Mercury in beef:*
> *Venus also, Cancer, Mars in Nonnay,*
> *Hail will fall larger than an egg.*

## C9 Q83

> *Sun twentieth of Taurus the earth will <u>tremble</u> very*
>     *mightily,*
> *It will ruin the great theater filled:*
> *To darken and trouble air, sky and land,*
> *Then the unbelievers will invoke God and saints.*

## C1 Q87

> *Volcanic fire from the center of the earth*
> *Will cause <u>trembling</u> around the <u>new city</u>:*
> *Two great rocks will make war for a long time.*
> *Then Arethusa will redden a new river.*

## C10 Q49

> *Garden of the world near the <u>new city</u>,*
> *In the path of the hollow mountains:*
> *It will be seized and plunged into the Vat,*
> *Forced to drink waters poisoned by sulfur.*

---

[2]All underlined words are author's emphasis only.

These four quatrains seem to have a connection with each other. They are known as the "Great Quake Quatrains." There is no absolute assurance that they are related, but when put together in a certain manner an interesting picture develops.

We can be reasonably sure that a city ("the new city") will undergo a natural disaster in the form of a massive earthquake. Look how the word *tremble* is used three times. "Two great rocks will make war for a long time"; what a perfect way of describing fault lines and the plate tectonic theory. Some commentators (E.L.) believe Arethusa to be a reference to the famous fountain of Arethusa at Syracuse in Europe. Others (E.C.) have said that it may be a variation of the word *Ares*, a god of war. The picture is about the same: two plates at war with each other and the lava boiling as a fountain and as a red river. The last line of the fourth quatrain indicates that the water supply will be contaminated.

The weather patterns will certainly be abnormal with hail larger than an egg in C10 Q67. In fact, there will be other atmospheric problems even more severe—C9 Q83: "To darken and trouble air, sky and land." Very strong suggestions of the dust plumes from volcanic eruptions and perhaps the ozone layer.

Before we tackle the problem of when, we need to look at where, and that is the new city. It has been argued back and forth that the new city must be either Los Angeles or New York. Certainly the mention of "hollow mountains" could be a reference to the skyscrapers of New York. Yet what is created on the Hollywood sets has been just as grand as mountains, but since they are unreal they are hollow. The central valley of California is the most productive piece of land in the world. This most certainly qualifies it as the "Garden of the world" (C10 Q49). The reference to the "great theater" in C9 Q83 can apply to both places. Yet in terms of influence and volume of activity, California wins again.

It has been suggested (E.L. and others) that the new city is really taken from the Greek term *Nea-polis*, the new city of Naples, Italy. The connection is made to the semi-dormant volcano Vesuvius, which is only 12 miles away. Edgar Cayce, the "sleeping prophet," said that before the great quake would take place in California either Vesuvius in Italy or Pelé on the Isle of Martinique in the French West Indies would have to erupt. Within 90 days the quake would occur. What an interesting way for Nostradamus to connect both of these locations. When many people thought that the quake would happen in May of 1988, I kept remembering what Cayce had said, and when there was no eruption I felt some relief.

Now comes the difficult part of predicting when this great earthquake will take place. After much thought and research, the best dates I can come up with are May 10 and 11, 1992, if it is actually going to occur in the near future.

We know from C9 Q83 that the Sun should be 20° Taurus, and this usually occurs on May 10. There is, however, another way of getting this date. In C10 Q67 it simply says May, but then the quatrain becomes a real puzzle. In the second line most authorities feel he means Saturn in Capricorn even though it says "Saturn, goat." Jupiter is then mentioned, but it's not clear whether he means it is in Capricorn or Taurus. I think he is saying that Jupiter is involved somehow. Mercury in Taurus (beef) seems like a definite. To me, "Venus also" says Venus is in Taurus. After the comma, Cancer is mentioned in much the same way that Jupiter was above. The next statement has really given everybody a headache—"Mars in Nonnay." I believe it has multiple meanings. First of all, it could be a variation on the French word *nonne,* meaning a "nun" or "virgin," thus Mars in Virgo. But Pisces rules nunneries.

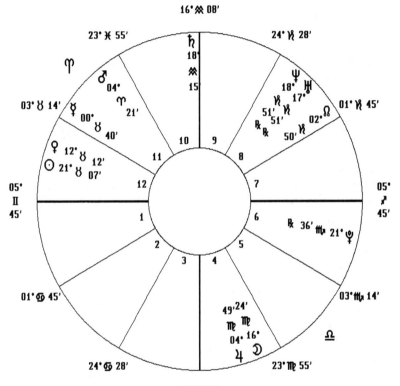

Chart 2
The Great Quake
May 11, 1992    6:49 A.M. PDT
118W15    34N04
Los Angeles, CA
Koch Houses

Another suggestion has been that *nones* is the name for the fifth canonical hour, or 3:00 p.m. Finally, it may simply mean that Mars is at "none" degrees, i.e., 0° of a sign, declination or right ascension.

Saturn in sidereal Capricorn, I believe, is the key position for the date I am using. The other two points are the positions of Venus and Jupiter. I differ from most; I think he means Venus in Taurus, not Cancer. Jupiter is involved, but not necessarily in Taurus.

Looking at Chart 2 for May 11, 1992, the Sun is less than two hours into the 21st degree of Taurus. C9 Q83 says the 20th degree of Taurus, but remember, this chart is just the best guess for any time late in the day on the 10th or the early morning hours of the 11th of May. Mercury is in Taurus trine Jupiter and opposing the Vertex, i.e., it is pointing due east. Does this mean that the major news releases will travel east? Mars, of course, is in the sign of the nun, Pisces, at the beginning of the month. It is also 0° declination, which fits with the "none" = zero theory.

The major focus in the chart is the T-square with the Sun/Venus and Pluto all square Saturn. In my proposed chart I put Saturn on the 10th House cusp so that the release point of the T-square is in the 4th House of land and nature.

In the Astro*Carto*Graphy map (Chart 3) there is a Saturn/Pluto crossing (paran) just east of the Los Angeles basin where many of the quakes are centered. There are also four other parans active (from other locations) for this area: Mars/Ura–31N35, Plu/Sat–32N23, Ven/Sat–33N04, and Mars/Nep–34N46. Also notice the almost exact conjunction of Uranus/Neptune over Washington, D.C.

In looking at the eclipse paths for the Northern Hemisphere in the near future (Chart 4), it is quite obvious that the Pacific plate between Hawaii and the West Coast of California and Mexico is filled with paths. Path number 2

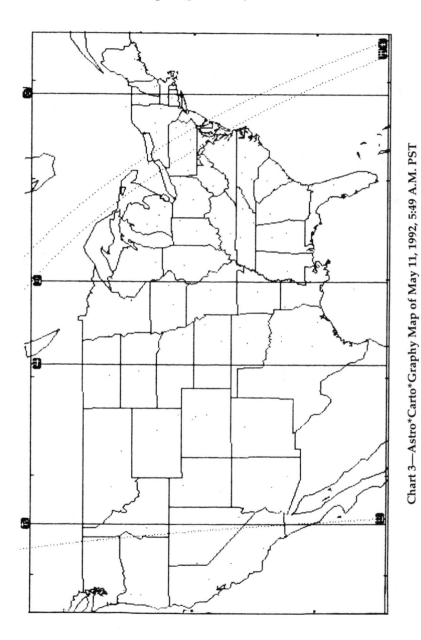

Chart 3—Astro*Carto*Graphy Map of May 11, 1992, 5:49 A.M. PST

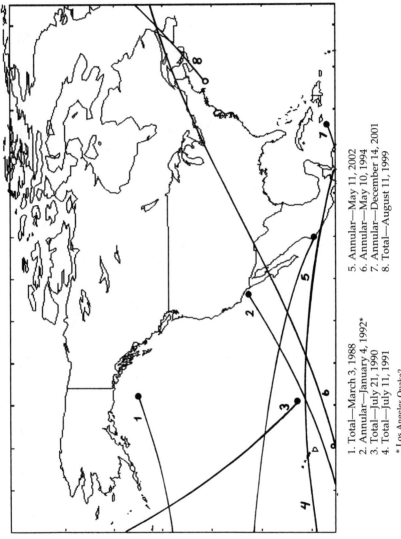

1. Total—March 3, 1988
2. Annular—January 4, 1992*
3. Total—July 21, 1990
4. Total—July 11, 1991

5. Annular—May 11, 2002
6. Annular—May 10, 1994
7. Annular—December 14, 2001
8. Total—August 11, 1999

* Los Angeles Quake?

**Chart 4—Eclipse Paths 1988-2002**

**Path of Totality (Complete path not shown)  o–Begin •–End**

ends right off the coast of greater Los Angeles!

The sign Cancer is mentioned, and Chart 2's South Node is placed at 3° Cancer. When five of the planets are in Fixed signs (including the key three) you get the impression that something very fixed is about to move, like a plate on the Earth's mantle. Venus is conjunct the New Moon for the month with Pluto conjunct the Full Moon. By the way, there is a period of about 12 hours where Mars is 0° declination, the Sun 20° Taurus and Mercury in Taurus, and that is the 10th and 11th of May as mentioned.

Let us turn our attention to the fixed stars and see if they confirm the above descriptions. Saturn is at 18° of Aquarius but also in sidereal Capricorn. It is opposite the fixed star *Merak*, said to have a Mars nature. This makes it potentially destructive; however, it is not connected with mass experiences or with natural cataclysms. The Sabian symbol says: "The skill and courage necessary to bring under control the destructive potential of carelessness of karmic visitations."

Pluto's position (21° Scorpio) also aspects a Mars-type fixed star, *Unukalhai*, with some Saturn influence. This star has a reputation for being very dangerous and destructive. There also is a connection with poisoning, which was alluded to in the fourth line of C10 Q49. The Sabian symbol says: "Obeying his conscience, a soldier resists orders," and the basis of this symbol is inner freedom.

The third part of this T-square is the Sun, and here we have *Zanrak*, which has a Saturnian character. Isolation, fear, and terror are some of the feelings associated with this star. The Sabian symbol for 19° Taurus (as the Sun is just separating from the square to Saturn and applying to the opposition with Pluto) says: "A new continent rising out of the ocean" and "The surge of new potentiality after the crisis."

There are no prominent fixed stars aspecting Venus

or the conjunction of Uranus/Neptune, but the Sabian symbol for the degree of Uranus/Neptune is interesting: "The protection afforded to individuals and groups by powerful institutions in charge of maintaining order."

The Sabian symbols seem to create a clear description of what would occur during an earthquake—the necessary control of destructive potentials, willful soldiers, land rising out of the ocean, new ideas after a crisis, police and government trying to maintain law and order.

I hope this journey into the past as a way to the future has been stimulating for you. It should, at the very least, cause us to think about the future as a series of choices. May the dreams of mankind and our personal dreams blend harmoniously.

## Abbreviations

A.P. = Arthur Prieditis
E.C. = Erika Cheetham, books 1 & 2
E.L. = Edgar Leoni
J.F. = Jean-Charles Fontbrune

## Bibliography

Cheetham, Erika. *The Further Prophecies of Nostradamus.* New York: Perigee Books, 1985.

———. *The Prophecies of Nostradamus: The Man Who Saw Tomorrow.* New York: Berkley Publishing Corp., 1981.

De Vore, Nicholas. *Encyclopedia of Astrology.* New York: Philosophical Library, Inc., 1958.

Ebertin, Reinhold. *Fixed Stars & Their Interpretation.* Tempe, AZ: American Federation of Astrologers, 1971.

Erlewine, Michael and Margaret Erlewine. *Astrophysical Directions.* Big Rapids, MI: Heart Center, 1977.

Fontbrune, Jean-Charles. *Nostradamus: Countdown to Apocalypse.* New York: Holt, Rinehart & Winston, 1978.

———. *Nostradamus 2.* New York: Henry Holt and Co., Inc., 1987.

Hogue, John. *Nostradamus and the Millennium: Last Predictions.* Garden City, NY: Dolphin Books, 1987.

Jansky, Robert. *Interpreting the Eclipses.* San Diego, CA: Astro Computing Services, 1979.

Leoni, Edgar. *Nostradamus and His Prophecies.* New York: Nosbooks, 1982.

Poulin, Maurice. "Decoding Nostradamus," *Considerations,* 1985.

Prieditis, Arthur. *The Fate of the Nations.* St. Paul, MN: Llewellyn Publications, 1982.

Rigor, Joseph E. *The Power of the Fixed Stars.* Hammond, IN: Astrology and Spiritual Publishers, 1978.

Robson, Vivian E. *The Fixed Stars and Constellations in Astrology.* Wellingborough, Northamptonshire, England: The Aquarian Press, 1969.

Rosenberg, Diana. "Nostradamus and the Great Quake," *Dell Horoscope* (October 1987), and personal correspondences.

Rudhyar, Dane. *An Astrological Mandala—Sabian Symbols.* New York: Vintage Books, 1974.

Sepharial. *Kabalistic Astrology.* North Hollywood, CA: Newcastle Publishing Co., Inc., 1981.

———. *The World Horoscope.* Brampton, Canada: Ballantrae, 1982.

Walker, Stuart. "Trouble in Paradise," *NCGR Journal,* 1986.

### Diana K. Rosenberg

Diana K. Rosenberg, a native New York Aries, studied astrology with Betty Lundsted, Joanna Shannon, Charles Emerson, Charles Jayne, Wayne Booher, and Olivia Barclay.

A member of the National Council for Geocosmic Research and its Helio and Mundane SIGs and the Astrological Society of Princeton, she is a charter member and Vice President of The Uranian Society.

She has written articles for the *NCGR Journal, Ingress, Heliogram, Mundane Journal, Urania*, and *Dell Horoscope* and is the author of a *Workbook and Correspondence Course in Fixed Stars and Constellations*.

# STALKING THE WILD EARTHQUAKE

In ancient times the Japanese, who live in one of the most earthquake-prone lands of our planet, had a tradition that the *namazu*, a mischievous giant catfish, lived in the mud beneath the Earth. The Kashima god kept the namazu pinioned under a magical rock to protect the Earth; if the Kashima god relaxed his vigilance, the impudent namazu thrashed about, causing a quake. . . .

*Japanese seismologists study catfish closely for behavioral patterns that might signal an earthquake: the usually sluggish fish become agitated before upheavals, possibly because they are extremely sensitive to vibrations and electrical impulses.*

In ancient Mongolia, the old storytellers told of a gigantic frog that carried the Earth on its back; every now and then, the frog itched, and when the frog itched, the frog twitched. . . .

*In Liaoning Province, during the winter of 1974-75, agitated frogs jumped out of the lakes through holes in the ice and froze in the snow. On February 4, a great earthquake hit, devastating the province. . . .*

In each quaint and amusing myth, there is a grain of truth . . . a core of ancient wisdom:

337

*In Babylon, astrologers believed that there was a rela-
tionship between the alignments of the Sun, the planets, and the stars and the trembling of the Earth. . . .*

*And there were voices, and thunders, and lightnings;
and there was a great earthquake, such as was not
since men were upon the earth, so mighty an earthquake, and so great.*

*—Revelation 16:18*

## THE GREAT LISBON EARTHQUAKE

November 1, 1755: Lisbon, thriving port and capital
of Portugal, teemed with activity: At the harbor, work
gangs unloaded vessels at the magnificent new gray marble Cays de Prada; merchants argued loudly over prices;
noisy children dodged the bellowing stevedores; but the
exquisitely clad aristocracy were not part of the crowd. It
was All Saints' Day, and Lisbon's six magnificent cathe-
drals were packed with kneeling worshippers. At 9:30 in
the huge Basilica de Sao Vincente de Fora, the chant of the
Introit had just begun. . . .

*A rolling, swaying surge ground marble and timbers
together; like a ship in a storm, the great church
groaned, heaved, and then crumbled, its huge stones
crushing the congregation. . . .*

For a relentless three-and-one-half minutes, a terrible
violence shattered Lisbon; gigantic fissures 15 feet wide
ripped through the center of the city. As aftershocks
heaved and rumbled, choking dust rose from more than
18,000 collapsed buildings. Fire licked, then roared
through the ruins. **In the first two  minutes, 30,000 died.**

*The terrified survivors rushed to open space of the
docks for safety . . . they stared at the ocean in stunned*

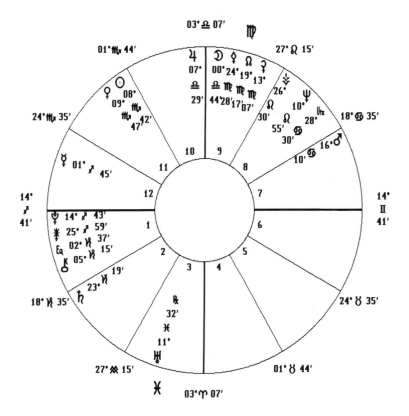

Chart 1
Great Lisbon Earthquake
November 1, 1755    9:30 A.M. LMT
38N43    9W10
Lisbon, Portugal
Placidus Houses

> *fascination as the water receded and the seafloor lay*
> *revealed, a litter of lost cargo and old shipwrecks.*
> *Suddenly someone screamed a warning, but it was*
> *too late. The withdrawn ocean had coiled and*
> *reared up into a huge wall of water, rushing to engulf*
> *them. In a moment, 20,000 more were gone.*

The proud Basilica de Santa Maria, Sao Paulo, Santa
Catarina, Sao Vincente de Fora, the Misericordia—all had
become a rubble of carved stone gravepiles for thousands
. . . hundreds of patients in the Hospital Real burned to
death. Out of a city of 230,000, about 90,000 were dead
(another 10,000 were killed across the Mediterranean in
Morocco); 85 per cent of the city's buildings were destroyed, including *all* of Lisbon's magnificent museums
and libraries. The king's palace, housing a 70,000-volume
library and hundreds of priceless works of art, including
paintings by Titian, Rubens and Correggio, burned to the
ground.

> *As the stunned survivors desperately tried to save*
> *their families, priests of the Inquisition roamed the*
> *ruins rounding up innocent people, dubbing them*
> *"heretics" and hanging them on the spot for angering*
> *God. . . .*

The shock waves of the Lisbon earthquake were felt
over 1,300,000 square miles through Europe and North Africa, and seitches (sea waves) up to 60 feet high hit a vast
area stretching from Finland to North Africa and across
the Atlantic to Martinique and Barbados. Vesuvius, which
had been in eruption, abruptly stopped! There were no re-
cording instruments in 1755, let alone a Richter scale, but
modern experts have estimated that the Great Lisbon
Earthquake may have been an incredible magnitude 9.
(See Chart 1.)

Other shock waves—philosophical, theological, and

intellectual—from this huge disaster spread through Europe as well. Many asked themselves why such a terrible event had struck during High Mass and questioned the authority of the Church (Lisbon was a bastion of the Inquisition); Voltaire had a field day mocking the 18th century's version of positive thinking that "this was the best of all possible worlds." The intellectual world mourned the loss to flames of Lisbon's great repositories of *incunabula* (rare ancient manuscripts) and priceless maps and charts of centuries of Portuguese exploration. Only science (still called "natural philosophy") gained; the Marquis de Pombal took charge of the rescue operations, planned and oversaw the rebuilding of the city (blaming the Church for its reaction, thereby weakening the Inquisition), and gathered a remarkable archive of hard data on the quake itself. This was the first of its kind and so thorough that it is consulted by scientists to this day.

"Natural philosophy" and newly discovered electricity were all the rage in 1755; when usually solid Boston was shaken by several quakes (the first and strongest just 17 days after the Lisbon disaster), Reverend Thomas Prince suggested in his sermon "The Works of God & Tokens of His Just Displeasure" that God might very well have been expressing His displeasure in the form of electricity, drawn to Boston by the forest of Ben Franklin's lightning rods on the roofs of the city!

Astrological tradition holds that predictions of mundane events can be made from an analysis of charts drawn up for the latitude and longitude of a given place for the exact time of an eclipse (especially one visible at that place), a Cardinal ingress, a lunation, planetary conjunction, transits to fixed stars, and for any unusual celestial event, such as the apparition of a comet. To these, modern astrologers have added planetary stations, the 90° dial (and dials for other harmonics), asteroids, planetary nodes

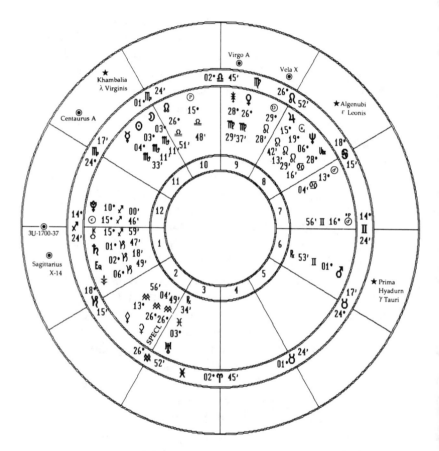

Chart 2
1753 Eclipse Over Lisbon
October 26, 1753    10:27 A.M. LMT
38N43    9W10
Lisbon, Portugal
Placidus Houses

and, of course, computers. In order to perceive earthquake patterns in predictive charts (as well as the charts of quakes themselves), we must revive some of the discarded traditional techniques and, at the same time, employ, and perhaps invent, new ones.

An eclipse in the third degree of Scorpio (dignity, triplicity, term and face of Mars, and the degree of the fall of the Moon), the sign of death, combust Mercury, of Mutable Earth, *passed directly over Lisbon* two years and six days before the Great Lisbon Earthquake. (See Chart 2.) Mars itself, co-ruler of the 12th House of misfortune and the ruler of the 4th House of landed property, both disposited and quincunxed (a death aspect) the eclipse. The antiscion, or solstice point, of the eclipse was 26 Aquarius 49, conjunct Earth-goddess asteroid Ceres on the cusp of the 3rd House of community in a death-quincunx to Venus in her fall in Mutable Earth, here ruling the 6th House of Mutable Earth. The rulers of the Earth houses (2, 6, 10) were afflicted: Saturn, approaching ascension, received a near-partile dexter quincunx from Mars, and Venus (terms of Saturn, face of Mercury), septsemioctiled (7 x 22.5° = 157.5°) Uranus. Mars adjoined the *Hyades, the powerful cluster of stars in the head of the Bull, in the Mutable Earth house; he ruled the 4th of homeland and squared Uranus. Pluto, lord of the underworld and co-dispositor of the eclipse, had just risen, co-ruling as well as inhabiting the 12th House of hidden dangers; the helio nodes of Uranus held the Ascendant/Descendant axis. Mercury ruled the 7th, the outcome 4th House from the 4th of landed property; he applied by dexter square to Neptune (god of earthquakes in ancient Rome) by 2°, a harbinger of the disaster two years later *at which the angles exactly matched the angles of the eclipse.*

Not only was the eclipse conjunct crippling *Khambalia, lambda Virginis, and black hole Centaurus A, but

Jupiter was transiting the stars of the fiery Lion's mane, Uranus was stationing conjunct the perihelion degree of Mars, Saturn was aligned with devouring black hole Sagittarius X-4, with the Ascendant, Ceres, Juno, Chiron, Jupiter's antiscia and the Arabian Part of Death also on black-hole degrees, and comet Chiron, associated with cracking, breaking and death, joined Pluto on the Ascendant (1990 precession correction 3°17'). The Uranus/S. Node midpoint was 0° Aries, sesquiquadrate Jupiter.

Even though black holes, asteroids, Uranus, Neptune and Pluto hadn't been discovered yet, an astrologer of the day would have been able to see that there was grave danger to the city: The Part of Commerce (ASC + Mercury – Sun) is on the Ascendant, exactly squared by the solstice point of the Arabian Part of Peril (ASC + Ruler of the 8th – Saturn); the "Mars Part," usually called the Part of Passion (ASC + Mars – Sun), is in a death-quincunx to the Ascendant/Part of Commerce conjunction, and its solstice point on the Descendant is sesquiquadrate the eclipse. The Moon, ruler of the 8th House of Death, is quincunx the IC, and the Part of Death squares Mars, its ruler. Although an astrologer would have realized danger, I doubt whether he could have foreseen an earthquake. (I would have guessed fire, and would have been partially correct.)

According to Barbara Watters, any planet in the degree of the Lunar Nodes is in a "fateful" and dangerous position; Venus culminated in the degree of the Nodes (in a death-quincunx to the S. Node) with Juno of helplessness; they squared the solstice point of Saturn, their antiscia embracing the IC. Ceres and the antiscion of the eclipse conjuncted in another "degree of the Nodes" on the cusp of the Placidian 3rd, the 12th House of misfortunes of the homeland 4th.

The solstice point of Uranus conjuncted the N. Node, and that of Mars conjuncted the vertex (fated, uncontrollable events in the immediate environment) in the house of death within 1° of a square to the Nodes; Jupiter (natural ruler of established religion), rich, fat and arrogant in Leo (terms of Venus, face of Jupiter), in dignity and triplicity, cast an apparently benevolent trine to the Ascendant he ruled. Jupiter was in the 8th House of death conjunct asteroid Gaea on cruel and destructive *Algenubi, epsilon Leonis, forming a sinister sesquiquadrate to Saturn; in a conflict between them, Saturn would eventually dominate, dignified by sign, and even though beneath the horizon, he's coming to ascension. A trine is not only a benefic 3rd harmonic aspect but is also 3 x 40°, the 9th harmonic of Plutonian endings.

In any eclipse the house with Leo on the cusp is automatically afflicted; the house behind it, ruled by Cancer, is intensified because the Sun, ruler of Leo, is being *eclipsed* by the Moon, ruler of Cancer. Here the 9th (church, concept of God) will be eclipsed by coming events; the abysmal behavior of the Inquisition during the disaster shocked Europe and resulted in the weakening of its power.

At the Libra Ingress immediately preceding the Lisbon quake (see Chart 3), the Ascendant was aligned in latitude, longitude and declination with *alpha Librae, the great "South Scale" star of karmic justice, long associated with the loss of possessions in time of war or disaster. (Pluto was at this star during the San Francisco quake of 1989; in ancient China the stars of the scales of Libra were called "The Foundation of Nature.") Neptune and Ceres culminated on cruel *Acubens and royal-and-violent *Regulus. The rulers of the Earth Houses were the natural Fire sign rulers—Mars, Jupiter, and the Sun; they were all afflicted, and in poor cosmic state. At the Ingress, the Moon, which in a mundane chart is the ruler of the common people and environmental conditions, was in the de-

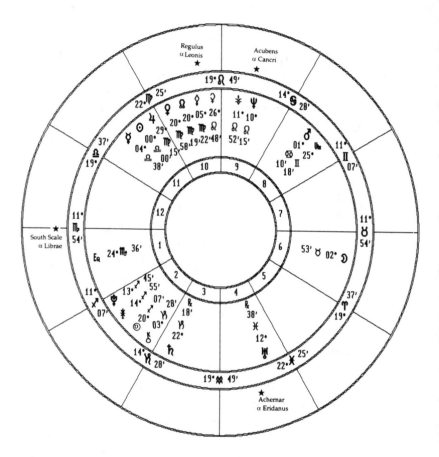

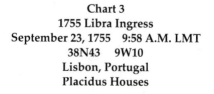

Chart 3
1755 Libra Ingress
September 23, 1755   9:58 A.M. LMT
38N43   9W10
Lisbon, Portugal
Placidus Houses

gree of her exaltation (opposing the eclipse degree) in the Mutable Earth house, in a death-inconjunct to Mercury, ruler of the 8th. She was last over the conjunction of Uranus (*Achernar, alpha Eridanus) and the S. Node, forming a dexter septile to them, next conjuncting Mars, whom she disposited, in the 8th House of death. Her dispositor Venus, in fall in Virgo, was fatefully conjunct the N. Node, squared by the Arabian Part of Death. As Lisbon is traditionally governed by Libra, the sign of Venus's dignity, and Portugal by Pisces, her exaltation, Venus's poor cosmic state at the eclipse, the ingress, and the quake itself seems significant. Mars and Saturn afflicted the Sun/Jupiter conjunction, all on the Aries (world) axis. There is no need for more. . . .

## Astrological Causes of Earthquakes

There is very little concerning earthquakes in traditional astrological literature that is helpful to modern astrologers. For one thing, catalogues of major quakes have become available only in the last two decades, and it is still difficult to get reliable data on ingresses and eclipses predating the 20th century. Astrological computer programs, as wonderful as they are, are not set up for rapid "scouting" of past celestial events so that locating pertinent eclipses, stations, lunar declinations, etc., can be extremely time consuming.

Raphael's *Mundane Astrology* lists of the effects of Solar Eclipses (amidst warnings of "seditions," "mischiefs" and "wontonness [sic] among women") the 2nd decanate of Aquarius for earthquakes, under Lunar Eclipses, the 1st decanate of Scorpio. Cornell's *Encyclopedia of Medical Astrology* holds that they are caused by planets transiting the Fixed signs as well as Virgo, Capricorn, and "violent signs," which would add Aries and Libra to those already listed. It also states that they occur at, or soon after, an eclipse of the Sun in Aquarius or Pisces, especially the 2nd decanate (the addition of Pisces here means that 9 of the 12 signs have now been named, leaving only Gemini, Sagittarius and Cancer "innocent" of causing earthquakes); when Jupiter is in Taurus or Scorpio aspecting Venus or Mercury; at the time of a Mars/Saturn conjunction in Taurus, Gemini, Leo or Scorpio in the 4th on the IC (a Mars/Saturn conjunction in Scorpio bracketed the IC at the eclipse over Mexico preceding the 1985 quake); or at the appearance of a comet.

I would have to say yes to all of these causes, and no as well. There are as many major quakes that do not fit these criteria as there are those that do. As for eclipses in Gemini, Sagittarius and Cancer, there have been several major quakes following eclipses in Gemini, and the March 26, 1872 8.5 Owens Valley, California quake came three months after a Solar Eclipse at 20° Sagittarius; the frightful MM XI quake near Naples on July 26, 1805 occurred just 30 days after an eclipse in Cancer, as have many other quakes. It may very well be that there is a statistically higher frequency of earthquakes after Fixed sign eclipses, but this has yet to be tested and would be of very little use in predicting them. As for comets, they turn up in interesting places in quake charts, especially those quakes that cause devastating fires. Halley's Comet, three years and five months before its 1909 recovery, *exactly* anti-culminated at the great 1906 San Francisco earthquake/fire. At the terrible Tokyo quake of 1923 (140,000 dead) it was conjunct Neptune, co-ruler of the IC, and quincunx Uranus, but this was *13 years* after its perihelion. In the 1836 quake in San Francisco, Halley's, just at the end of its apparition, was opposite Uranus and quincunx Neptune, and in 1985 Halley's culminated at the Mexico City quake, but these patterns are not consistent or frequent enough to be useful in prediction.

*We must suppose the action of the wind in the earth
to be analogous to the tremors and throbbings caused
by the force of the wind contained in our bodies. Thus
some earthquakes are a sort of tremor, others a sort of
throbbing.*

*—Aristotle*

For all the efforts of Aristotle, Sir Francis Bacon, Pombal, John Mitchell and many others, no better understanding of the processes that lead to upheavals in the Earth developed until 1912 when German astronomer/meteorologist Alfred Wegener postulated a theory of "continental drift." The scientific community hooted, sneered and mocked; one colleague wrote that it was typical of the kind of thinking that "took an idea, searched selectively for corroborative evidence, ignored facts opposed to the idea, and ended in auto-intoxication, convinced that the subjective idea is objective fact." *It took the once-every-127.2794-year conjunction of Uranus and Pluto in Virgo, the sign of "Mutable Earth" (their first conjunction in an Earth sign in 2,286 years!), in 1965-66 to finally break the geologists' fierce devotion to their traditional myths.* Acceptance of the possibility that continents might move led to the discovery of tectonic plates and subduction, and thus study of the structure of our apparently *very mutable* Earth has been given an entirely fresh perspective.

### Predicting the Where of Earthquakes

As difficult as it is to tell when an earthquake will occur, it is even harder to tell where it will happen. Even now, with a world network of data available and knowledge of tectonic plates, localizing the probable event is extremely difficult.

*Geodetics*, in astrology, is a technique that postulates that major events on Earth will occur when celestial events "tick off" local angles calculated with the longitude of

Greenwich, England as a fiducial: that is, using Greenwich as 0° Aries and moving east from there, each locality's longitude is used as a fixed MC for the place in question. For instance, Paris at 2E12 would have a geodetic MC of 2 Aries 12; then the rest is calculated as an ordinary chart, using the local longitude as MC and calculating the other angles and cusps (including the vertex and the equatorial Ascendant, two highly sensitive points) as you would for any horoscope; Michael Munkasey has pioneered the addition of the co-Ascendant and the polar Ascendant. Although they are conventionally calculated east of Greenwich (for areas beyond 180°, subtract the longitude from 360°), it has been noted that calculating *west* of Greenwich also gives results; New York at 74W therefore has a geodetic MC of either 14° Gemini (74°) or 16° Capricorn (360° minus 74° is 286°, which equals 16° Capricorn). Paris's MC (rounded off) can be either 2° Aries or 28° Pisces, or both. It is important to note that there is no geophysical basis for this technique, and it is only valid for events after 1883-4 when international time zones were established, thereby (theoretically) setting up morphogenetic fields that might affect events on Earth. So now we have a structure like this:

|  | EAST (of Greenwich) : | WEST (of Greenwich) |
|---|---|---|
| from longitude: | MC: | : MC: |
| from latitude: (using MC) | ASC: | : ASC: : |
| from co-latitude: (90° minus lat.) | CO-ASC: | : CO-ASC: : |
| from 0° latitude: | EQUAT. ASC: | : EQUAT. ASC: |
| from latitude: (using IC) | POLAR ASC: | : POLAR ASC: : |
| from co-latitude | VERTEX | : VERTEX |

Geodetic points were activated at the October 17, 1989 7.1 San Francisco quake. The August 16, 1989 Lunar Eclipse at 24 Aquarius 12 occurred *on* the Santa Cruz/San Francisco east geodetic equatorial Ascendants (this, the first Total Lunar Eclipse clearly visible over North America in nearly seven years, occurred at moonrise in California); a Solar Eclipse two weeks later (no path) conjoined the east and squared the west geodetic vertexes of the earthquake. At the quake itself, the Sun was on San Francisco's west geodetic co-Ascendant, and the Lunar Nodes aligned with the east geodetic equatorial Ascendant/Descendant axis. (See Chris McRae's "The Geodetic Equivalent Method of Prediction" in this volume for more information.)

In a Special Report published in January 1989, the Foundation for the Study of Cycles published a comprehensive review and bibliography of studies of seismic periodicities related to solar and lunar cycles. Among their findings:

• There is a relationship between the periodicity of quakes and variations in the gravitational constant; several studies found a direct effect between changes in the Earth's rotation rate, axis of rotation, moment of inertia, and quakes.

• Earthquakes relate to solar cycles and tend to be more frequent at sunspot maxima and minima (solar activity changes the Earth's rotational rate; quakes increase when solar activity is high and fluctuating).

• 4.42- and 9.3-year periodicities in quakes (and volcanic eruptions) were found in six separate studies. These apparently relate to the 18.6-year lunar declination cycle which moves tidal bulges north and south (every 18.6 years the Moon reaches extremes of declination north and south of the equator; the most recent extrema occurred September 15,1987, 4:22 UT).

• Highest tidal potential (New or Full Moon at perigee) and lowest tidal potential (quarter phase at apogee) both tend to trigger seismic activity; however, Ritter (1987) found unusually high global earthquake activity when the Moon was at quarter phase, at apogee, and at maximum declination.

• Four separate researchers found a pattern of lunar-solar angles of 455, 1355, 2255, and 3155 (8th harmonic peaks from 05 Aries) in quakes of the Parkfield segment of the San Andreas and Imperial faults.

• Global torsions: There is a rival theory to thermal convection and plate tectonics as the source of seismic energy. The Earth is expanding, and since the Northern Hemisphere is mostly continent and has greater inertia with the Southern mostly oceanic, expansion would cause the Northern to slow down more than the Southern, creating a torsion with most of the motion at the equator. This energy would be intermittently manifested by changes in the Earth's rotation and by tidal bulges triggering quakes.

• One of the most important findings came from the fact that studies showing a positive correlation between tidal triggering and quakes tended to focus on very limited regions, while studies showing a negative correlation were global in scope or averaged over large areas, strongly implying the necessity for localized research. Bagley (1970) introduced the concept of an "earthquake signature" for a given locale; certain areas tend to have quakes at the same Sun-Moon alignment and/or level of solar activity; these "signatures" could be identified and tested.

• Kokus (1988) reported an unusually high incidence of quakes near eclipses, which ties in with astrological tradition and folk mythology; it is important to note that changes in the Earth's curvature, as well as relative extremes in its acceleration and rotation rate, occur near eclipses, especially when they take place at equinoxes and solstices.

This summary closes by noting that these studies are in direct contradiction to the bulk of research done in the field of earthquake prediction and that there appears to be a bias against papers on solar and lunar triggering of seismic events by the referees of scientific journals.

In a major statistical study of earthquakes and planetary positions related to geographic regions (*NCGR Journal*, Winter 1986-'87), Judith Hill and Mark W. Polit found that earthquake dates demonstrated *more than twice the frequency of planetary chart similarities* when grouped by region than did random dates for both fast- and slow-moving planets. This breakthrough study proved what many had suspected for some time—that individual "degree areas" recur in earthquake events at specific locations. At the 1989 7.1 San Francisco quake, Mars and Venus were again in characteristic degree areas for this locale. (See Figure 1.)

In the science journal *Nature* (July 7, 1983), Knopoff and Kilston reported statistically significant 12-hourly, lunar-fortnightly, and 18.6-year periodicities in 35 large (greater than magnitude 5.3) earthquakes in Southern California between 33° and 36°N. Smaller quakes did not display these periodicities. They concluded that within a few years of each lunar declination maxima, sometimes near a New or Full Moon, near sunrise or sunset, there would be a higher-than-average likelihood of one or more large earthquakes in Southern California. (The 6.1 Whittier Narrows quake of October 1, 1987, 7:42 PDT, 14:42 UT, 33N58 118W03, and the 7.1 San Francisco quake, October 17, 1989, 17:04 PDT, 10/18, 0:04 UT, 36N58 122W01,

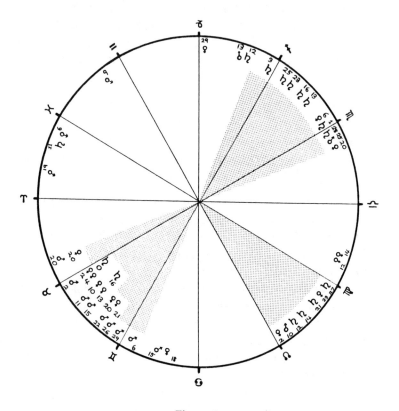

**Figure 1**
**Longitudinal Positions of Venus, Mars & Saturn**
**at 15 Earthquakes greater than Magnitude 6**
**in San Francisco Bay Area 1800-1984**
**(Shaded Area: Fixed Cross)**

| | | |
|---|---|---|
| 10/11/1800 (M6.0) | 10/08/1865 (M6.5) | 03/31/1898 (M6.5) |
| 06/21/1808 (M6.3) | 10/21/1868 (M6.8) | 04/18/1906 (M8.3) |
| 06/10/1836 (M6.8) | 04/10/1881 (M6.0) | 07/01/1911 (M6.6) |
| 06/??/1838 (M7.0) | 05/19/1889 (M6.1) | 10/22/1926 (M6.1) |
| 11/26/1858 (M6.3) | 04/24/1890 (M6.0) | 04/24/1984 (M6.1) |
| | Added: 10/17/1989 (M7.1) | |

This graphic courtesy of Judith Hill and Mark W. Polit, "Correlation of Earthquakes with Planetary Position—The Regional Factor," *NCGR Journal*.

though slightly farther north than the scope of their study, fulfilled these expectations.) However, as Kokus and Ritter found (*Cycles*, March 1988), there are areas where quakes have no correlation with the lunar phase, and two-thirds of those chosen for their study in the southeastern U.S. occurred at the first or last lunar quarter. (The declination maxima of the Moon coincides with the return of the North, or ascending, Lunar Node to 0° Aries.)

Confirming Knopoff and Kilston's work, the author found roughly a 19-year pattern of major quakes, primarily in Southern California, counting from 1781, the year Los Angeles was incorporated: 1800: Santa Barbara; 1819: no record; 1838: (only one recorded, San Francisco region); 1857: Great Fort Tejon quake; 1876: (1877—Imperial County quake); 1895: (late 1894—San Diego); 1914: (January 1915—Los Alamos); 1933: Long Beach quake; 1952: Kern County quake; 1971: San Fernando quake. The next year in this pattern is 1990. . . .

In an exploratory study of 238 quakes 7.5 or greater between 1930 and 1950 (*Kosmos*, Winter 1984-'85 and *Heliogram*, August 1988), Scott G. Vail found that Saturn was preferentially concentrated near the event charts' Gauquelin angles, especially in the 9th, 3rd and 12th Houses, and that aspects in heliocentric coordinates gave results more consistent with traditional aspects; from then on, all work was done in helio. Separating hard aspects (45° and multiples), especially of Saturn and Mercury, occurred with greater-than-random frequency, while applying aspects in the same series appeared with less-than-random frequency. Minor fractions of 45° appeared significant; 30°, 60° and 90° aspects did not. He also found minor aspects significant in earthquake timing.

## Ancient Universes & Earthquakes

*To the Hindus, the universe, at bottom, was a sea of milk; the foundation of the world was a great turtle who swam in the sea; on the back of the turtle were four elephants who supported the disk of Earth, and when an elephant shook his head (as elephants do from time to time), there was an earthquake. . . .*

*In an ancient Mayan legend the world was a cube of earth supported at each of its corners on the shoulders of four gods, the Vashakmen. If the weight of increasing population became too heavy, the Vashakmen shifted their heavy load, ridding the world of people and thus easing their burden. . . .*

These ancient "four-cornered" universes were based upon the four Cardinal points of the solar-terrestrial year: North (0° Cancer), the Sun's "solstice" or standstill on the horizon, at midsummer in the Northern Hemisphere and midwinter in the Southern; South (0° Capricorn), its opposite; East (0° Aries), the Vernal Equinox (equal length of day and night) in the Northern Hemisphere, which is the Autumnal Equinox south of the equator; and West (0° Libra), its opposite. It is only in the last two decades that proof has been found that *these Cardinal points have been the basis for sacred structures in every civilization of which we have record* and among so-called "primitives" as well. The Temple of Abu Simbel and the great Sun temple of Amon-Ra at Karnak in Egypt; the Guo Shou jing Observatory Tower in Henan Province, China; Peru's Machu Picchu and the Temple of the Sun at Cuzco; Templo Mayor at Tenochtitlan; Uxmal and the Caracol at Chichén Itzá in the Yucatan Peninsula; Uaxactun in Guatemala; Chaco Canyon and the "Hall of Mirrors" of Alta Vista, New Mexico; Fajada Butte at the Utah/Colorado border; Cahokia in Illinois; Wyoming's Bighorn and Montana's Fort Smith Medicine

Wheels; Saskatchewan's Minton Turtle and Moose Mountain wheels; the stones of Scotland's Kintraw, Callanish and others; Carnac in Brittany; Newgrange in Ireland; Gors Fawr in Wales; and England's Long Meg, Woodhenge, Castle Rigg, and, of course, Stonehenge—all of these, and many, many more, were constructed, at least in part, *to locate and delineate the position of the Sun at the solstices.*

## Using the 90° Dial

This axis of 0° of the Cardinal signs (called "Aries"), derived from the four ancient solsticial and equinoctial "pillars" of the solar year, is the basic focus of the 90° dial. This dial is an indispensable tool for astrological research; the 8th harmonic (semi-squares and sesquiquadrates, also known as octiles), 16th (semi-octiles, 22.5° and multiples thereof), and further minor hard-aspect harmonics, as well as midpoints, hard aspects to midpoints, antiscia and contrantiscia, can be immediately and visually perceived on the dial, laying bare the major and minor "bones" of a chart. In a study of 44 extremely powerful "superquakes" (8.5 or higher) worldwide, all but three had planet(s), Lunar Nodes or angles within 1.5° of a hard aspect (conjunction, square, opposition, octile or semi-octile) to "Aries" (the 4 Cardinal points). In other words, within 1.5° of: 0° Aries, Cancer, Libra, or Capricorn; 15° Taurus, Leo, Scorpio, Aquarius; 22.5° Aries, Cancer, Libra, Capricorn; or 7.5° Gemini, Virgo, Sagittarius or Pisces. (See Figure 2.)

The heliocentric nodes of the planets are powerful points of energy and are validly used with *both geocentric and heliocentric* planetary positions; each node functions not only in its own degree but is highly sensitive to hard aspects on the 90° dial. The 1990 positions and yearly motion (forward), in seconds, of the ascending nodes are:

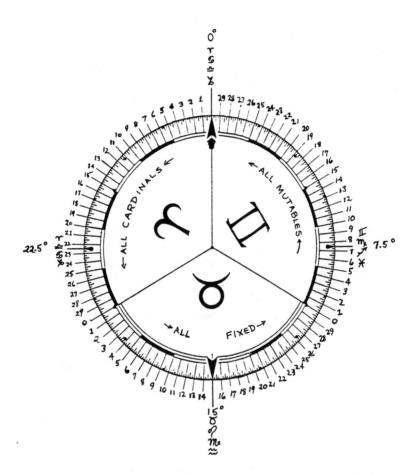

**Figure 2**
**World Axis Points on 90° Dial**

Use of 90° dial compliments of Gary Christen and Astrolabe.

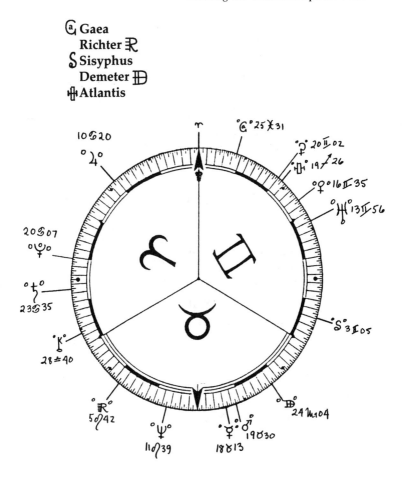

Figure 3
1990 Heliocentric Planetary Nodes

Use of 90° dial compliments of Gary Christen and Astrolabe.

| Mercury: | 18 Taurus 13 42.66" | Saturn: | 23 Cancer 35 31.43" |
|----------|---------------------|---------|---------------------|
| Venus: | 16 Gemini 35 32.39" | Uranus: | 13 Gemini 56 18.38" |
| Mars: | 19 Taurus 30 27.75" | Neptune: | 11 Leo 39 39.66" |
| Jupiter: | 10 Cancer 20 36.39" | Pluto: | 20 Cancer 07 48.00" |

Used on the 90° dial (Figure 3), which displays all major and minor hard aspects, the *heliocentric planetary nodes are invariably transited at major mundane events*; indeed, in 1934 E. H. Bailey published an article in the British *Journal of Astrology* proposing that they be used for a "Universal Horoscope." At the Lisbon quake, both Mars and the Sun/Venus conjunction hit the nodes of Neptune and Pluto (which were in semi-octile aspect then); the Moon was on Mercury's node, Pluto on Venus's node, and Chiron, Uranus, and the vertex on Jupiter's. (See Figure 4.)

In an intensive study of 11 of California's greatest quakes undertaken in 1987, it was found that six occurred following, and a seventh the same day as, eclipses on the 16th harmonic axis (22.5°) of the nodes of Uranus (Figure 5).

### Solar Eclipses
9/28/1856  6 Lib 11:   8.0 Fort Tejon Quake 1/09/1857
6/29/1927  6 Can 31:   IX-X Pt. Arguello Quake 11/04/1927

### Lunar Eclipses
2/09/1906 19 Leo 40:   8.3 San Francisco Quake 4/18/1906
12/28/1917  6 Can 07:   6.8 Riverside Quake 4/21/1918
2/10/1933 21 Leo 22:   IX Long Beach Quake 3/10/1933
2/10/1952 21 Leo 14:   7.7 Kern County Quake 7/21/1952
2/10/1971  20 Leo 55:  6.6 San Fernando Quake 2/09/1971

(The 1971 San Fernando quake occurred 6.66 hours *before* the eclipse.)

California's statehood chart (September 9, 1850) has a Uranus/Pluto conjunction at 29° Aries *on the Uranus nodal axis,* and the New Moon preceding the 1989 7.1 San Fran-

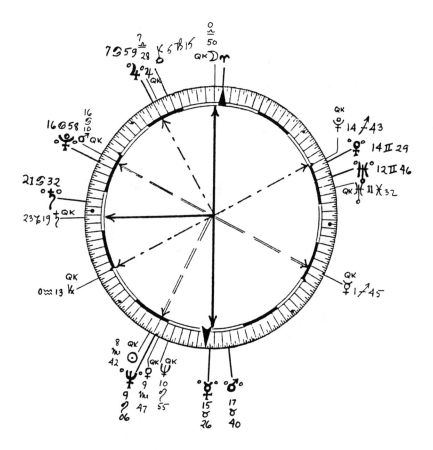

**Figure 4**
**90° Dial showing Lisbon Quake Positions**
**with Heliocentric Planetary Nodes, 1755**
**(°Circles° = Nodes)**

Use of 90° dial compliments of Gary Christen and Astrolabe.

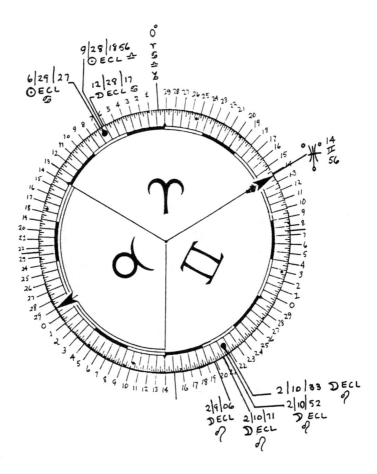

**Figure 5**
**7 Eclipses preceding Great California Quakes**
**on 22.5° Axis of Node of Uranus**
**and New Moon preceding 1989 San Francisco Quake**

Use of 90° dial compliments of Gary Christen and Astrolabe.

cisco quake was 6 Lib 43 on this same axis. On February 9, 1990, there was a Lunar Eclipse at 20 Leo 47; on July 21, 1990, a Solar Eclipse at 29 Cancer 04; on November 13, 1993, there will be a Solar Eclipse at 21 Scorpio 32, and on May 10, 1994, a Solar Eclipse at 19 Taurus 48 (over Southern California). All aspect the Uranus node. In an unusual intersection of eclipse paths in a relatively short period of time, two others touch Southern California during the early 1990s: the Solar Eclipse of July 11, 1991, crossing Baja, California, will hard-aspect the nodes of Neptune and California's natal Saturn, and the eclipse of January 4, 1992 (conjunct Uranus), which sets at Southern California, affects Los Angeles' chart harshly.

The most sensitive midpoints thus far discovered in major (larger than MM 6 or 7.0 Richter) earthquakes worldwide are Sun/Jupiter, Mars/Saturn, Uranus/Neptune, and Transpluto/Admetus. (Transpluto is a speculative 10th planet beyond Pluto's orbit. Admetus is one of the Uranian system's "transNeptunian" planets having to do with density, core, rotation, enclosure, weight, entrapment and death; its nature is Saturnian.) It has also been noted that the Sun/Moon midpoint of the previous Cardinal Ingress is highly sensitive and often "ticked off" at the event.

### Earthquake Power

There are two major scales delineating the power of earthquakes. The *Richter scale* is a logarithmic measurement of magnitude, or size of the seismic waves generated by a quake at its source; each increase of a whole number in the Richter scale represents an increase of 60 times in the energy of the tremor and of 10 times in the extent (size) of the seismic wave, as measured by seismograph. Therefore, a magnitude 8.0 is not twice that of a 4.0, it is *ten thousand times* as great (the famous 1906 San Francisco quake was an estimated 8.3), and the energy generated in an 8.0 is *10 million times* that of a 4.0.

The older *Mercalli scale* (and an updated "MM" or "Modified Mercalli") describes intensity, or the amount the ground shakes at a given location, which is judged primarily by observation of local structural damage and the tremor's effect on the local population. The MM scale uses Roman numerals from I to XII; at V, the quake is "felt by everyone, many awakened; dishes broken, plaster cracked, clocks stop"; at VIII, "damage considerable in ordinary buildings, some partially collapse; slight in specially designed structures, great in poorly built structures; fall of chimneys, etc." At XI, "few structures remain standing; bridges destroyed; broad fissures in ground; underground pipelines completely out of service; rails greatly bent; earth slumps, soft ground slips." At XII, the top of the scale, "Damage total; waves seen on ground surfaces; lines of sight and level are distorted, objects thrown upward into air," and there is "general panic."

The two scales cannot really be correlated, but a *very rough* estimate of magnitude vs. intensity would be something like this:

| Magnitude | | 2 | 3 | 4 | 5 | 6 | 7 | 8 | 8.9 |
|---|---|---|---|---|---|---|---|---|---|
| Maximum Intensity | I-II | III-IV | | V | VI | VII-VIII | IX-X | XI | XII |

In the *Catalog of Significant Earthquakes 2000 B.C.-1979*, there are no quakes of magnitude 9 listed. Only two are 8.9's—Sanriku, Japan, 1933 and Cabo de San Francisco, near the border of Ecuador/Colombia, in 1906; five are estimated to have been intensity XII: one in China in 1668, the three at New Madrid, Missouri in 1811-12, Fort Tejon, California, 1857, and the above-mentioned Ecuador/Colombia quake of 1906.

## THE 1964 ALASKA EARTHQUAKE

*Under the waters, deep in the bay, were great hollow caverns; a huge and jealous demon lived in the caverns and guarded them fiercely; he feared and hated outlanders. If strangers came near, the demon raged with fury; he thrashed, he stormed, he clamored, he roared; the air thundered and cracked, the land heaved and shook and buckled and the waters rose into great high mountains; then, when the intruders were frightened and helpless, he captured and tamed them. . . .*

*—Myth of the Tlingit Indians of Alaska*

In the early 1960s, men came to Alaska's North Slope to search for oil. They were strangers to the land. . . .

In the teeming, boom-town atmosphere of Anchorage, Alaska in 1964, few, if any, of the inhabitants cared that ancient Indian myths told of land devastated by massive upheavals or of sea waves the size of mountains drowning the land. Fishermen, wildcatter oilmen, lumberjacks, hard-hat construction workers, daredevil bush pilots, and hardy citizens jostled one another in the rapidly expanding city; sometimes the ground trembled, but that was nothing to these proud, roughhewn 20th-century pioneers.

Good Friday, March 27, 1964, 5:36:14 p.m. (3/28/64, 3:36:14 UT), 61.4N, 147.73W (the head of Prince William Sound, about 80 miles east of Anchorage), see Chart 4. The Lunar Nodes engaged the semi-octile axis of the nodes of Uranus *on the Ascendant/Descendant of the 1963 eclipse over Alaska;* the setting Sun and a not-yet-risen Full Moon squared them, semi-octile the "death axis" (0° of the Fixed signs) of the 90° dial. The angles were just past the Cardinal axis, semi-octile the nodes of Saturn; the Sun had reached asteroid Richter on earthquake star *Al Pharg,

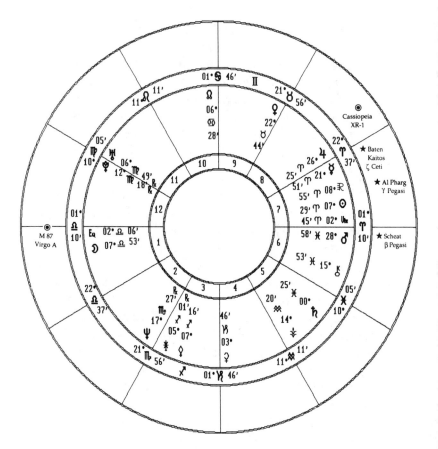

**Chart 4**
**1964 Alaska Earthquake**
**March 27, 1964   5:36 P.M. AHST**
**61N24   147W43**
**Prince William Sound**
**Placidus Houses**

gamma Pegasi, and Mercury conjoined *Baten Kaitos, shipwreck star zeta Ceti; Jupiter squared the 1963 eclipse degree.

> *At first, the ground rocked gently; used to small tremors, people in Anchorage went about their business, waiting for the shaking to stop—but instead it grew more intense. Suddenly, the entire south-central coast of Alaska convulsed. The land surged in huge undulating waves, shocking and splitting the terrain.*

Anchorage, about 80 miles northwest of the epicenter, suffered the greatest damage; most of the city lies on an oleaginous substratum of clay, which turned into an unstable and slippery fluid that slid toward the sea, with huge sections of the city riding upon it. A new unoccupied six-story apartment house collapsed into rubble; the facade of concrete panels fronting the new J. C. Penney department store sheared away from the structure, crushing passers-by. Part of Fourth Avenue, Anchorage's main street, dropped 11 feet straight down, taking with it stores, automobiles, and people. One wing of the elementary school dropped 20 feet into a crevass, tearing the structure apart; the 68-foot airport control tower went down, killing the controller. In all, about 30 city blocks were completely destroyed. At suburban Turnagain Heights, a section of bluff 8,600 feet long collapsed, destroying 75 homes.

For 500 miles, from Cordova to Kodiak Island, the great quake ravaged south-central Alaska; roadways crumbled, bridges collapsed; one ship's captain at Valdez reported seeing the land "jumping and leaping in a terrible turmoil." The combination of low population density and time (late afternoon, when most schools and businesses had already closed) kept the death toll to a remarkably low level: 131. Of these, 121 were killed by the huge

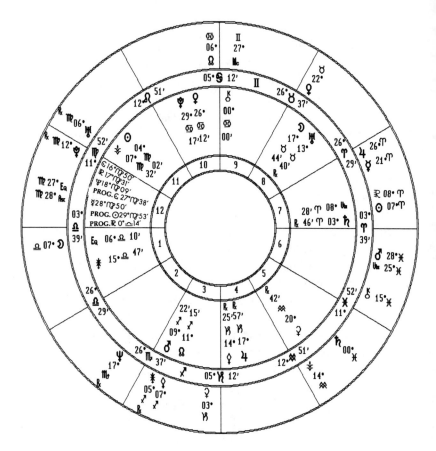

**Chart 5**
**Quake Victim Relocated to Kodiak, Alaska**
**August 27, 1937   8:10 A.M.   AHST**
**57N48   152W24**
**Outer Ring: Alaska Quake at Kodiak**
**Placidus Houses**

tsunami that followed the shock, which wiped out small settlements and Eskimo villages; 9 people at Crescent City, California died when waves from the quake hit their shore (Mars aligned with *Scheat, beta Pegasi, a star since ancient times associated with sorrow, suffering, and drowning).

At Kodiak, southwest of Anchorage, a young woman was thrown against a piece of factory machinery which mangled her arm; fortunately, she received immediate medical attention and survived, though the arm had to be amputated. Born August 27, 1937 at 10:10 a.m. PST at 46N59, 123W50, she had relocated to Kodiak, 57N48, 152W24. (See Chart 5.) At the time of the quake, transiting Neptune opposed her Moon and Mars opposed her Mercury, squared Chiron-of-crippling and trined Pluto (which was on her relocated 12th cusp). The Lunar Nodes conjuncted her local MC/IC, and the Full Moon at the quake was on her relocated vertex/antivertex, affirming the "fated-out-of-control-events-in-the-environment" interpretation of these angles; Saturn was sesquiquadrate her natal Juno and semi-square her Jupiter/Pallas conjunction in Capricorn. She was born on a Gaea/Richter/Neptune conjunction in Virgo; at the quake, her progressed Sun was on the Cardinal axis at 29 Virgo 53 conjunct progressed Richter at 0 Libra 14, and solar arc Chiron conjoined her ruler, Venus. These aspects suggest that danger from an earthquake might be seen in an individual's chart through the use of natal, progressed, and solar arc asteroids!

Buck Helm, the trapped, injured longshoreman of the 1989 San Francisco quake, was born on a Richter/Sun conjunction with Jupiter, Mercury, Mars, Venus and Gaea all aspecting the nodes of Uranus. At the quake, besides a progressed conjunction of Sun/Saturn, solar arc Richter opposed natal Pluto and quincunxed natal Jupiter, and so-

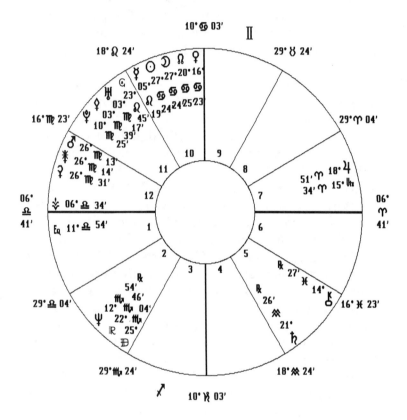

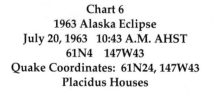

Chart 6
1963 Alaska Eclipse
July 20, 1963   10:43 A.M. AHST
61N4   147W43
Quake Coordinates:  61N24, 147W43
Placidus Houses

lar arc Gaea septsemioctiled natal Saturn. Transiting Saturn was semi-square his natal Richter, and the 6 Libra 43 New Moon quinsemioctiled his natal Gaea. Data: November 19, 1931, no time given, probably Oakland, CA.

The extraordinary length, complexity, and strength of the Great Alaska Quake made it the most powerful ever recorded on the North American continent; it also made it very difficult for seismologists to analyze. Out of about 800 seismographs around the world, only a few yielded usable seismograms (some technicians thought that if the armatures had not been under restraint, the tracing pens might have traveled about a foot off the paper); the resulting estimated magnitude was between 8.3 and 8.6—but 8.6 is *double* the magnitude of 8.3! The energy released was equal to 12,000 atomic bombs, or 240,000,000 tons of TNT, and the area of land surface deformed by the quake was "larger than any such area known to be associated with a single earthquake in historic time"; more than 100,000 square miles of the surface of the Earth had either been thrust up or dropped down; more than 25,000 square miles of land had moved laterally to the southeast; Anchorage shifted 6 feet, Valdez, 33 feet, and Seward, 47 feet. Detailed maps of Alaska have had to be redrawn. At Montague Island, the seafloor had lifted 38 feet, and on a parallel fault between Montague and Kodiak Islands, an area of the seafloor suddenly lifted 50 feet, causing the great tsunami that followed. The tsunami, in turn, raised such a huge mountain of water that it caused an atmospheric disturbance in the air above it, affecting the ionosphere 50 miles above the Earth!

On July 20, 1963, eight months before the quake, the path of a Solar Eclipse (Chart 6) cut across Alaska. Unlike the eclipse preceding the Lisbon quake, traditional astrological techniques yield less-than-satisfactory results on this chart; thus, new ones must be tried. Using the earthquake's epicenter of latitude 61N24, 147W43.8, the following are the geodetic angles and eclipse "hits":

West MC: 27 Leo 44
Asc.: 6 Scorpio 22
Co-Asc.: 21 Scorpio 50          Eclipse Saturn: 21 Aquarius 26
Equat. Asc.: 1 Aquarius 48
Polar Asc.: 16 Cancer 36        Eclipse Venus: 16 Cancer 23
Vertex: 14 Gemini 33            Eclipse Chiron: 14 Pisces 27
East MC: 2 Scorpio 16
Asc.: 13 Sagittarius 24
Co-Asc.: 15 Capricorn 27        Eclipse Vertex: 15 Aries 28
Equat. Asc.: 28 Capricorn 00    Degree of Eclipse: 27 Cancer 24
Polar Asc.: 23 Leo 40
Vertex: 8 Leo 11

(At the quake itself, helio Saturn was 26 Aquarius 55, *on the west geodetic IC* and the midpoint axis of geo Uranus/Neptune and geo Transpluto/Admetos.)

In spite of prejudice to the contrary, I believe that helio and geo positions can and should be combined; our universe is, apparently, a primarily cognitive construct.

The next Solar Eclipse (no path) on January 14, 1964, two-and-one-half months before the quake, also hit the area's geodetic angles: Mars at 1 Aquarius 15 was on the west geodetic equatorial Ascendant square the eclipse's local Ascendant at 0 Taurus 01; Saturn, which had been retrograde, returned to its position at the previous eclipse, 21 Aquarius 54, square the west co-Ascendant; both Saturn and the MC/IC (which matched the Ascendant/Descendant of the first eclipse) were in hard aspect to the nodes of Uranus; since Saturn and Uranus co-ruled the 12th and Jupiter (at perihelion) in the 12th conjoined the solstice point of Neptune, the devastating tsunamis were presaged. Pluto at 14 Virgo 01 squared the west geodetic vertex (the vertex and anti-vertex, loci of "fated, out-of-control" events in the environment, are the points of intersection of the great circles of the prime vertical and ecliptic); Venus was on the west geodetic IC at 27 Aquarius 14, conjunct black hole/pulsar Cygnus X-3. While geodetics are still experimental, there are enough contacts to warrant further research in this area.

Although syzygies do not usually accompany quakes (with a few notable exceptions), in a preliminary examination of the 44 previously mentioned "superquakes" of magnitude 8.5 or higher, about two-thirds showed a modified "bowl" pattern, that is, planets tended to range more or less on one side of the Earth, within a range of about 240°-260°.

## Harmonic Clusters

In an exploratory study of harmonic clusters occurring in 103 major California quakes from 1769 to 1980, using the harmonic clusters option in the *CCRS Horoscope Program*, the traditional "hard" aspects were unexpectedly weak; the first harmonic (i.e., conjunctions) predominated, but this may have been due to the program setting for orbs of three per cent of the harmonic circle, which gave the conjunctions a very wide 10.8° orb. Next, surprisingly, came (close together) the 17th harmonic and the 19th (consider that 19 x 19 = 361, the number of degrees of the Earth's daily rotation, and that the square root of 360 is 18.973666). Then came the 11th, 13th, 7th (the septile), 5th (the quintile) and 23rd. All these harmonics have two things in common: they are all odd numbers and they are all "primes," numbers that are evenly divisible only by themselves and one. There is a near-conjunction of the 17th and 19th harmonic at about 170 degrees: 9 x 18.947368 (19th harmonic) = 170°31'34" and 8 x 21.176471 (17th harmonic) = 169°24'42". *Since anything that is 10° from one end of an axis is 170° from the opposite axis, this is one "warning*

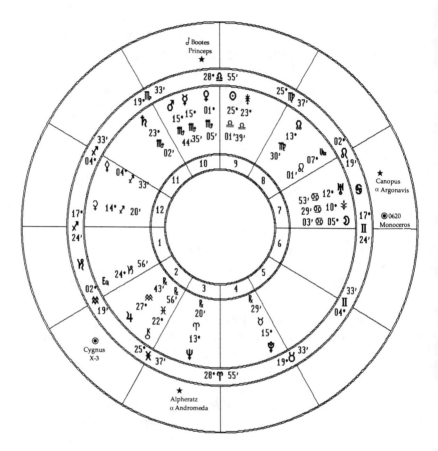

Chart 7
Purchase of Alaska
October 18, 1867   12:00 P.M. LMT
57N3    135W20
Sitka, Alaska
Placidus Houses

*sign" that is easy to see visually on any predictive chart, such as
an eclipse or an ingress.*

In the Alaska eclipse, the Lunar Nodes were 10° from
the MC/IC axis, which means that each node was 170°
from the opposite angle, and Mars was 10° from the Ascendant, therefore 170° from the Descendant. At the Libra
Ingress preceding the Lisbon quake, Neptune was 170°
from the IC. At the Full Moon immediately preceding the
1989 San Francisco quake, the Sun and Moon were each
10° from the MC/IC axis, which meant that each was 170°
from the opposite angle. These examples indicate that
both the 17th and 19th harmonics were in play. These harmonics might be explored further with a modification of
orbs, the addition of more axes (antivertex as well as vertex, IC, DSC, and the four Cardinal points), a larger sample, and controls.

### Using the Locality Chart

In Mundane Astrology, it is useful to work with a
chart for the locality, if one is extant, and the earliest available horoscope is usually (though not necessarily) the best.
Alaska (from *Alayeska*, "the great land") was purchased
from Russia for $7,200,000 on October 18, 1867 (Chart 7)
during a station of Uranus on the U.S. Sun with Neptune
square it. No time is available, but it has often been demonstrated that the angles of noon charts are valid and powerful; Noon LMT at Sitka has been used. Both geo and
helio asteroid *Juno* conjoined the Sun; nearby *Juneau* later
became the capital. Jupiter, ruler of the chart, is on black
hole Cygnus X-3, trined by Sun/Juno and squared by Saturn. Venus rules the MC and disposits the Sun; she culmi-
nates in exile (detriment) in the Fixed Water sign Scorpio
(ice), disposited by a dignified Mars opposing an exiled
Pluto, with whom she is in mutual reception. Neptune is
on Jupiter's perihelion degree, the fixed star *Alpheratz,

alpha Andromeda/delta Pegasi; the midpoints of Neptune/Pluto and Transpluto/Admetus meet at the IC in the longitude of the extreme variable *Mira, omnicron Ceti, an infrared source of "demonic power" in the constellation of the whale. The Moon is in her dignity on Black Hole 0620 Monoceros; these positions evoke both the cold isolation of the state and its extraordinary beauty and complexity.

The July 20, 1963 eclipse over the state squared the purchase Sun/MC, octiled the nodes and semi-octiled (22.5°) the Moon. The eclipse's MC/IC were on the helio nodes of Jupiter; the Ascendant/Descendant were on the previously noted semi-octile axis of the nodes of Uranus. Eclipse Saturn, exactly one septile from 0° Capricorn and in the ("fated") degree of the Lunar Nodes, squared natal Saturn and sesquared the Moon; eclipse Uranus was on the contrantiscion (3 Virgo 39) of the precession-corrected Sun (26 Libra 21). **When using charts more than 50 years old, it is important to include precession-corrected positions.** Eclipse Mars, on the descending node of asteroid Gaea, was in the 12th House of hidden dangers quincunx Jupiter of the purchase chart, and Neptune was approaching a sinister conjuction with the state's natal Mercury/Mars in Scorpio opposite Pluto in Taurus, a clear warning of future danger from the sea. (Neptune, the god ancient Greeks called Poseidon, was known as *Enosichthon*— "Earthshaker.") Eclipse Jupiter, co-ruling the Mutable Earth 6th, conjoined the antiscia of the state's mean N. Node, while Pluto approached it (it is vital to include antiscia on mundane charts!); the vertex/equatorial Descendant conjunction bracketed Alaska's natal Neptune. Mercury, ruler of the eclipse 12th House, was on the ascending node of asteroid Richter.

Asteroids and their helio nodes are a promising area of research; of those tried so far, the most useful in earthquake prediction are:

| 0001 Ceres | N. Node 20 Gemini 02 |
| 3338 Richter | N. Node 5 Leo 42 |
| 1184 Gaea | N. Node 25 Pisces 31 |
| 1198 Atlantis | N. Node 19 Sagittarius 26 |
| 1108 Demeter | N. Node 24 Scorpio 03 |
| 1866 Sisyphys | N. Node 3 Gemini 05 |

(Sisyphus is a mythological resident of Hades eternally condemned to roll a great rock up a slope, which then (eternally) rolls right back down.)

At the Alaska eclipse, Atlantis and Gaea were conjunct at 23 Leo 22 and 23 Leo 45, respectively, square Richter at 22 Scorpio 46 and Demeter (on her own node) at 25 Scorpio 04; they formed a T-square with Saturn, which ruled the 4th. The IC was the solstice point of the N. Node of Atlantis.

If one lives in an earthquake-prone area, it would be wise to check the positions of these asteroids, along with their antiscia and nodes, at each ingress and eclipse. As for the more familiar asteroids, an afflicted Vesta can indicate danger to the security and safety of a community and its "vested interests," Juno can represent helplessness and, for some undetermined reason, Pallas is often very prominent in these charts.

*In Indonesia, if the demon who carried the Earth was not satisfied that sufficient sacrifices had been made to him, he shook with rage. . . .*

Computers and catfish, elephants and asteroids, freezing frogs, lightning rods, planets and winds and demons and nodes and turtles swimming in milk . . . will we ever be able to reliably predict earthquakes? Probably not.

When we study the chart of an earthquake, we are looking at the *end result* of patterns of energies, rather than their initial stages. Astrology is a discipline that analyzes potentials that emerge out of *beginnings*. However, with new techniques and access to data and computers, it is becoming possible to perceive planetary "earthquake weather"—periods of increased likelihood of major Earth upheavals—and if that ability is put together with developments in other disciplines, then warnings like those given for storms and tornadoes may become possible, and one of the great natural scourges of mankind might be alleviated. To this end, we continue our work.

## Bibliography

Allen, Richard Hinckley. 1899. Reprint. *Star Names: Their Lore & Meaning*. Mineola, NY: Dover Publications, Inc., 1963.

Campion, Nicholas. *The Book of World Horoscopes*. Wellingborough, Northamptonshire, England: The Aquarian Press, 1988.

Coffman, J., von Hake, C., Stover, C., eds. *Earthquake History of the United States*. U.S. Dept. of Commerce, NOAA, Boulder, CO, 1982.

Cornell, H. L., M.D. *Encyclopaedia of Medical Astrology*. York Beach, ME: Samuel Weiser, Inc., and St. Paul, MN: Llewellyn Publications, 1972.

Cornell, James. *The Great International Disaster Book*. New York: Simon & Schuster, 1976.

Dobyns, Zipporah P. *The Node Book*. Rev. Los Angeles: TIA Publications, 1979.

Fairbridge, Rhodes W., General Consultant. *The World Around Us.* New York: Reader's Digest Assn., Inc., 1972.

Ganse, Robert A. & Nelson, John B. *Catalog of Significant Earthquakes 2000 B.C.-1979.* World Data Center A for Solid Earth Geophysics, U.S. Dept. of Commerce, NOAA, Boulder, CO, 1981.

Gribbin, John. *This Shaking Earth.* New York: G. P. Putnam's Sons, 1978.

Hand, Robert & Sweeney, W. J. *Nova Astrological Computing Program.* Orleans, MA: Astro-Graphics Services, Inc., 1988.

Hawkins, J. R. *Transpluto.* Dallas, TX: Hawkins Enterprising Publications, 1976.

Hill, Judith & Polit, Mark W. "Correlation of Earthquakes with Planetary Positions—The Regional Factor," *NCGR Journal,* Winter 1986-87, pp. 9-16.

Kilston, S. and Knopoff, L. "Lunar-solar periodicities of large earthquakes in southern California," *Nature,* Vol. 304, 7 July 1983, pp. 21-25.

Kokus, Martin S. "Earthquakes, earth expansion, and tidal cycles," *Cycles,* November 1987.

Krupp, E. C., ed. *In Search of Ancient Astronomies.* New York: Doubleday & Co., Inc., 1978.

Lehman, J. Lee. *Asteroid Names & Nodes.* New York: National Council for Geocosmic Research, 1981.

Lilly, William. *Christian Astrology.* 1647. Reprint. England: Regulus Publishing Co., 1985.

MacCraig, Hugh. *The 200 Year Ephemeris: 1800-2000.* Richmond, VA: Macoy Publishing Company, 1949.

Michelsen, Neil F. *The American Ephemeris of the 20th Century 1900-2000.* San Diego, CA: ACS Publications, Inc., 1980.

―――. *Comet Halley Ephemeris 1901-1996.* San Diego, CA: ACS Publications, Inc., 1985.

―――. *Uranian Transneptune Ephemeris 1850-2000.* Franksville, WI: Uranian Publications, Inc., 1978.

Negus, Dr. Kenneth G. "The Moon's Nodes, the Nineteen-Year Transit Cycle, and the U.S. Presidents," *Journal of the Astrological Society of Princeton, Inc.,* 2, 1981.

von Oppolzer, T. R. 1887. Reprint. *Canon of Eclipses.* Trans. by Owen Gingerich. Mineola, NY: Dover Publications, 1962.

Pottenger, Mark. *CCRS Horoscope Program.* Orleans, MA: AGS Software, 1988.

Raphael. *Mundane Astrology.* London: W. Foulsham & Co., 1910.

Rosenberg, Diana K. *Correspondence Course in Fixed Stars & Constellations.* New York, 1989.

Sheldrake, Rupert. *A New Science of Life: The Hypothesis of Formative Causation.* Los Angeles, CA: J. P. Tarcher, Inc., 1981.

*Special Report: Seismic Periodicities Than Can Be Related to Lunar and Solar Cycles.* Foundation for the Study of Cycles, Irvine, CA, January 1989.

Staal, Julius D. W. *Stars of Jade.* Decatur, GA: Writ Press, 1984.

Tarsaidze, A. *Czars and Presidents.* New York: McDowell/Obolensky Enterprises, Inc., 1958.

Vail, Scott G. "Planetary Motions and the Occurrence of Earthquakes: An Exploratory Study," *Kosmos,* Winter 1984-85, reprinted in *Heliogram,* August 1988, pp. 12-14.

Walker, Bryce. *Earthquake.* Alexandria, VA: Time-Life Books, 1982.

Watters, Barbara H. *Horary Astrology and the Judgment of Events*. Washington, D.C.: Valhalla Paperbacks, Ltd., 1973.

Yeomans, Donald K. & Kiang, Tao. *Two Body Ephemeris for Comet Halley 240 B.C.-1911*. Jet Propulsion Laboratory, NASA, Pasadena, CA, 1981.

### Caroline W. Casey

A native of Washington, D.C., she has a degree in symbol systems from Brown University and has studied esoteric traditions in London, India, California, the Yucatan, New England and Washington, D.C.

The primary astrological consultant for Time-Life Books' *Cosmic Connections*, she has appeared on ABC's *Nightline*, CNN's *Crossfire*, and frequently on CBS's *Nightwatch*. She also has been interviewed on *USA TODAY TV* and by *People* magazine.

Her clients come from all branches of government as well as from among the media and include artists, foreign diplomats, Wall Street businesspeople, and metaphysical colleagues.

# DREAMS AND DISASTERS: PATTERNS OF CULTURAL AND MYTHOLOGICAL EVOLUTION INTO THE 21ST CENTURY

Astrology is at least threefold in its purpose and practice. One, we can use it to *describe the characteristics* of a person, event or time period. Two, astrology is *instructive* as to how to play the energies, to perceive the patterns, viewing them as instructions; it reveals how to cooperate with the larger process, remembering that *disaster* means literally "against the stars," and three, it's *celebratory and devotional* as we celebrate the divine order. . . .

In our imaginative travels from present time into the 21st century, we will be playing with all three aspects of this symbolic language in the following way: The late great mythologist, Joseph Campbell, bequeathed to us the task of co-creating with the Magical Transcendent a global mythology. We need a collective dream, a synthesis of multicultural aspiration, to inspire and guide us through the enormous challenges we face. With devotional hearts, we can use astrology as a descriptive and instructive language to delineate that dream.

Astrology's view of free will is that we, individually and collectively, have the free will to follow our instructions, or to blow it. The stakes are high now, nothing short of planetary and species survival. We are entrusted with carrying the sacred burden of the past into a safe and beneficent future.

In astrology we are not dealing with a fixed future

model. The more we collaborate with the future, the greater flexibility we have as individuals and as a culture. *The primary function of astrology is to discern the pattern of Evolutionary Intelligence and cooperate with it.*

Now, in the late 20th century, the alignment of Uranus and Neptune makes it possible for us to break free from the matrix of broken dreams and disappointments, allowing for something which does not merely seem new, but is new. . . .

We are called upon to experiment with time and our concepts of time. Let's talk to ourselves in the future. Let's write history backwards. What year was it when all nuclear weapons were banned? Onward peace wagers. Let's take a testdrive into future possibilities as opposed to indulging ourselves in paralytic nostalgia, animals frozen in the glare of the onrushing future.

In Philip Dick's brilliant novel *Now Wait For Last Year* (DAW Books, 1981), an acutely toxic and addictive drug allows for forward and backward time motion, but without an evolutionary mindset this freedom becomes a prison. One of the characters asks another, "Are you waiting for last year to come by again or something?"

"That's exactly right, I've been waiting a long time for last year. But I guess it's just not coming again."

We can reach back into the past for strength and inspiration from enlightened traditions, but not to live there. We are time travelers into the future, into different possible futures . . . . Our task is one of scouting ahead and taking responsibility for our Vision (Neptune in Capricorn), returning and pulling the switch on the tracks for the Reality Train (Saturn).

We will use the planetary patterns to describe the extraordinary upheavals we have all been experiencing in our personal lives since 1988 as well as their significance and relationship to collective world events. We will also discern instructions as to how to play the energy in this increasingly wild force field.

The following prophecies are intended as guides to consensus reality, remembering that if we can imagine it we can pull it off. I refer to these offerings as "prophecies" rather than predictions. *Predictions* and *predicament* come from the same Latin root *dicere*, meaning "to say." Prophecy has an aura, a connotation of divine cooperation, and thus expresses a path by which we can avoid predicaments, which are nearly always unpleasant. *Dream* comes from the Old English *drieman*, "to make music or melody, to play on an instrument, rejoice"; "to behold or imagine in sleep or vision"; "to think or believe a thing to be possible."

We can now dream the dream together and form a vessel into which the collaborative creativity of the Magical Transcendant can pour. *Dream* can also mean "to act drowsily or indolently, to procrastinate". . . and that would be a disaster.

So now, let's take this prophetic testdrive into the middle of the 21st century. How can we imagine a future worth living in which the Earth can be restored and death is not imminent? When we return from this exercise in future dreaming, we will concern ourselves with the shadows we must face in order to get there.

The primary astrological tool for timing and prophecy is the tracking of the movement of the planets from Saturn on out—Uranus, Neptune and Pluto—each representing an evolving form of cultural intelligence.

*Neptune represents the Intelligence of Vision*—how a culture seeks its Vision, its primary mythology, and how it turns imagination into reality.

Neptune was in Scorpio from 1957-1970, and the culture sought its Vision through drugs, the occult and ways relating to Scorpio's intensity of investigation. Neptune was in Sagittarius from 1970-1984, seeking its vision through Sagittarian means: endless enlightenment trainings, the age of the guru, exploration of philosophies from other cultures. Neptune was in Capricorn from 1984-1998, foreshadowing the dissolution of the economic structure and its culture of narrow self-interest and greed, as well as the movement of visionaries into the corporate global structures.

As we remember, it was the great financial restructuring of the 1990s which drove most of the polluting industries (especially chemical and nuclear power) into bankruptcy, giving the Earth and its inhabitants some literal breathing space in which to implement the solution-oriented visions of the Neptune in Aquarius period (1998-2011). In the 1990s, all of the world's ecological, political, economic, and spiritual bills came due. The collapse of the global economy gave rise to the necessary development of micro-economies. These fostered privately sponsored breeding grounds for scientists, artists, and visionaries to collaborate on the solutions to the myriad irreverent problems created by a world suffering under the influence of a narrow form of "scientific" superstition, which believed the universe to be dead. This belief had allowed unspeakable insensitivities to be committed.

The year 1992 was pivotal on so many levels. Not only was it the year of the coming together of the European Common Market, it was also the 500-year celebration of the so-called "discovery" of the "New World" by the "Old World." And it heralded the beginning of the Neptune/Uranus conjunction (which actually occurred in 1993), a time of the building of bridges and the forming of significant alliances and workable prototypes—the matrixes of collaboration which would prove to be the making of the real New World from the Old. The 500-year-old promise of New and Old World cross-fertilization and creative symbiosis flowered at last—economically, spiritually, metaphysically and even (the last sphere of human activity to register any interesting change of consciousness) politically.

*Loa* is the Voudoun term for the force of invisible spirit, the gods. It is said that the loa ride on the visible; they piggyback on apparently mundane forms of human exchange, especially cross-cultural exchange. The invisible rides on the visible. Spirit is smuggled across borders under the guise of "business." This is a description and an instruction of the Neptune in Capricorn era. It is definitely something to celebrate. Until 1992, 1492 had been the most extravagant encounter of foreign cultural interaction on Earth. In 1992, under the guise of business ventures, all borders were flung open, all markets became common markets. And mythologically, all the gods were dancing.

On an individual level, the '90s were a time of each person finding his/her unique contribution and cultural work, ritually offering talent to the Evolutionary Conspiracy. The heartening principle was understood; it really takes only one-tenth of one per cent of the population to change history, to act as a fulcrum, if that percent has a focused Vision and a willingness to collaborate with the loa, the gods, the planetary Intelligences of the Best that wants to take place.

Many individuals felt a sense of mission, that (metaphorically) they had parachuted down to this planet in its time of crucial need to collaborate with the Magical. Those who could wake up did wake up in 1992-93, and by concentrating on their aspirations they polished their emanations, allowing them to be drawn into place through the principle of creative affinity. Like was drawn to like, deep called unto deep, and so the teams were formed, comprised of individuals with non-redundant, symbiotic capacities. It was only retroactively that the turbulent individual and collective changes from 1986-1988 (Saturn/ Uranus effect) made sense as people were being jockeyed and bumped into their correct places for the dance of the '90s to begin. These Visionary Activists formed projects, often disguised as business ventures, which served as vessels or event designs into which the loa could incarnate. The Loa-Visionary Activist Alliance was unbeatable. All the gods were invited. Those who embodied principles of imaginative and pragmatic compassion, so long relegated to the fringe of the culture, moved into the centers of power and the creation of policy, propelled by their own aspiration and the backing of the loa of that specialized domain.

With the revelations of intelligent extraterrestrial life, brought about in the early period of the 21st century (Neptune in Aquarius, 1998-2011), through the Earth's deep-space listening programs came an end to Earth's isolation from larger galactic community. Life and patterns of life were found everywhere. Conscious participation, cooperating with life throughout space, became necessary. The advances in physics and the proof of the unified field theory (and Guts, the Grand Unified Theory System) revealed the universe as an organic, unfolding and continually evolving Intelligence. We humans serve this larger order by becoming increasingly conscious, increasingly cooperative and respectful of all of creation, having at last understood that everything is conscious, everything is alive, and everything is related and deserves respect.

Once physics had produced the unified field theory (everything is in communication with everything else) and there was meaning to the patterns, the argument between ancient metaphysics and modern physics was over. The wedding of ancient metaphysics (of which astrology is a primary surviving system) and modern physics produced a child—Reverent Science.

*In the fall of 1989, Jupiter (the Intelligence of Interdisciplinary Synthesis) in Cancer (the Intelligence of Appropriate Response) had opposed the lineup of Uranus, Saturn and Neptune in Capricorn.* The kind of solution-oriented structures that would have to be implemented by the millennia had become devastatingly clear to enough people at that time. And they were aware that time was short. Relaxed urgency became the tone. It was becoming apparent that certain environmental global changes set in motion by human greed and folly were irrevocable (like global warming and species devastation), while some could be reversed with swift, appropriate response. Organizational seed structures were planted then that would not fully take root or be visible until the end of the century.

On December 23, 2012, the Great Mayan Calendar came to its completion, signaling the end of human history as we had known it. This date written in Mayan as 13.0.0.0.0 is the completion of the cycle of 13 Baktuns, each of which is 144,000 days. The above date is the culmination of their calendar, which began with their calculation of the beginning of time—August 13, 3,114 B.C. In astrological terms, this represented the end of human history confined solely to the planet Earth as Earth released its human seeds out into the galaxy.

With the pragmatic development of superconductors and antigravity as a source of transport, travel (both global and space) became near instantaneous. (This rendered fascism and totalitarian control impossible as no one had to stay in one place long enough to be arrested.) *Pluto is the Intelligence of Death, Rebirth and Renewal.* With its passage through Capricorn from 2008-2024, we see the increasing irrelevance and death of the State as the preferred model of social organization. Clans (modern tribes by choice) develop without any spatial boundaries.

In the fall of 2012 with Neptune at the threshold of its

own sign Pisces trine Saturn in Scorpio, music and the arts are increasingly potent magical vessels for positive catalytic change. We remember that the word *dream* originally meant to play music. The clue is that the making of music is an instrumental part of dreaming the world into existence, a way of aligning with the harmony of the spheres. Neptune in Pisces is a furthering of the alliance between the scientific and the mystical, the aboriginal and the ultramodern, as what was previously relegated to the realm of esoterica—the power of tones, chords and colors to heal and create—is increasingly embraced by science.

In the late 19th century it was the dream of such composers as Scriabin to write the symphony that would bring harmony and invoke universal peace. The early 21st century may well be the time for the realization of such dreams, and not a moment too soon. At the same time, Uranus is square Pluto in early Cardinal degrees, triggering a violent release of energy that needs the wise guidance of these magical arts. In fact, Uranus, the Promethean Intelligence, is square its station point of 1989, opposing its station point of 1970. The integration of the intuitive arts, which began in 1970 and was further stabilized and integrated in 1989, is urgently needed in 2012. Those who began their training in 1970 and deepened it in 1989 are the necessary leaders during this wild time. This year reminds us of the saying that riding the wild tiger is easy enough; it's mounting and dismounting that are the tricky parts. Meanwhile, Pluto stations at Saturn's station point of 1989, further testing the structural decisions and assumptions of the late 20th century, especially in regard to the State, power elites and economic and class structures. Whatever stood in the way of massive change in 1989 is blasted into oblivion. As class structures fall and we see the end of the hegemony of the white race, the atmospheric quality of this transition is in the hands of the artist-scientist-musician-magicians. Their work before (starting in 1989), during, and after determines whether this is a time of literalized or ritualized violence.

It brings us to Pluto in Aquarius (2024-2044) and the widespread beginnings of global families developing through creative affinity. All of the above helps to create consensus reality. However, this transition was staged— everyone who is still around has really gone through something together from which true global community, true participatory democracy, was/will be forged. This is the fulfillment of the Dream which blossomed in 1989 when, as in the time of the French Revolution, the Goddess of Democracy appeared in one place (Tiananmen Square in China in 1989, Paris in 1779) and then was everywhere.

In 2020 we may see the breakdown of culture into two main groups. *Uranus*, representing the *Intelligence of Radical Change and Innovation*, is in Taurus, the realm of the traditional and the biological. One group is the Radical Traditionalists (Rad Trads) whose function is the restoration of the Earth to its pristine state. They are stewards of the gene pool, human history and culture. They are the seed people. The second group of people are the Visionary Technocrats, a movement begun when Neptune was in Aquarius (1998-2011), gathering momentum as those born during that time period entered their precocious maturity. These Visionary Technocrats (Vis Techs) started the colonization of outer space, beginning with the Moon, Mars, the asteroids and the L5 point, which is the orbit point between Earth and the Moon where the two gravity fields cancel each other out thus allowing for permanent orbiting colonies.

Biology and physics meet. Biological organisms are created which devour the Earth's remaining toxic waste.

Children are born in increasing numbers with irrefutable telepathic capacities (as well as other talents previously described as "paranormal"). This allows for the understanding that technology is but a crude literalization of innate capacities of the human brain. The Rad Trads opt for brain cultivation and pragmatic mysticism and prefer to communicate with their Vis Tech siblings through astral travel and home-grown metaphysics.

By 2025-2038 with Neptune in Aries, we see the beginning of a massive exodus from the home planet into outer space (starting with the above points of colonization). This exodus of Star Voyagers reduces the population stress on Earth, allowing the Rad Trads to get on with their work of restoration and healing. They are aided in their task through the development of perpetual motion and clean energy technologies (fuel from salt water). This is the *Age of Marvelous Solutions and Healing*—more energy with less matter and waste. The increasing cultural understanding of electromagnetic fields, both around the Earth (how to heal its ruptured ozone layer) and the human body, allows for the regeneration of limbs and the elimination of crude surgical techniques. The *Age of Regeneration* arrives in which plant and animal species thought to be extinct are re-animated with the gene seeds salvaged by those with foresight in the early '90s. A cultural understanding emerges that the Earth, people—all life forms—have magnetic fields and that efficient healing starts there. The physical follows the energetic.

More things with less matter. The end of the Age of Materialism. The year 2025 begins a whole new cycle of humanity, the Age, once again, of the Pioneer, the Heroine, the Hero. . . .

The initial conflict between the Rad Trads and the Vis Techs must come to a resolution and wedding around the mid-21st century as each realizes the symbiotic necessity of the other. The Rad Trads must steward and restore the gene pool to provide grounding in order for the Vis Techs to fly and travel. More exchange through the Summit Conferences of Visionaries in both groups, the Traditional Shaman culture of elders and the Visionary Technocrats, allows for more fluidity of exchange between the two groups on a voluntary basis so that individuals can rotate in from the outer colonies to touch base with their Mother Planet.

By 2038-2052 with Neptune in Taurus, the Earth should be well on its way to full healing. The survival of a rich gene pool is assured. At this time we also see the stabilization of the outer-space colonies—the cities on Mars, the Moon, asteroids—and further expansion begins. . . .

With Pluto in Aries from 2067-2097, we have the beginning of star travel and the infinite opening universe in which to play. . . . Initial physical contact with extraterrestrials occurs in a large-scale societal way, full on cultural exchange and encounters with creatures from the core of the Milky Way similar enough in structure so that there can be breeding and intercultural marriage. . . .

Thus, life continues to serve the Great Order with increasing love and efficiency, with rapid, accelerated evolution in consciousness. And it only gets more far out after that. . . .

Here we are back in present time . . . . The task at hand is to elaborate on what we must do to get to the future we've just experienced or, indeed, to any future. What are the shadows we must bring to light, the demons with which we must wrestle? In astrological language, each part of the grammar (the planets, the signs, the houses, the aspects) has virtues to aspire to, instructions to fulfill— and demons to wrestle. One earns the virtues by wrestling with the demons. A related astrological principle is that solutions are always contained within the problems, with the corollary that whatever we reject or suppress will get hurtled back at us with equal force.

We must embrace and dance with the demons. A Tibetan meditation consists of visualizing the demons on the other side of a locked door. Then we imagine a laser beam (Plutonian energy) streaming from our third eye, shattering the lock, whereupon we invite the demons to "come on out, no one's as ugly as Yamantaka (the Lord of death)." The demons then emerge sheepish, rather than terrifying. The terror lies in their presence behind the locked door.

Let's go back to 1988, the time of the Saturn/Uranus conjunction, for a reminder of the language of our primary demon. *Uranus is the Intelligence of Freedom, Intuition*—the accurate sensing of possibilities. *Saturn* in its darker shadow and most constrictive form is *fear*. The sentence structure says that if you buy into the agenda of fear then you have given up your freedom, your Uranus, your intuitive grasp of the future. Fear is the primary demon we all must wrestle with and transcend, the guardian on the threshold, the keeper of the dark night, for it is fear that would keep us separate in non-collaborative isolation. Astrology says that whatever you don't find inside you'll find outside in a form you won't like so much. It is incumbent upon each of us to find our inner Saturn, our own form-giving, inner guide, father authority. Or else we will create an outer bossy, state-authoritarian structure where he who hesitates gets bossed. Saturn's traditional association with fear is derived from the outer projection of the unintegrated Saturn—something to engender fear, indeed. Fear allows the lie that we can profit from another's pain. Triage (the writing off of certain peoples, continents or species deemed "unsalvageable" by those who call themselves "realists") is not an acceptable attitude. Realists are simply those still numbed by a narrow World Bank bureaucratic mindset. They are not unredeemable either. We must fight for the joy and survival of all. The odious concept of "cost-benefit analysis" (the lie that a certain amount of fellow creature violence is "acceptable" if it yields sufficient profit) is to be banished.

A truism in the field of mythology is that its study is not some esoteric and/or academic indulgence but crucial to our survival, for unless we have a living vital mythology and rituals to make it meaningful, we will project shadow (unintegrated aspects of ourselves and our culture) onto others and other races, resulting in war—the ultimate expression of the illusion of isolation. Or, and this is just as crazed, we will project those unintegrated aspects of ourselves onto outer forms or people (like the State or leaders) to which we would like to give our power and responsibility. Gandhi said, "If I could lead people out of the forest, someone else could lead them back in."

Wrestling with the demon is a colloquialism because another method of relating to a demon is holding the other polarity in consciousness. The polarity to fear is love or unity, poignant kinship, integration, wholeness. Reverence is the form of relating which expresses and inspires love. Reverence is a ritual. Neptune is often called the higher octave of Venus, the amplification of the principle of relatedness, the yearning and aspiration for the emotional experience of unity. The instruction of Neptune is to cultivate devotion to living from that truth.

The Saturn/Neptune conjunction of 1989 was experienced by many as a time full of hard Saturnine lessons as each of us had our own obstacles to unity finely etched. The hunger for things to be different was also sharply defined. A Saturnine principle is that hunger precedes fulfillment. When we say "I'm hungry for this specific thing," by definition we have formed an imaginative vessel into which the Magical Transcendent (the energy we identify with the positive aspects of Neptune) can pour. We're all hungry and yearning for more loving paradigms in which to relate.

The years 1988-1993 can be viewed as one important unit of time: 1988, the Saturn/Uranus conjunction; 1989, the Saturn/Neptune conjunction; 1993, the Uranus/Neptune conjunction—all of which are in Capricorn, representing the real structure of the world and our responsibility for designing its next adaptation. As Saturn/Uranus told us that if we buy into the agenda of fear we are not free, so Saturn/Neptune told us that fear will rob us of our creative power to dream our lives, private and collective, into being. It is significant that studies have shown that watching television diminishes dream activity at night. Do you want the culture of infantile glamour to do your dreaming for you? In 1993, the coming together of Neptune and Uranus in Capricorn is the celebration of our freedom to create a visionary reality as well as the banishing of the illusion under which humanity has suffered throughout this Dark Age that there exists contradiction between pragmatism and idealism. And 1993 will be a great time for rituals in inner cities throughout the world of casting off the gold chains of bondage. Those gold chains (designer cars, clothes, lifestyle, drug money—all expressions of glamorous nihilism) have shackled some of the most imaginative, creative elements of youth culture to unwitting servitude of the State. Similarly, yuppie culture has addicted former idealists to lifestyles of greedy, fearful isolation. These are the gross shadow manifestations of Neptune in Capricorn, the worshipping of Soul-dead Television "Culture." Gotham's shopping nightmare. Voluntarily or violently, that climate of selling one's soul for momentary and fragmentary addictive satisfaction will climax and explode in the early '90s. The Uranian shock to Neptunian spiritual narcolepsy reminds us that massive, internal evolutionary leaps tend to occur in times of massive external breakdown.

We are reminded of the Russian scientist Pavlov who conditioned dogs to salivate at the sound of a bell and other primitive behavioristic outrages. When there was a flood in Pavlov's laboratory, none of the dogs who survived retained the least trace of their elaborate conditioning. Can the great tide of human catalytic breakdown have less effect on humans than a flood on dogs? Crisis can liberate us from shadow if the invitation to be initiated and to participate in the most dynamic and creative aspects of cultural evolution is extended. As crises increase, more events and projects must be invoked to invite in those previously excluded.

The crisis of the illusion of waste: As our dump sites are overflowing, so are our prisons. We can no longer exile our cultural failures. There isn't room anymore. The negative, shadow aspects of Neptune, Pisces and the 12th House refer to what the culture relegates to the realms of exile. But the repressed always return, with a vengeance. What does it say about a culture that creates massive amounts of toxic waste with no idea what to do with it? And that presumes to deal with a considerable proportion of its alienated youth in the same manner? It says that this is a culture with no future.

Neptune in Capricorn (1984-1998) is the era when ideals are finally recognized as necessities. (Environmental concerns are finally being recognized by economists.) Principles are becoming pragmatics. Businesses which reorganize along more sensitive (Neptunian) lines thrive. Businesses which do not go under.

In the summer of 1989 (the second sweep of the Saturn/Neptune conjunction) a study published in the journal *Nature* and reported in the *New York Times* (July 4) proclaimed "Rain Forest Worth More If Uncut." This study delineated the facts that not only is the annual loss of 28 million acres of forest around the world a spiritual and ecological disaster—it is also an economic disaster. Immorality is ultimately a bad investment. We realize that self-interest and common interest are, in fact, the same if we look deeply enough into the apparent conflict. Once again, we understand the simple truth that there is no future in nihilism.

The rain forest is a central reality and symbol. Moist, luscious, teeming with an exotic and mysterious profusion of life forms that have evolved over millions of years, this surely is the habitat of the Earth's soul. The cornucopia of nature's abundance—the Grail—throughout core Western mythology has always been contrasted with its demonic polarity—the Wasteland. The lesson has always been and will always be one of reversal. Neptune. It is not that the Grail serves us but it is we who serve the Grail as wise stewards. When we violate this trust, it makes us crazy and ill. It sends a convulsive shudder down our collective backbone. From Wall Street to the inner city and on into our bedrooms, how we treat the rain forest, the Grail, is how men treat women, is how we treat our souls. Everywhere we feel a crisis of the soul, a crisis of that Vision, a crisis of Neptune. Dealing junk bonds on Wall Street and crack on the corner or trading sex without reverence is both a reflection and acceleration of soul death based on a spiritual alienation from our task as compassionate stewards and our truth as one unified being. The whole of creation groans and celebrates together. We cannot pluck one strand of creation without resonating the whole. There is no joy or pain anywhere in which we do not partake consciously or subliminally. Poignancy is the experience of kinship.

Astrology is the language of this interrelatedness, an articulation of correlation and resonance, embedded in the natural world. As such, it is called now to its most sacred use—to provide us with the overview so sadly lacking in conventional public dialogue with its addiction to fragmentary sensationalism in which each crisis is viewed as "news," an isolated crisis rather than a crisis of isolation.

All of the problems we face in creating a non-catastrophic future are interrelated. We face a crisis of Neptune, a crisis of Vision in a culture of complicitous addiction to narrow self-interest and short-term greed.

Neptune is called the ruler of oil (presumably because it rules anything intrinsically addicting). On the second sweep of the Saturn/Neptune conjunction of 1989, within a day there were three major oil spills following the disastrous Exxon Valdez spill several months earlier (the investigation of which had prompted the Alaska oil spill coordinator to remark that "It wasn't that it was Captain Ahab on the bridge; it was that it was Curly and Moe in the Exxon boardroom." Our cultural addiction to oil, our addiction to immediate gratification without long-term Vision, is related to the crisis of the Earth's rain forests, the strip-mining of collective resources, with the Earth's abundance meant for all of which we are meant to be stewards rather than ravagers and bandits. When such atrocities are committed, we need to take drugs to numb ourselves to the pain.

Our addiction to beef consumption, the cow, the Great Mother, the drinking of milk, are emblematic of cultural infantilism that places pressure on men to clear-cut rain forests—millions of years of evolution, untapped wealth, wisdom, beauty and magic—for several seasons of hamburgers. The greed of multinational bankers compels Latin America to do this desperate short-term self-ravaging to alleviate the pressures of debt repayment. Each violence committed against the natural world is a violence committed against the feminine and does damage to each man's soul, manifesting in the relationships between men and women. The disintegration of the social fabric and the male and female wounding are all echoes of the pain of the natural world and the traditions of our ancestors howling in outrage down the corridors of equinoxes and solstices . . . and this resonates in our psyches. The unintegrated masculine or feminine is always technically mythologically "monstrous" and terrifying. . . .

Joseph Campbell said that the good news is we're free; the bad news is that we don't know what to do with our freedom, having thrown out all our systems of guidance and mocked and trivialized our languages of the Soul.

In the outer rain forest and the inner rain forest, our soul's domain, lie untold medicinal plants . . . plants that could well heal the plagues like AIDS with which humanity is afflicted. The literal and symbolic question, then, is: Will we find the thing that heals us before we kill it?

The task before us is great. It is, as the I Ching says in its final hexagram, nothing short of leading the world out of confusion and back to Order. On one level, we are all in the court of the Evil Emperor. The drive of the unleashed unconscious is towards mass extinction and genocide to compensate for the unbearable, unchecked increases in population. The unconscious lumbers towards the precipice of disaster and catastrophe (both words having their root in the Latin *aster*, "star"). But consciousness can always be interjected into any cyclical process. Our task, perhaps the task of life, is to make the unconscious conscious.

We can dance or crawl into the 21st century. It's our choice. We each carry the task of being a Visionary, a pragmatic functioning in the real world.

Now Neptune, representing the intelligence of Dreams, Vision, Illusion, Addiction, is also symbolic of *Water*. Water reflects a reverse image. So Neptune comes to represent the *principle of reversal*. Most people take Saturn, the "reality" principle, to be the determining factor. But Neptune says, "No, the reverse is true: structure follows Vision." The environmental revelations of 1988 (Saturn/Uranus) led to the understanding in 1989 (Saturn/Neptune) of the enormous structural and attitudinal reversals required in our collective consciousness. We must regear, reverse industrialism and linear notions of progress from a war economy to an environmental effort based on cyclical understanding. . . .

We are at the collective crisis of the death of the "cowboy myth," whose essential shadow is one of rootless extraversion, the lone unrelated male laying waste to the land and indigenous cultures which had embodied an appropriate pragmatic mysticism. Ronald Reagan rode this myth into the sunset. Now we need a better mythos.

Neptune, being the principle of living vibrant mythology, also describes what happens to a person, a family, a culture when there is no vital mythology. That person, that family, that culture becomes hooked (the glyph or visual representation for Neptune is the trident) on anything that will numb the pain of alienation from the Divine. Addiction is the repetition of any innately unsatisfying experience in which one says, "Gee, that didn't really work. Let's try more." As Carl Jung and Bill Wilson, the founder of AA, remarked to each other in their correspondence, there is no cure for addiction without a spiritual experience since addiction is a pure drive for transcendence that became twisted in an inappropriate direction.

How can we not fear when we look, clear-headed, at the craziness of the situation? And what is a better myth?

What is the cure, the thing that will heal us, the plant that lies waiting in the rain forest—the symbolic plant in our psyches that we must find to manifest—the wedding of polarity? Any unintegrated half of a polarity is a rogue element and bound to be crazy. . . . The feminine, the voice of the Soul, says reverence is the antidote to fear. Increase reverence rather than fear, the major demon to passing our collective evolutionary initiation through which we are all now traveling.

*Astrology trains the mind to think symbolically*—to dignify outer events by understanding that they are always reflective of inner process. An astrological chart is a real map, a symbolic map of the instructions of that moment, just as everything in our lives is real and symbolic. Everything has resonance and meaning. Symbols are the language of the soul. Chance is the category of the alienated mind. What one ritualizes one need not melodramatically enact. Melodrama is expensive to the creative life, whereas ritual contributes, catalyses, amplifies. . . . We integrate those aspects of ourselves to which we can give outer representation. An initiation is the outward mythological and ritual enactment of inner material.

We are all candidates for Initiation into the new Myth. Whether we heed the call is the issue. Some hear and talk over it, uncomfortable with the tension, seeking to control it, to make it go away, to trample on the mystery rather than offering themselves—quiet, alert, relaxed but vigilant.

Our old paradigms are dying. We must die *to* them if we are not to die *with* them. This strips us temporarily of guidance systems and Soul takes over—the Real Work begins. Being defeated by our souls (we are still so willful) allows us to become more ourselves. Compassion comes from being eaten alive. Initiation entails terror, but initiatory terror is distinguished from fear because it is wedded to Faith. Simplistic New Age dogma says it's all for free. (The unintegrated-male-leave-the-planet ideology.) Space without stewardship is an infantile reinvocation of the dead "cowboy myth." We can't have Vis Techs without the Rad Trads. In fact, we can't have either unless each person acknowledges and consciously reverences both in the psyche in a light and dark, extroverted and introverted, way.

The new ancient myth we are called upon to reinvoke, to celebrate and to offer our imaginative talents to creating is the Wedding, the Conjunction, the Sacred Marriage, the Fifth Act, the redemptive Vision, the True Myth. Reverent relating creates a vessel into which life-spirit can pour. The great tool that lies not in our modern memory but in our primeval, rain forest, ancestral memory is magick—the collaboration of our dreams bridged to the spiritual life force of what wants to be. This alliance can heal and save us all.

We are called now to the grand conspiracy (*conspire* means literally *con spiro*, "to breathe together") of collaboration, of offering the best in us to the Grand Design and extending the invitation to others to act similarly. By doing this we form a vessel into which grace can pour.

Life turns into the mystery play—dangerous and flashy . . . dangerous and wonderful. . . . Good luck to all of us.

## STAY IN TOUCH

On the following pages you will find listed, with their current prices, some of the books and tapes now available on related subjects. Your book dealer stocks most of these, and will stock new titles in the Llewellyn series as they become available. We urge your patronage.

However, to obtain our full catalog, to keep informed of new titles as they are released and to benefit from informative articles and helpful news, you are invited to write for our bi-monthly news magazine/catalog. A sample copy is free, and it will continue coming to you at no cost as long as you are an active mail customer. Or you may keep it coming for a full year with a donation of just $2.00 in U.S.A. ($7.00 for Canada & Mexico, $20.00 overseas, first class mail). Many bookstores also have *The Llewellyn New Times* available to their customers. Ask for it.

Stay in touch! In *The Llewellyn New Times'* pages you will find news and reviews of new books, tapes and services, announcements of meetings and seminars, articles helpful to our readers, news of authors, advertising of products and services, and much more.

### *The Llewellyn New Times*
**P.O. Box 64383-Dept. 384, St. Paul, MN 55164-0383, U.S.A.**
• • •

### TO ORDER BOOKS AND TAPES

If your book dealer does not have the books and tapes described on the following pages readily available, you may order them direct from the publisher by sending full price in U.S. funds, plus $2.00 for postage and handling for the first book, and 50 cents for each additional book. There are no postage and handling charges for orders over $50. UPS Delivery: We ship UPS whenever possible. Delivery guaranteed. Provide your street address as UPS does not deliver to P.O. Boxes. UPS to Canada requires a $50 minimum order. Allow 4-6 weeks for delivery. Orders outside the U.S.A. and Canada: Airmail—add retail price of book; add $5 for each non-book item (tapes, etc.); add $1 per item for surface mail.

### FOR GROUP STUDY AND PURCHASE

Because there is a great deal of interest in group discussion and study of the subject matter of this book, we feel that we should encourage the adoption and use of this particular book by such groups by offering a special "quantity" price to group leaders or "agents."

Our Special Quantity Price for a minimum order of five copies of *The Astrology of the Macrocosm* is $44.85 cash-with-order. This price includes postage and handling within the U.S. Minnesota residents must add 6% sales tax. For additional quantities, please order in multiples of five. For Canadian and foreign orders, add postage and handling charges as above. Credit card (VISA, Master Card, American Express) orders are accepted. Charge card orders only may be phoned free ($15.00 minimum order) within the U.S.A. or Canada by dialing 1-800-THE-MOON. Customer service calls dial 1-612-291-1970. Mail orders to:

### LLEWELLYN PUBLICATIONS
**P.O. Box 64383-Dept. 384 / St. Paul, MN 55164-0383, U.S.A.**

## SPIRITUAL, METAPHYSICAL & NEW TRENDS IN MODERN ASTROLOGY
**Edited by Joan McEvers**

This is the first book in the Llewellyn New World Astrology Series. Edited by well-known astrologer, lecturer and writer Joan McEvers, this book pulls together the latest thoughts by the best astrologers in the field of Spiritual Astrology.

She has put together an outstanding group of informative and exciting topics.
- Gray Keen: Perspective: The Ethereal Conclusion
- Marion D. March: Some Insights into Esoteric Astrology
- Kimberly McSherry: The Feminine Element of Astrology: Reframing the Darkness
- Kathleen Burt: The Spiritual Rulers and Their Practical Role in the Transformation
- Shirley Lyons Meier: The Secrets behind Carl Payne Tobey's Secondary Chart
- Jeff Jawer: Astrodrama
- Donna Van Toen: Alice Bailey Revisited
- Philip Sedgwick: Galactic Studies
- Myrna Lofthus: The Spiritual Programming within a Natal Chart
- Angel Thompson: Transformational Astrology

**0–87542–380–9, 288 pgs., 5 1/4 x 8, softcover**　　　　　**$9.95**

## EARTH MOTHER ASTROLOGY
**by Marcia Starck**

Now, for the first time, a book that combines the science of astrology with current New Age interest in crystals, herbs, aromas, and holistic health. With this book and a copy of your astrological birth chart (readily available from sources listed in the book) you can use your horoscope to benefit your total being—body, mind and spirit. Learn, for example, what special nutrients you need during specific planetary cycles, or what sounds or colors will help you transform emotional states during certain times of the year.

This is a compendium of information for the New Age astrologer and healer. For the beginner, it explains all the astrological signs, planets and houses in a simple and yet new way, physiologically as well as symbolically.

This is a book of modern alchemy, showing the reader how to work with Earth energies to achieve healing and transformation, thereby creating a sense of the cosmic unity of all Earth's elements.

**0–87542–741–3, 288 pgs., 5 1/4 x 8, illus., softcover**　　　　**$12.95**

## PLANETS: THE ASTROLOGICAL TOOLS
### Edited by Joan McEvers

This is the second in the astrological anthology series edited by respected astrologer Joan McEvers, who provides a brief factual overview of the planets.

Then take off through the solar system with 10 professional astrologers as they bring their insights to the symbolism and influences of the planets.

- Toni Glover Sedgwick: The Sun as the life force and our ego
- Joanne Wickenburg: The Moon as our emotional signal to change
- Erin Sullivan-Seale: Mercury as the multi-faceted god, followed with an in-depth explanation of its retrogradation
- Robert Glasscock: Venus as your inner value system and relationships
- Johanna Mitchell: Mars as your cooperative, energizing inner warrior
- Don Borkowski: Jupiter as expansion and preservation
- Gina Ceaglio: Saturn as a source of freedom through self-discipline
- Bil Tierney: Uranus as the original, growth-producing planet
- Karma Welch: Neptune as selfless giving and compassionate love
- Joan Negus: Pluto as a powerful personal force

**0–87542–381–7, 380 pgs., 5 1/4 x 8, charts, softcover          $12.95**

## THE SUN AT THE CENTER
### by Philip Sedgwick

Geocentric (Earth-centered) astrology dates back to the days when astrologers and astronomers were one and the same—when it was believed that the Earth was the center of the universe. Those that first proposed that the Sun was at the center were labeled frauds and heretics, denounced by their peers and by the Church.

Now renowned astrologer Philip Sedgwick breaks new ground in astrology with the first book based exclusively on the heliocentric theory. He demonstrates how this system is particularly useful in discovering one's life purpose, as well as for understanding the significance of major world events.

This is not a refutal of astrology's geocentric findings, but an expansion of astrological thought that includes new astronomical findings. *The Sun at the Center* will help the reader understand how to interpret heliocentric horoscopes with exploration of heliocentric nodes, eclipses, the actual motion of the planets, and aspects unique to this system.

**0–87542–738–3, 208 pgs., 6 x 9, softcover          $12.95**

**FINANCIAL ASTROLOGY FOR THE 1990s**
**Edited by Joan McEvers**
Favorably reviewed in the *Wall Street Journal* by financial expert Stanley W. Angrist! This third book in Llewellyn's anthology series edited by well-known astrologer Joan McEvers explores the relatively new field of financial astrology. Nine respected astrologers share their wisdom and good fortune with you.

Learn about the various types of analysis and how astrology fine-tunes these methods. Covered cycles include the Lunar Cycle, the Mars/Vesta Cycle, the 4 1/2-year Martian Cycle, the 500-year Civilization Cycle used by Nostradamus, the Kondratieff Wave and the Elliott Wave. Included topics are:

- Michael Munkasey: A Primer on Market Forecasting
- Pat Esclavon Hardy: Charting the U.S. and the NYSE
- Jeanne Long: New Concepts for Commodities Trading Combining Astrology & Technical Analysis
- Georgia Stathis: The Real Estate Process
- Mary B. Downing: An Investor's Guide to Financial Astrology
- Judy Johns: The Gann Technique
- Carol S. Mull: Predicting the Dow
- Bill Meridian: The Effect of Planetary Stations on U.S. Stock Prices
- Georgia Stathis: Delineating the Corporation
- Robert Cole: The Predictable Economy

**0–87542–382–5, 368 pgs., 5 1/4 x 8, illus., softcover**      **$14.95**


**HORARY ASTROLOGY**
**by Anthony Louis**
This new book delves deeply into the heritage and the modern applicability of the horary art. Author Anthony Louis is a practicing psychiatrist, and he brings the compassion and erudition associated with his field to this scholarly textbook.

Written beautifully and reverently in the tradition of William Lilly, the book translates Lilly's meaning into modern terms. Other features include numerous case studies; tables; diagrams; and more than 100 pages of appendices, including an exhaustive planetary rulership list, planetary key words and a lengthy astrological/horary glossary. Dignities and debilities, aspects and orbs, derivative houses, Arabic parts, fixed stars, critical degrees and more are explored in relation to the science of horary astrology. Worksheets supplement the text.

**0–87542–394–9, 600 pgs., 6 x 9, softcover**      **$18.95**

## THE HOUSES: POWER PLACES OF THE HOROSCOPE
**Edited by Joan McEvers**

This volume combines the talents of 11 renowned astrologers in the fourth book of Llewellyn's anthology series. Besides compiling all this information into a unified whole, Joan McEvers also contributes her viewpoint and knowledge to the delineation of the 12th House.

Each house, an area of activity within the horoscope, is explained with clarity and depth by the following authors:
- Peter Damian: The 1st House and the Rising Sign and Planets
- Ken Negus: The 7th House of Partnership
- Noel Tyl: The 2nd House of Self-Worth and the 8th House of Values and Others
- Spencer Grendahl: The 3rd House of Exploration and Communication
- Dona Shaw: The 9th House of Truth and Abstract Thinking
- Gloria Star: The 4th House of the Subconscious Matrix
- Marwayne Leipzig: The 10th House of the Life's Imprint
- Lina Accurso: The 5th House of Love
- Sara Corbin Looms: The 11th House of Tomorrow
- Michael Munkasey: The 6th House of Attitude and Service
- Joan McEvers: The 12th House of Strength, Peace, Tranquillity

**0–87542–383–3, 400 pgs., 5 1/4 x 8, charts, softcover**     **$12.95**

## THE ASTRO*CARTO*GRAPHY BOOK OF MAPS
**by Jim Lewis and Ariel Guttman**

Everyone believes there is a special person, job and *place* for him or her. This book explores those special places in the lives of 136 celebrities.

The maps, based on the time of birth, graphically reveal lines of planetary influence at various geographic locations. A planet affecting a certain area is correlated with a person's success, failure, or activities there. Astro*Carto*Graphy can also be used to bring about the stronger influence of a certain planet by showing its angular positions. Angular positions involve the Ascendant, the IC, the Descendant and the Midheaven. The maps show where planets would have been had you been born at different locations than at your birthplace.

Charts and maps of personalities in the entertainment field, such as Joan Crawford, Marilyn Monroe, Grace Kelly, James Dean, John Lennon and David Bowie, are included in this compilation. Activists like Martin Luther King, Jr. and Lech Walesa, spiritual pioneers like Freud, Jung and Yogananda, and events in the lives of painters, musicians and sports figures are explored as well as the successes, problems and tendencies of such politicians as FDR, Harry Truman, JFK, Richard Nixon, Ronald Reagan, George Bush, and Margaret Thatcher.

**0–87542–434–1, 300 pgs., 8 1/2 x 11, charts, softcover**     **$15.95**

# THE LLEWELLYN ANNUALS

**Llewellyn's MOON SIGN BOOK**: Approximately 400 pages of valuable information on gardening, fishing, weather, stock market forecasts, personal horoscopes, good planting dates, and general instructions for finding the best date to do just about anything! Article by prominent forecasters and writers in the fields of gardening, astrology, politics, economics and cycles. This special almanac, different from any other, has been published annually since 1906. It's fun, informative and has been a great help to millions in their daily planning.

**State year $4.95**

**Llewellyn's SUN SIGN BOOK**: Your personal horoscope for the entire year! All 12 signs are included in one handy book. Also included are forecasts, special feature articles, and an action guide for each sign. Monthly horoscopes are written by Gloria Star, author of *Optimum Child*, for your personal Sun Sign, and there are articles on a variety of subjects written by well-known astrologers from around the country. Much more than just a horoscope guide! Entertaining and fun the year around.

**State year $4.95**

**Llewellyn's DAILY PLANETARY GUIDE and ASTROLOGER'S DATEBOOK**: Includes all of the major daily aspects plus their exact times in Eastern and Pacific time zones, lunar phases, signs and voids plus their times, planetary motion, a monthly ephemeris, sunrise and sunset tables, special articles on the planets, signs, aspects, a business guide, planetary hours, rulerships, and much more. Large 5 1/4 x 8 format for more writing space, spiral bound to lay flat, address and phone listings, time zone conversion chart and blank horoscope chart.

**State year $6.95**

**Llewellyn's ASTROLOGICAL CALENDAR**: Large wall calendar of 52 pages. Beautiful full-color cover and color inside. Includes special feature articles by famous astrologers, introductory information on astrology. Lunar Gardening Guide, celestial phenomena, a blank horoscope chart for your own chart data, and monthly date pages which include aspects, lunar information, planetary motion, ephemeris, personal forecasts, lucky dates, planting and fishing dates, and more. 10 x 13 size. Set in Central time, with conversion table for other time zones worldwide.

**State year $8.95**